hope this
keeps you [illegible] your best memories
lots of love
Jane December 95

COLLINS

PHOTOGRAPHY HINTS & TIPS

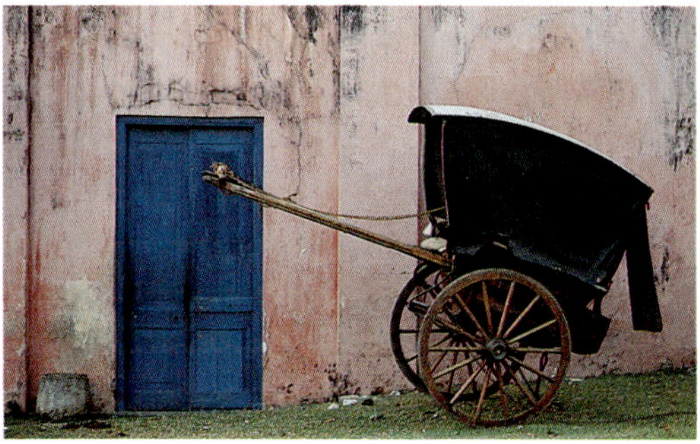

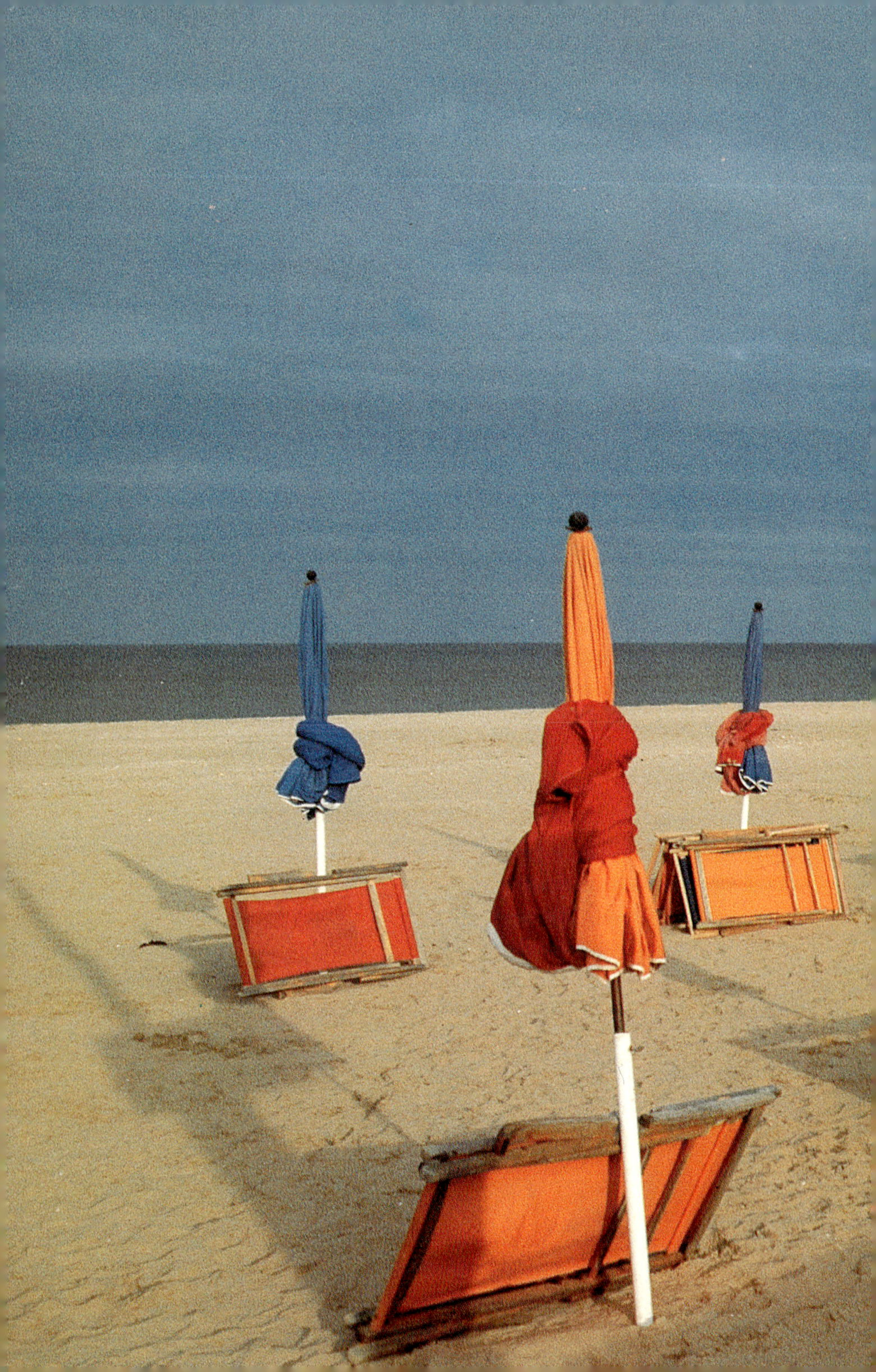

COLLINS

PHOTOGRAPHY HINTS & TIPS

MICHAEL BUSSELLE

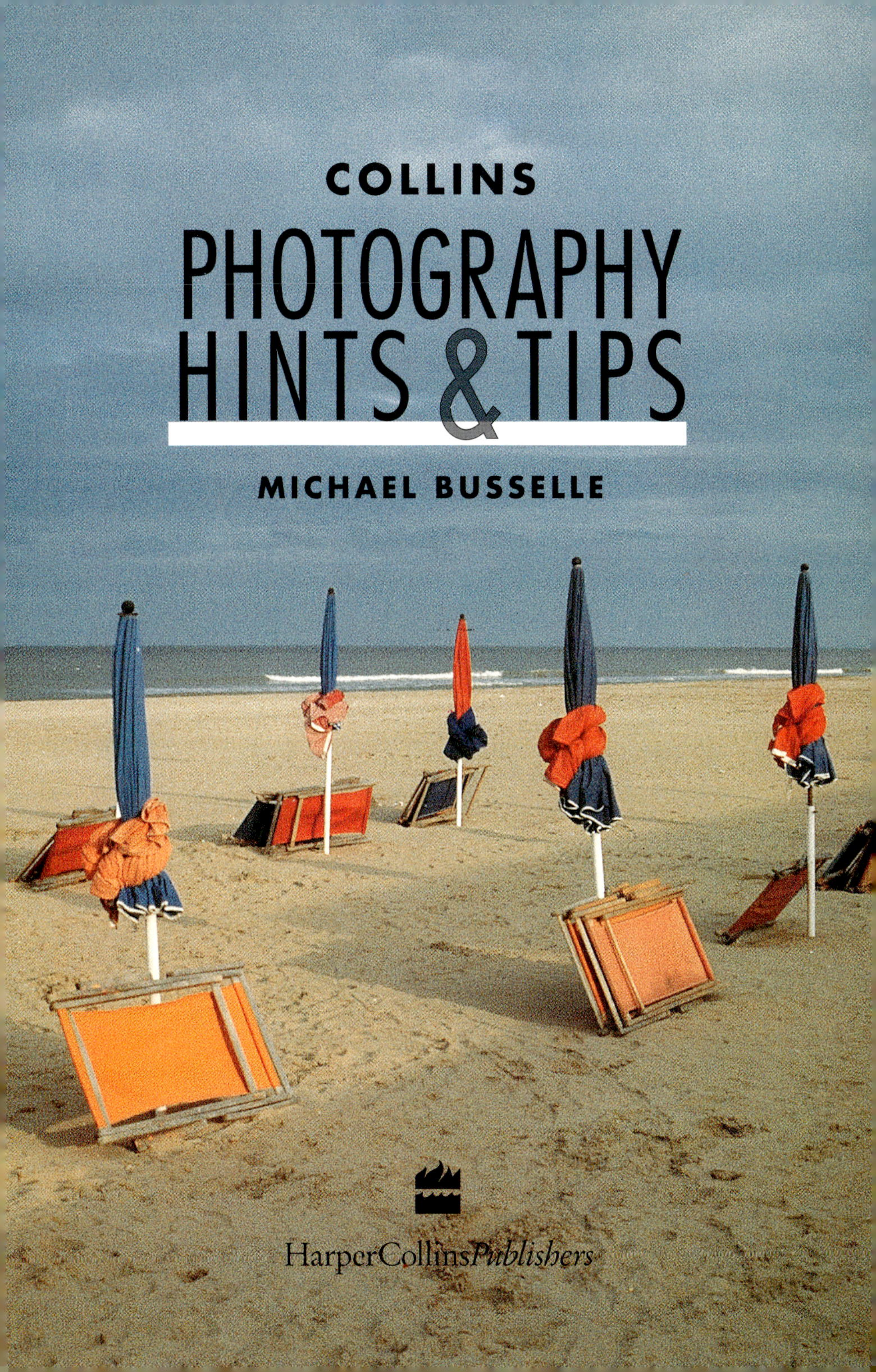

HarperCollinsPublishers

First published in 1995 by
HarperCollins Publishers

This book was created exclusively for
HarperCollins Publishers by Pardoe Blacker Publishing Ltd
Design: Grant Bradford, Dawn Brend, Jon Eland
Editors: Jon Williams, Linda Williams
Illustrations: Simon Roulstone

For HarperCollins Publishers
Commissioning Editor: Polly Powell
Project Editor: Barbara Dixon
Art Editor: Caroline Hill

**A catalogue record for this book is available from
the British Library**

ISBN 0 00 412726 9

Colour reproduction in Singapore, by Colourscan
Printed and bound in Italy

The author and publishers gratefully acknowledge the
assistance of **Nikon UK Limited**, Nikon House,
380 Richmond Road, Kingston upon Thames,
Surrey KT2 5PR

All photographs were taken by Michael Busselle
with the exception of the following:
Julien Busselle 6 (top), 51 (bottom), 103, 129 (bottom), 130.

Contents

Introduction

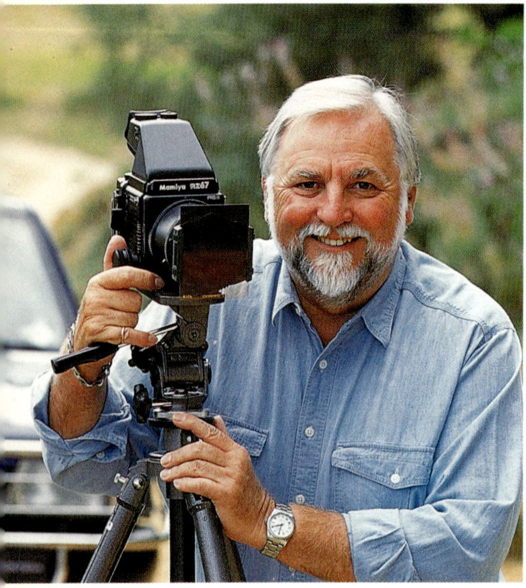

Most people learn how to take good photographs simply by trial and error. Taking photographs, making mistakes, understanding why they occurred and finding ways to avoid them in the future are all essential if you want to become a better photographer. Books and articles on photographic techniques can help, but only by exposing film will you begin to understand fully how the processes work and how to produce satisfying pictures on a regular basis.

General books on photographic technique tend to focus on the broader aspects and processes. Often it is not until you try a particular shot that you realise how you have to discover some of the more mundane and practical techniques for yourself, or learn them from somebody else. A knack is involved, and improving your photography is a learning process.

I have been taking photographs for more than 40 years, and I'm still learning. Most of the knack I've acquired has been hard won; watching other photographers more experienced in a particular field, finding ways, often in desperation, to overcome problems which could ruin a shot and learning how to prevent the repetition of annoying and potentially costly errors.

There are numerous bits of advice and shortcuts which can be applied usefully by photographers at all levels of experience, making good results far easier and more reliable to achieve. This book distills the fund of experience that I have gained, both from my successes and from my failures, into a collection of practical hints and tips. If only some of these make you think 'That's a good idea,' or help you to overcome a particular problem, then I feel that this book will

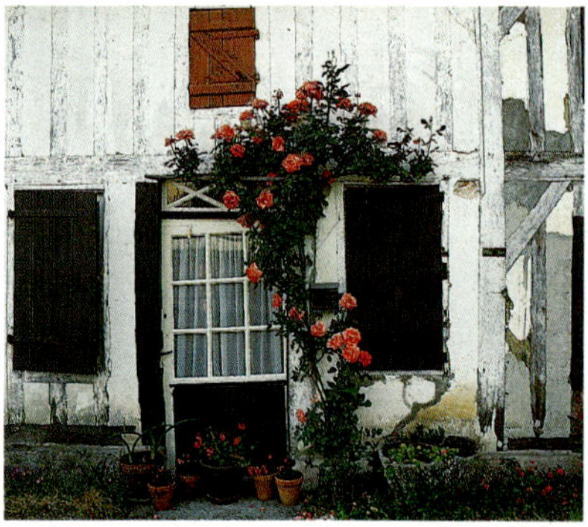

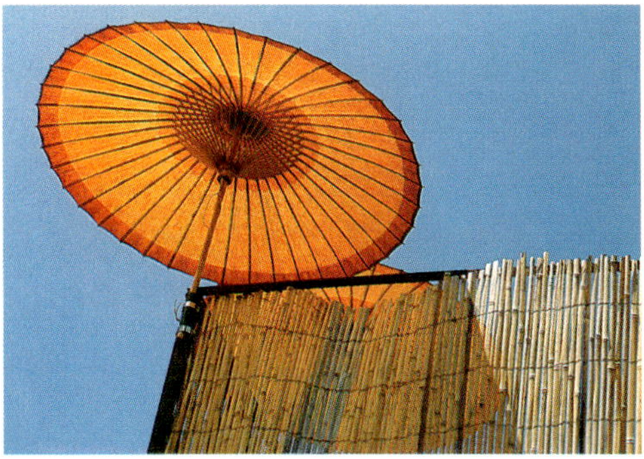

have achieved its goal. You may be surprised exactly how much the success of a picture can depend on the knowledge of simple 'tricks' which are taken for granted by more experienced photographers, and are not included in many books that cover general techniques. The ease with which it is possible for even inexperienced photographers to shoot most subjects using today's automatic cameras leads many people to believe that a successful photograph is guaranteed but, in spite of the considerable technological advances made since the mid 1980s, there is still a knack to taking good photographs, and this book will help you to acquire that knack.

Photography Hints and Tips is arranged into eight chapters, each focussing on a particular aspect of photography. If you are interested in a certain type of subject, such as portraits or landscapes, or in using particular equipment, for example long lenses or flash, you can refer quickly and easily to the hints and tips which are most relevant to you. Each of the numbered paragraphs is graded with one, two or three 'bullets' reflecting the level of expertise that is recommended to enable you to employ that technique successfully. There is also a comprehensive glossary where technical terms that might be unfamiliar are explained in more detail.

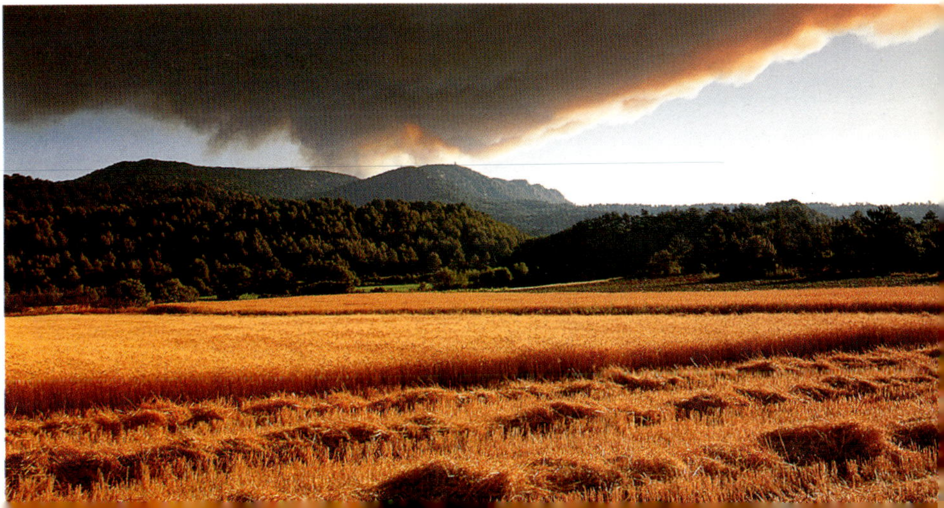

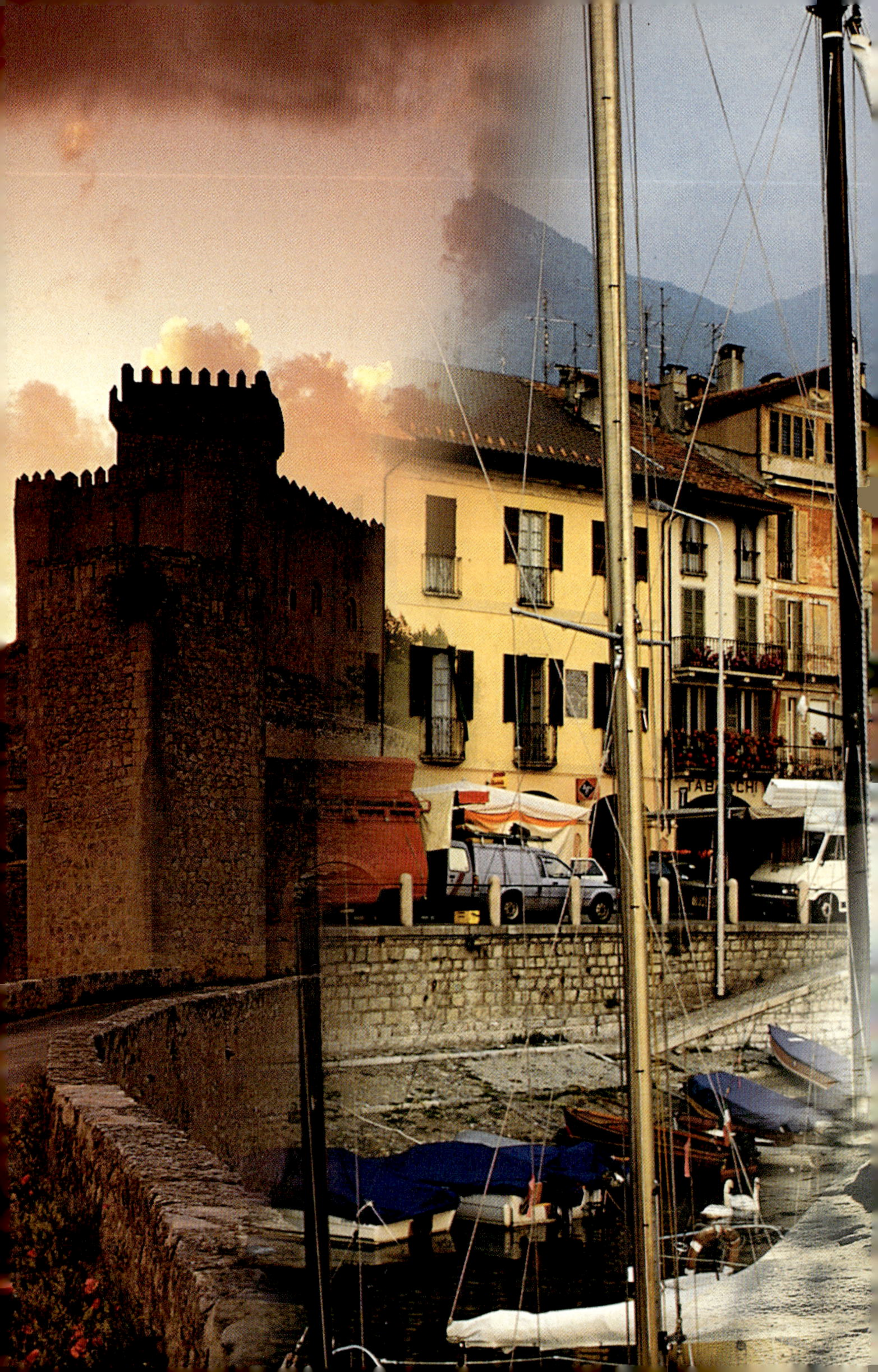

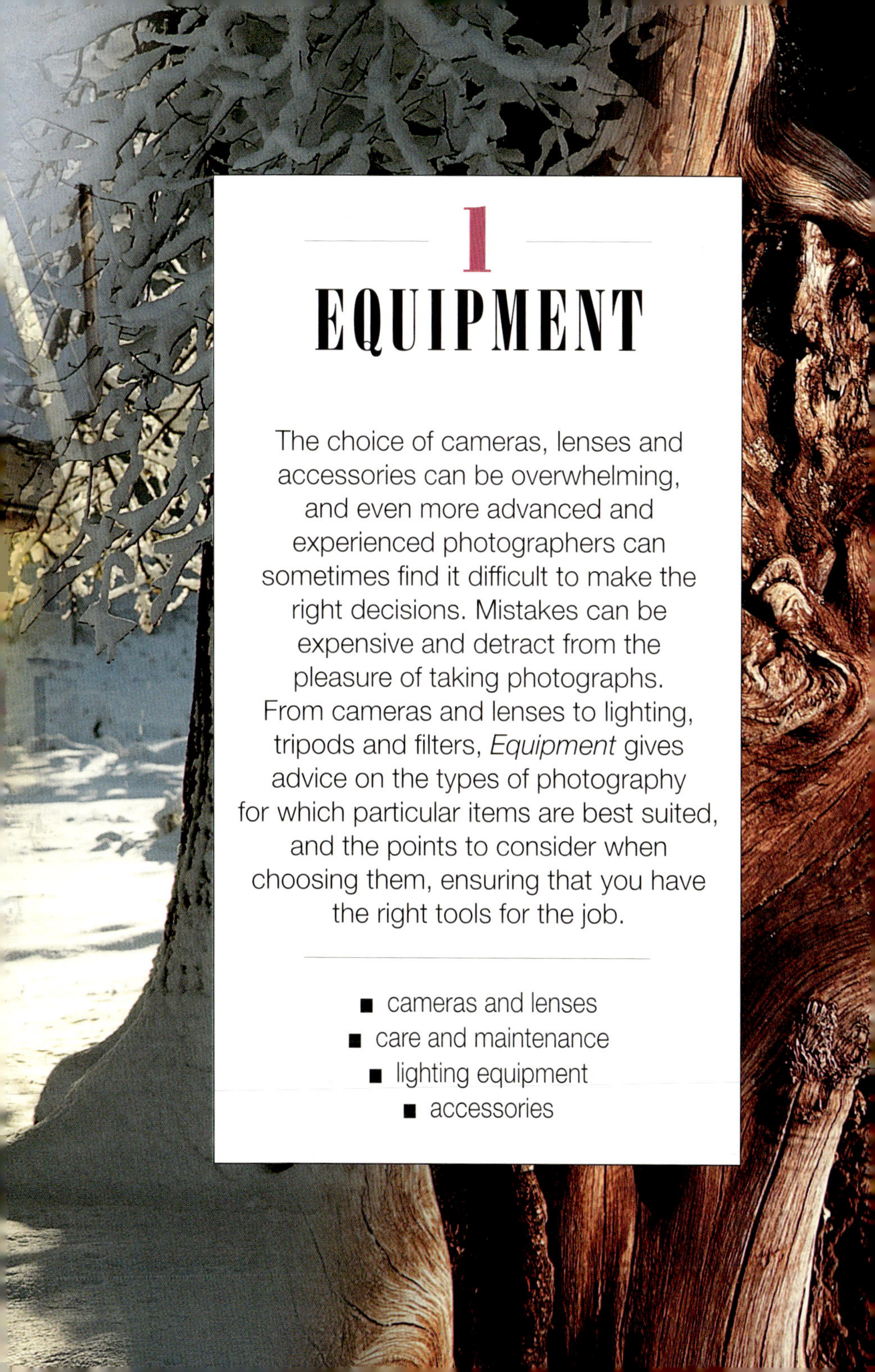

1

EQUIPMENT

The choice of cameras, lenses and accessories can be overwhelming, and even more advanced and experienced photographers can sometimes find it difficult to make the right decisions. Mistakes can be expensive and detract from the pleasure of taking photographs. From cameras and lenses to lighting, tripods and filters, *Equipment* gives advice on the types of photography for which particular items are best suited, and the points to consider when choosing them, ensuring that you have the right tools for the job.

- cameras and lenses
- care and maintenance
- lighting equipment
- accessories

1 Cameras and Lenses

1.01 ● When choosing a camera, bear in mind that many less-expensive compact cameras have quite simple, less critical exposure systems. These tend to give more reliable results when used with colour negative film which has a much wider tolerance to exposure error than colour transparency film.

1.02 ● If you want to take your photography seriously, choose a camera which has a manual mode. These are often more straightforward to use than automatic programme modes, and allow you much greater control over image quality, abnormal lighting conditions and varied subjects. A manual mode should help you to understand more clearly how your camera works and how it can be used to control the quality and effect of your photographs. ▼

1.03 ● Check second-hand lenses carefully: some abrasions can adversely affect image contrast and definition. Make sure that the internal surfaces of the lens mount are matt black and have not worn shiny. Hold the lens obliquely towards a light source and view it by both reflected and transmitted light to reveal any flaws. Check also that the focussing mechanism runs smoothly but is not too loose – this indicates excessive wear. Hold one-touch zoom lenses vertically: if the focussing collar slides forwards under its own weight it may be badly worn.

1.04 ●● Test the camera's exposure system periodically. Although you can check its meter against another, this will not take into account the efficiency of the shutter, iris mechanism and the light transmission of the lenses. Try to check the complete system in a

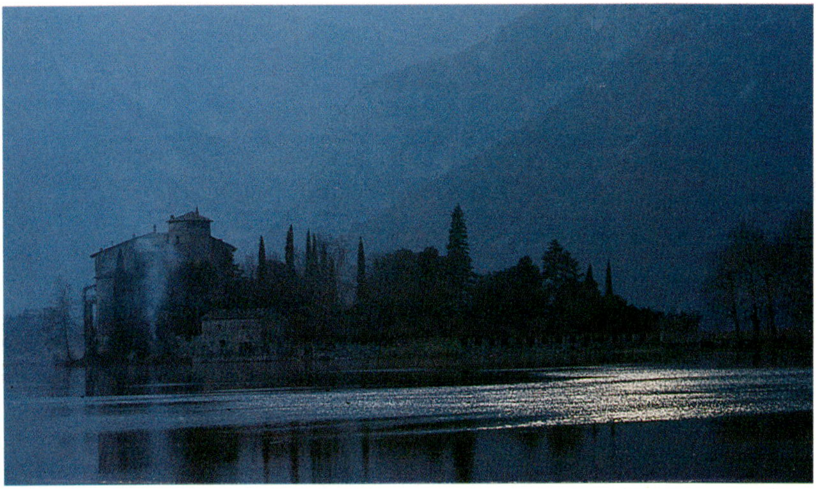

practical situation. Photograph a Kodak test card which incorporates a grey scale and colour swatch. Set the camera to the correct film speed and make a bracket of exposures in one-third of a stop increments; you can then make a direct comparison with the test card. Remember that individual lenses can vary and that f8, for instance, with one lens may pass less, or more, light than f8 with another. Moreover, the colour quality can vary with different makes and types of lens, so you should extend testing to all lenses in your system.

1.05 ●● For photographing subjects like wildlife or sport, when a long-focus lens with a wide aperture is often needed, it is worth considering an Apo (Apochromatic) lens. This uses special glass elements which bring all the wavebands of light into sharp focus on the same plane. It produces critically sharp images without having to be stopped down, allowing sharper enlargements to be made.

1.06 ●●● If you are especially interested in architectural photography and enjoy photographing buildings, a perspective control, or shift, lens will prove to be an invaluable accessory. It is a wide-angle lens designed in a way that enables the optical axis to be raised so that more of the image can be included at the top of the frame while keeping the camera level. Many of the major 35mm and medium-format camera systems include such a lens, but they are more expensive than a standard wide-angle lens. ▲

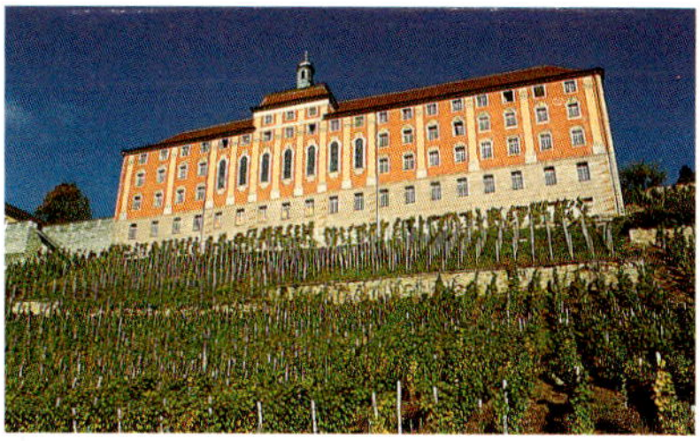

An upward camera tilt causes converging verticals.

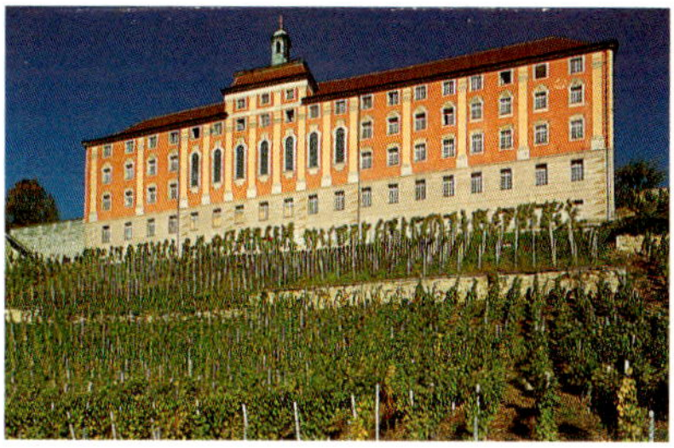

Using a shift lens has avoided the problem.

1.07 ●● Autofocus lenses can be both useful and effective for many everyday subjects. There are occasions, however, when it is easier and more satisfactory to focus manually, for example when using a tripod-mounted camera for subjects with poor contrast, with little detail or in low light. For this reason, when choosing autofocus lenses, make sure that the manual focus facility is easy and convenient to use, even if you intend to use the autofocus mode for much of the time.

1.08 ● One simple way to test a new camera or new lenses is to find a subject of average tone and contrast, with angular lines and lots of fine detail – I tend to use the front of my house, shot from across the road. Mount the camera on a tripod, then take a series of exposures at a wide aperture, at f11 and at minimum aperture to check the sharpness, distortion and colour quality of your lenses. A bracket of seven exposures in one third-stop increments (one stop over and one stop under) will reveal whether the camera's exposure meter is calibrated correctly: the best exposure should be the one in the middle. A sequence of the same exposure at different combinations of shutter speed and aperture will help you to check if these settings are constant; in practice they should all be identical. Use colour transparency film and a high-powered magnifier to judge the results. ▶

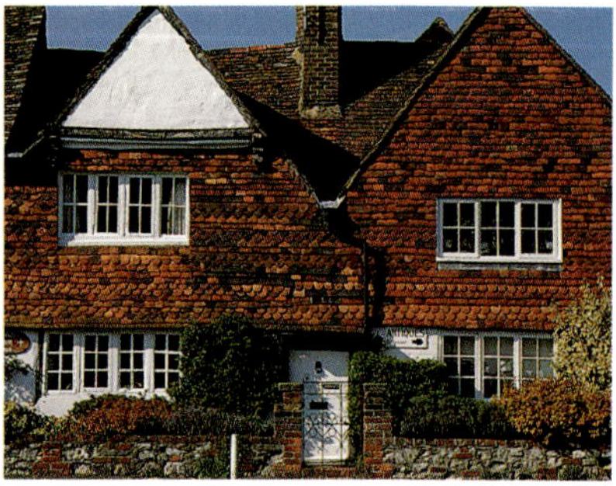

Underexposed transparency.

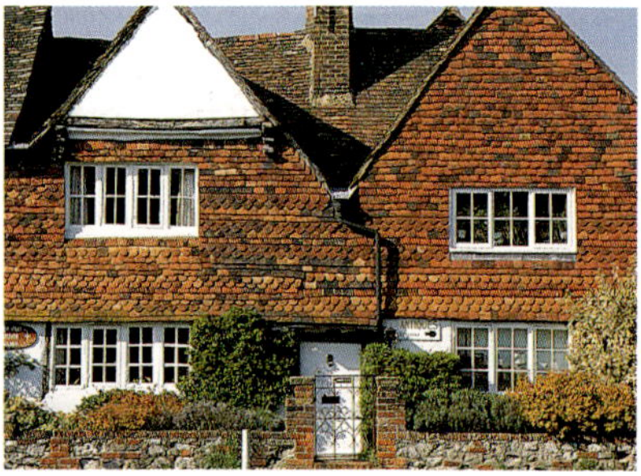

Correctly exposed transparency.

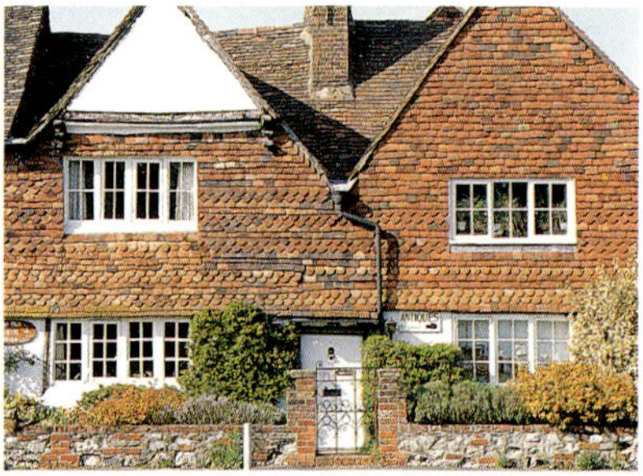

Overexposed transparency.

1.09 ●● The shutter speed at which a camera will synchronise with flash can vary widely, from 1/30 sec to 1/1000 sec. For normal flash pictures it is not particularly relevant, but when flash is combined with ambient light, for example when fill-in flash is used, it is often necessary to use fast shutter speeds, and the ability to synchronise flash at speeds of 1/250 sec or less can be vital. Many cameras with focal plane shutters will synchronise at speeds of only 1/60 sec or slower, but some manufacturers of these types of camera make special lenses with leaf shutters, which will synchronise at all speeds in order to overcome this problem.

1.10 Photography on trips or holidays, when you are away from home for a fairly long time, makes the periodic checking of cameras and equipment essential if you want to avoid potential problems. The following routine will help:

- Every other day or so, when you have unloaded the camera, look through the open back and fire a few frames to check that the shutter is opening and closing as it should. In the case of an SLR, check that the mirror is flipping up correctly and the iris is stopping down to its selected setting.
- Change the shutter speed as you do the above checks to ensure that there is a corresponding change in the time the shutter remains open.
- Check that no hair is trapped in the film gate and the lens and filter surfaces are free from smears and dust.
- When using flash, check through the open back of the camera to make sure that the flash is synchronising correctly with the shutter opening and closing.
- If you have more than one camera, cross check the exposure readings given from the same subject with the same film speed setting.
- If you have only one camera body, periodically take a reading from an average-toned distant scene in bright sunlight to ensure that the reading indicates something in the region of 1/250 sec at an aperture of f11 with the film speed set to ISO 100.

1.11 Don't wait until the penlight batteries in your camera or flash gun become too weak to power the camera's functions or the flash. Once the batteries become sluggish, replace them with fresh cells and use up what remains of the power in the old batteries in something much less demanding, like a pocket calculator.

1.12 When you buy a camera bag, choose one which has a little more space than you need. Although a neatly packed bag may seem ideal at the beginning of a session, it is hard to keep it that way during a shoot and you may find that things will not fit back easily into it while you are in the throes of inspiration.

PRACTICAL HINTS

- ☐ I carry a couple of polythene bags in my camera bag, a black one in which to store exposed films (the liner from a packet of bromide paper is ideal) and another for keeping all the empty packaging that is invariably generated by a busy day's photography.
- ☐ A useful tip to enable you to save space in your camera bag is to fit two small lenses into the same compartment, whenever possible. Super glue the small lenses' rear lens caps together, back-to-back, thus effectively making one lens out of two.

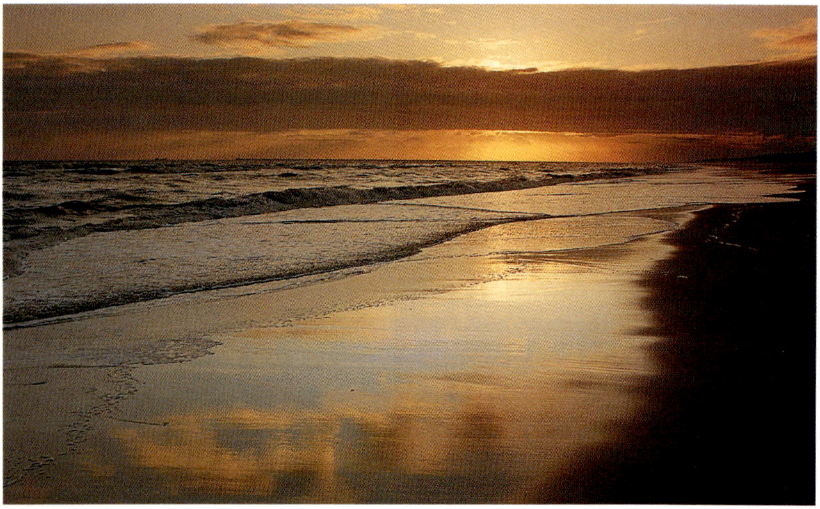

The beach is a hazardous environment for camera equipment.

PRACTICAL HINT

- To protect your camera from possible damage by water, cover the camera with a plastic bag leaving only a hole for the lens to see through. Hold the bag in place with a rubber band. Cling film is also useful in this context.

1.13 ● Water can harm modern cameras, and shooting in rain requires some special consideration. Sea spray, in particular, can seriously damage equipment because salt water is corrosive. ▲

1.14 ● A useful way to unscrew a stuck filter or lens attachment is to press its front rim firmly on to a soft, gripping surface, like a rubber mat, and twist. Holding the edges can distort the shape of a thin metal filter holder and make it more difficult to remove.

1.15 ● In hazardous or dusty environments, such as a beach, place each individual piece of equipment inside a polythene bag within your camera bag, removing them only when needed and replacing them immediately afterwards. At the end of a session like this, turn out the bag completely and remove all traces of dust, sand and debris, then carefully clean surfaces and contact points of loose grit, first with a blower brush or an aerosol Dust Off, and second with a cleaning cloth like selvyt or microfibre. For stubborn smears, sealed sachets of moist tissues can be very useful.

1.16 ● It is a good idea, when your cameras and accessories are not in use regularly, to tape over the electrical connections, for example the motor drive terminal and the camera flash synchronisation socket.

1.17 ●● The small diffusion boxes, sold to fit over on-camera flash guns to provide a softer source of light, are really only effective when used quite close to a subject. At distances of more than 50cm, a 30cm-square diffuser, for instance, will become progressively harder until, at about 3 metres, its effect will be little different from the undiffused flash. Small diffusion boxes can, however, help to overcome the problem of red eye. ▼

1.18 ● When choosing a flash gun, buy the most powerful you can afford. Although many small flash guns have an adequate guide number when direct flash is used at reasonably close quarters, their limitation soon becomes apparent when you wish to use bounced flash, a soft-box or to photograph more distant subjects. In addition, when a flash gun is constantly discharging its maximum power the recycling time can become unbearably long, especially when you are photographing people or events.

1.19 ● Many cameras now have a hot shoe instead of a socket for a flash lead, preventing the use of off-camera flash lighting. You can buy a simple, inexpensive adapter which slips into the hot shoe, providing a conventional socket for greater flexibility.

1.20 ●● While flash equipment is by far the most popular choice for studio photography, don't overlook the advantages of continuous light, like

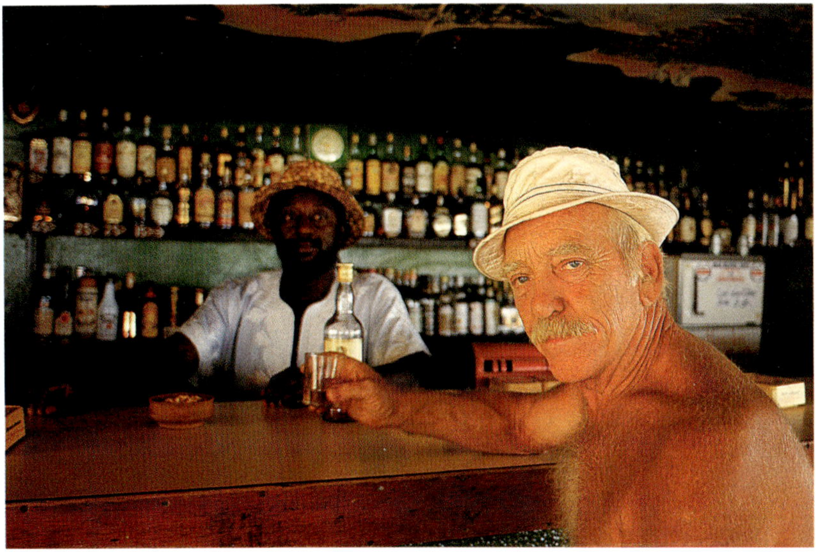

A diffused flash creates a more pleasing light, but needs quite a powerful flash gun.

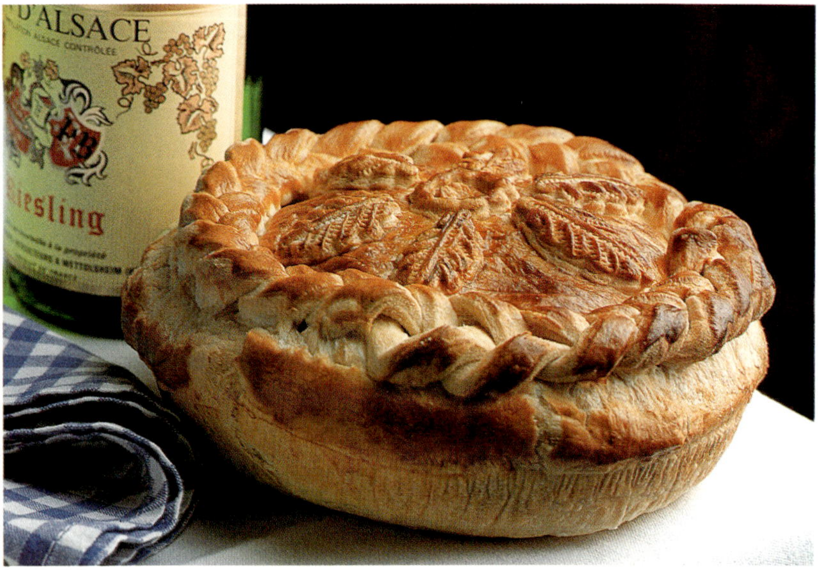

photofloods, especially if you are interested in still-life and close-up photography. The power of a particular flash unit determines the aperture needed to give the correct exposure, and small monobloc units may not allow a small enough aperture to obtain sufficient depth of field. With halogen or tungsten lights, however, you can select the preferred aperture and use a longer exposure to compensate. Remember that you can use a conventional exposure meter with continuous lighting, but you will need a special meter for flash. ▲

1.21 • For some makes of flash gun it is possible to purchase separate rechargeable power units which allow a much faster recycling time and many more flashes per charge than either batteries or the normal rechargeable nickel cadmium cells supplied with the flash gun.

PRACTICAL HINT

- Cameras with small built-in flashes can be used to fire a separate flash gun for angled or bounce flash lighting by the use of a slave cell. This is a small light-sensitive cell with fits into the separate flash gun's synch-lead socket and which will trigger it instantaneously when the small in-camera flash is fired. If you do not want the light from the in-camera flash to influence the picture, use a piece of tracing paper, or tissue, to reduce its brightness.

1.22 ●● Shooting into the light can produce pictures with a distinctive and very pleasing quality, but you will need to take measures to avoid the potential hazard of lens flare. While a lens hood or compendium is adequate for many situations it may not provide sufficient shading when the sun is very close to the edge of the frame. I have made up a small gadget using a flexible arm (the type used for table lamps) and a couple of bulldog clips. One of these holds the device on to the camera or tripod and the other end grips a large piece of black card or plastic. I can then bend the flexible arm so that the card is held right up to the edge of the frame, providing the maximum possible protection. ▼

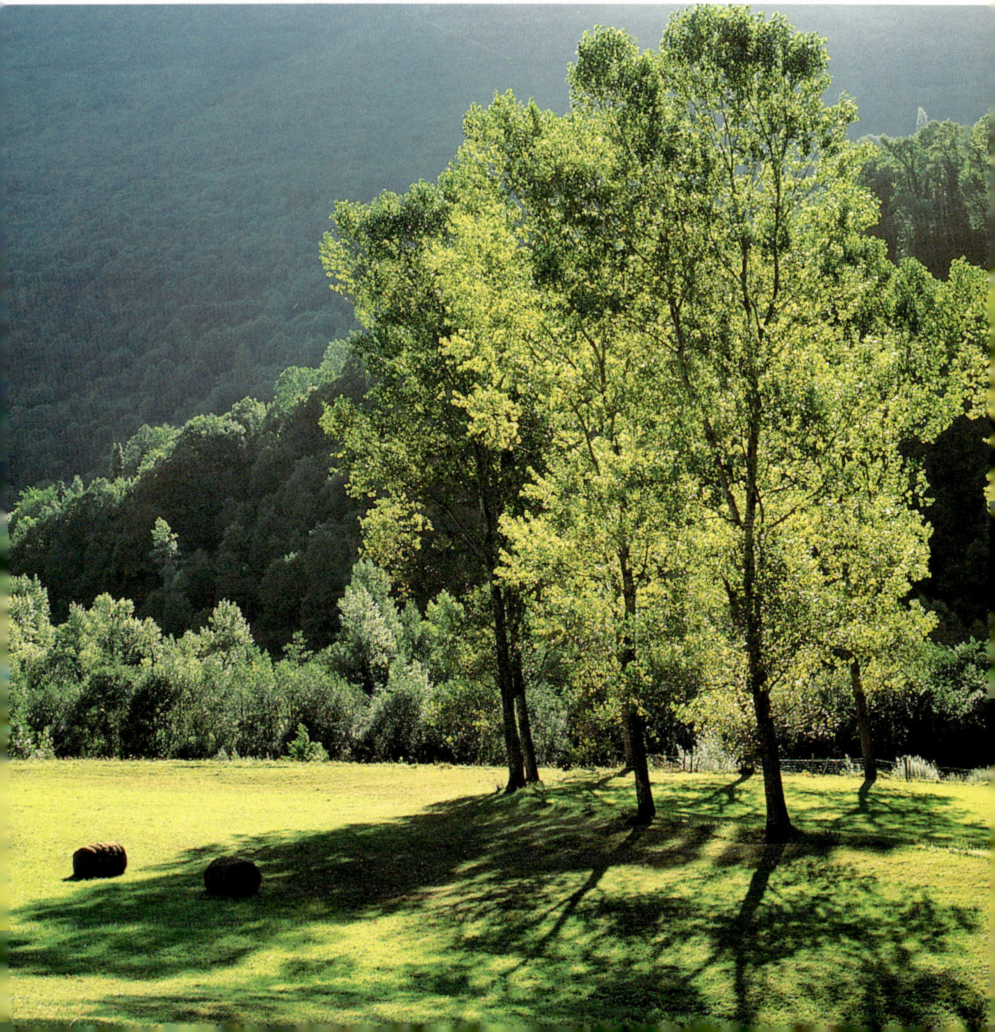

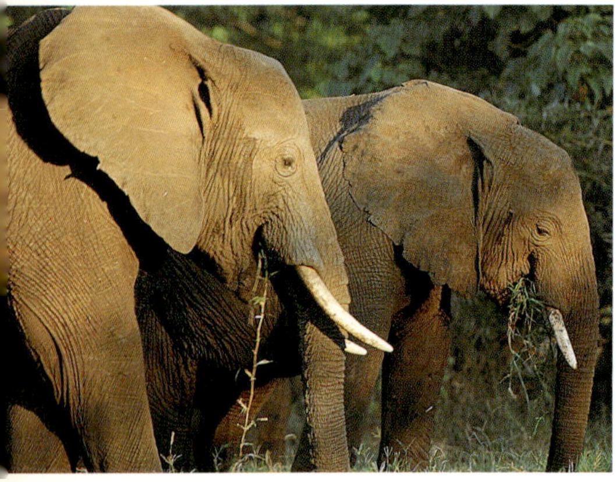

1.23 ● There are a few items that I always carry in my camera bag, which have proved invaluable from time to time:

- A couple of jeweller's screwdrivers, including a Phillips, for tightening loose fittings on lenses and on camera bodies
- Piece of lens cleaning cloth and a few sachets of moistened tissues for removing stubborn smears
- Small roll of gaffer tape, a chinagraph pencil and a felt-tip pen for marking exposed films
- Small torch for those occasions when the light level is too low to read the camera settings
- Note book
- Mini tape-recorder
- Spirit level
- Compass
- Small plastic mirror for reading the settings when the camera is up high on the tripod
- Swiss army knife which, among other things, has a magnifying glass, a small pair of pliers, tweezers and a corkscrew!

1.24 ● A bean bag can be useful for helping to steady a hand-held camera against a support, like a car window, a tree or wall, when slow shutter speeds are used and when it is not convenient to use a tripod. ◀

1.25 ●● One of the main advantages of a view camera is that the front and rear movements can be used to create a wide range of sharp focus images, much more than can be obtained by using a small aperture for maximum depth of field. You can achieve a similar effect with roll film and a 35mm camera by using a split close-up lens

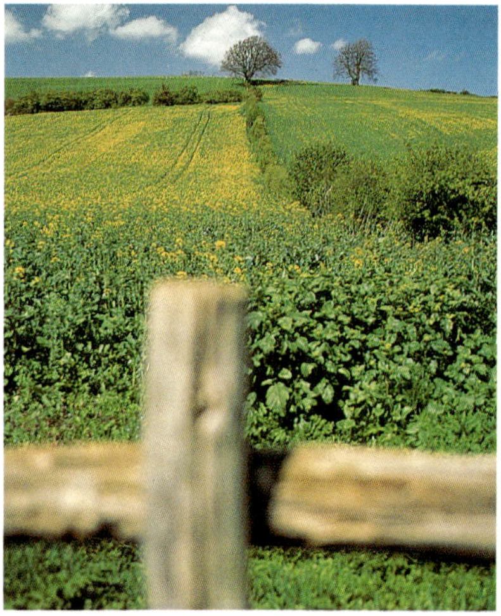

Limited depth of field has resulted in the foreground of this shot being unsharp.

which works in a similar way to bifocal spectacles. Take care, when you frame the shot, to ensure that you position the cut edge of the close-up lens over an area of the image where it will not be noticeable. The 'join' will be less obvious if you select a fairly wide aperture. ▼

1.26 ● Many photographers, including the most experienced, worry that they have not packed everything needed for a day's shoot, or a trip away; the omission of even small, seemingly insignificant, items can cause major problems. A check list is the one certain way to overcome such difficulties and will help to ensure that you have appropriate equipment to hand for every task. As well as using a list to help you pack your camera bag, you can also have lists for more specific shoots. For a small cost, these can be laminated, then you can tick specific items with an erasable marker pen as you pack them.

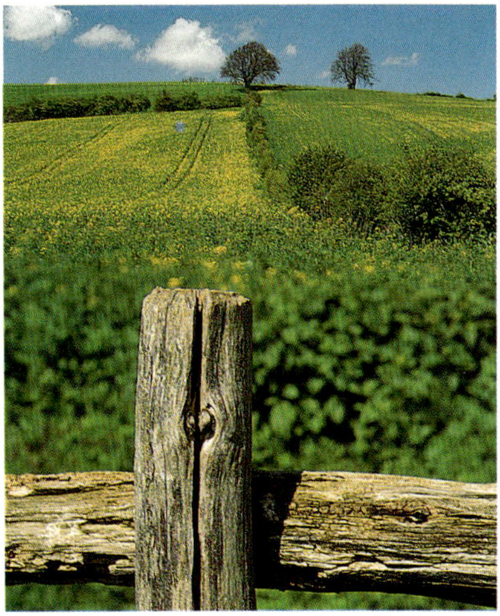

Using a split close-up lens enables foreground and distant details to be recorded sharply.

TECHNICAL TIP

- If you shoot in colour when making tests, it is best to use transparency film since subtle variations in image quality and exposure are much easier to see and assess than when viewing colour negatives or prints. Record the information concerning each exposure, with the appropriate frame number, before you make the tests and shoot to the list. This avoids the risk of subsequently forgetting the order in which the tests were carried out.

1.27 ● For each new piece of equipment you acquire, I would advise you to make tests. Whether it is a lens, a filter or a new camera, the information gained can be very useful and you will lessen the risk of disappointing results, or making mistakes, when using the item to take an important shot. Just a dozen or so exposures of an average subject on a roll of film is often enough.

PRACTICAL HINT

- When you choose a tripod, ensure that you can use it comfortably at eye level for most subjects without having to use the centre column. Tripods are much less rigid when the centre column is extended.

1.28 ● A tripod is the one accessory which can make the greatest difference to image sharpness. Few of the photographers who habitually hand-hold their cameras have any idea of exactly how sharp their lenses really are. If you do not have a tripod, any form of solid support is better than hand-holding when using slower shutter speeds. Prop the camera against a tree or fence, or support it on one knee, and rest your elbow on the camera, for example.

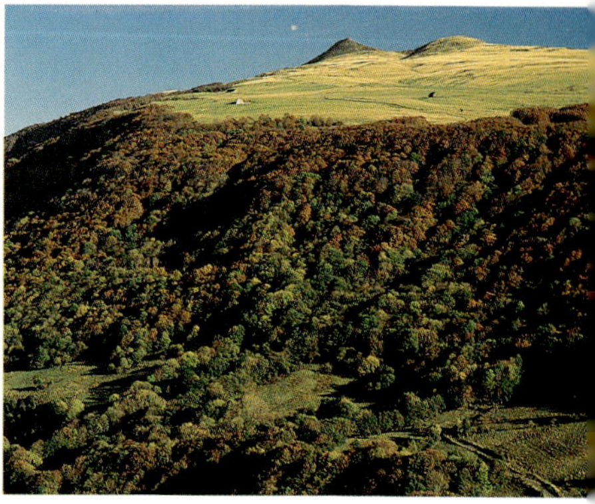

This was shot on a long-focus lens, with the camera tripod mounted, to ensure a critically sharp image.

1.29 ●● Although a ball and socket tripod head offers the maximum flexibility of adjustment, a pan-and-tilt top gives more precise control and is a better choice for static subjects like still-life and landscapes. You can use the sideways tilt to ensure that the horizon is level and then lock it before using the forward tilt and pan movement to adjust the image's lateral and vertical framing independently.

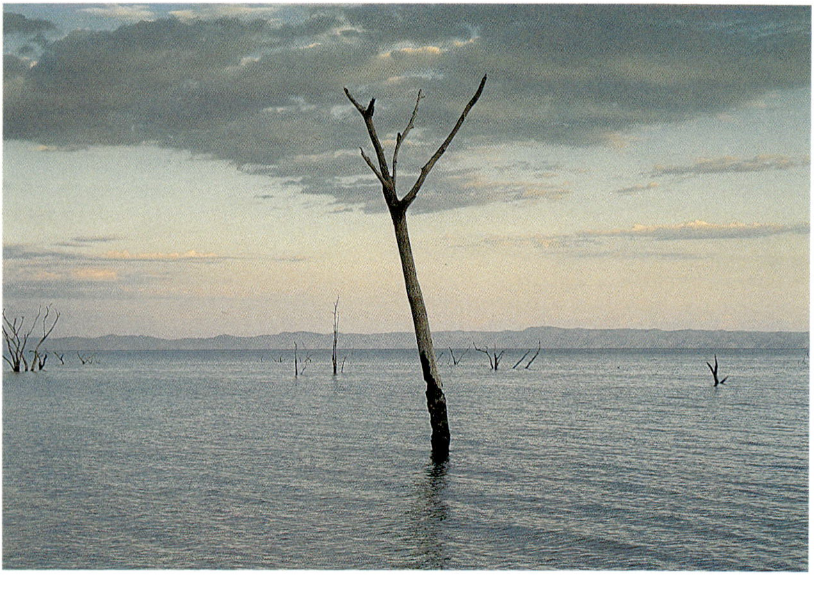

1.30 ● You can improve the effectiveness of a tripod when using long-focus lenses by taking up play with a hooked elastic rope (the type used for securing luggage on car roof-racks). Simply hook one end on to the bottom of the tripod's centre column, take it round the lens barrel and then hook the other end on to the same place. This is particularly useful in windy conditions, and you can gain extra stability by making a strong wire hook and suspending your loaded camera bag from the centre of the tripod. ◀

1.31 ● Many tripods do not readily allow the camera to be supported close to the ground, so for this purpose a small table-top tripod is more convenient, especially as it fits easily into a small camera bag. If the table-top tripod is fitted with a ball-and-socket head, it is also a useful way to hold a camera firm against a vertical surface, such as a wall or tree trunk, when a conventional tripod is not available.

1.32 ● Photographs of subjects such as landscapes can be spoilt if the horizon line is not completely level. A spirit level will help to avoid this hazard but, if you have a camera with a removable viewfinder screen, replace it with one which has a grid. Alternatively, simply draw a thin pencil line across the centre of the screen, ensuring that it is completely parallel to the sides. ◀

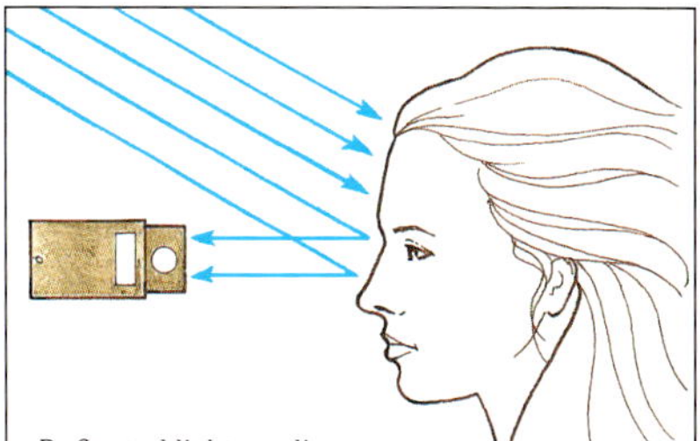
Reflected light reading

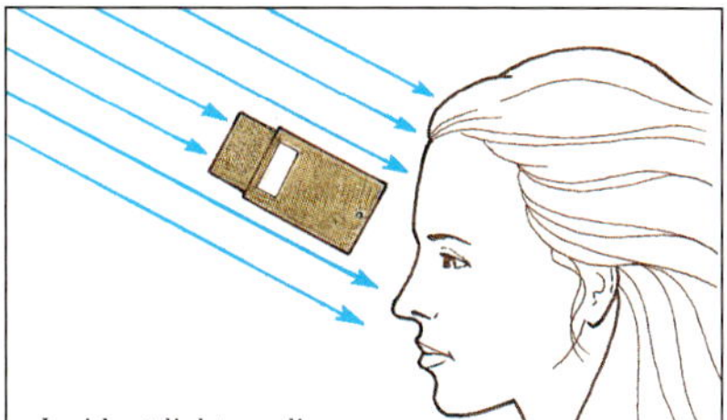
Incident light reading

1.33 ●● Although most modern cameras are equipped with a built-in exposure meter, a separate hand-held meter can be useful for taking an incident light reading from subjects which are abnormally dark or light in tone. The meter measures the light that falls on an object rather than the light reflected from it, a measurement that is especially useful for close-up subjects like portraits, copies and still-life. Hold the meter directly in front of the subject and aim it towards the camera or light source. ▶

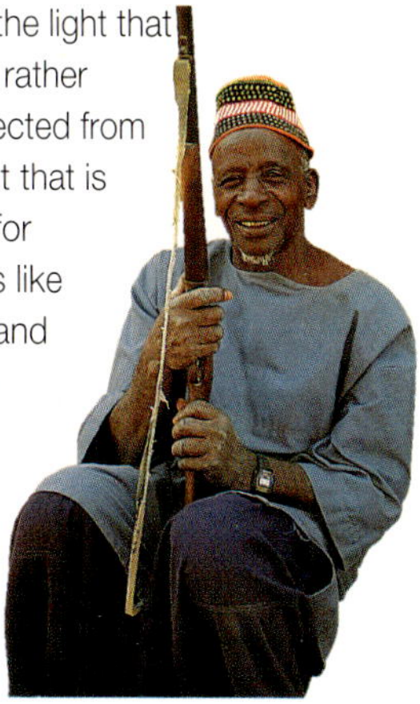

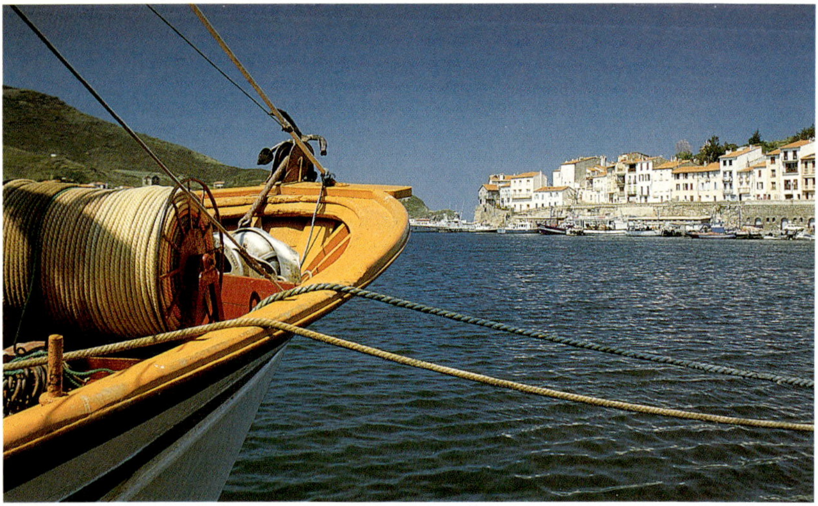

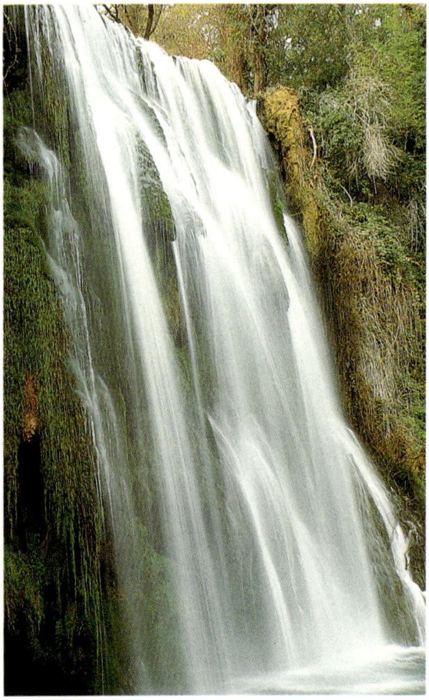

Two crossed polarising filters were used to allow an exposure of several seconds on this shot.

1.34 Using filters with wide-angle lenses can often cause vignetting, (the darkening of the corners of the image), especially when more than one filter is used or with ultra wide-angle lenses. You can buy special wide-angle filters from some manufacturers; B&W for instance, has a filter size significantly larger than the lens and filter thread diameter. Alternatively, buy filters of a larger diameter and use step-up rings so that you can fit them to a smaller-sized lens. ▲

TECHNICAL TIP

- Use two polarising filters placed one in front of the other and rotated as a continuously variable neutral density filter in situations when a slower shutter speed is required than is permitted by the lighting conditions.

1.35 ●● Polarising filters are some of the most useful accessories, but they can influence the metering and autofocus systems of some cameras. This is most likely to occur with a linear polariser and you may, therefore, find it preferable to use a circular polarising filter to overcome this problem.

1.36 ●● If you use a warm-up filter, such as an 81C, to reduce a blue cast in the foreground of landscape pictures, it can sometimes make the sky too yellow. Some manufacturers make graduated colour balancing filters; these can be useful in altering the colour of the foreground without affecting the sky.

1.37 ● A good stock of spare batteries is vital for today's photographer. Buy a well-known brand from a reliable supplier who has a fast turnover, and mark each packet clearly with the date of purchase to ensure that you use them before they become stale.

1.38 ●● Some manufacturers produce dual-function filters, for example a polariser or neutral density graduated filter combined with a warm-up filter. You may find this preferable to using two separate filters, as a number of filters placed in front of the lens can have an adverse effect on the definition, particularly with long-focus lenses. ▼

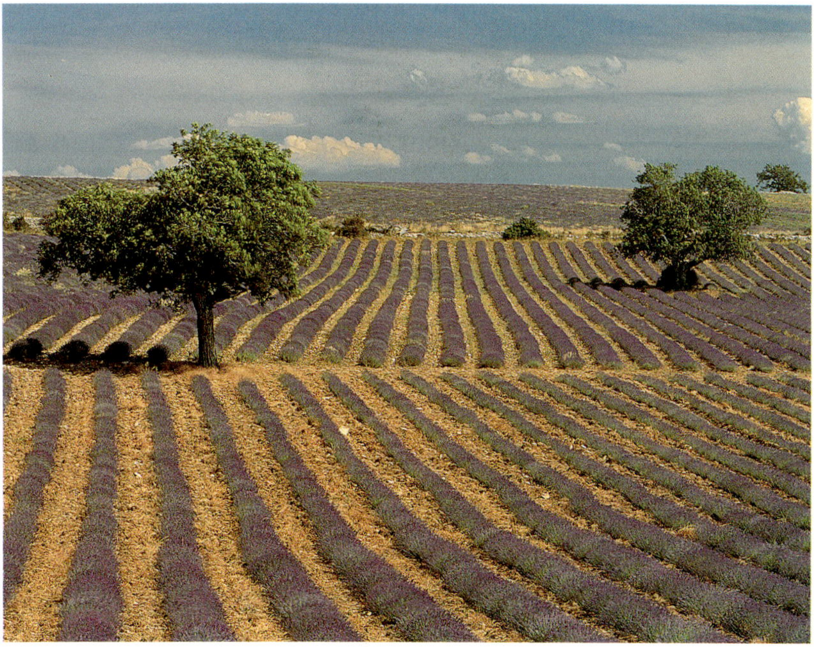

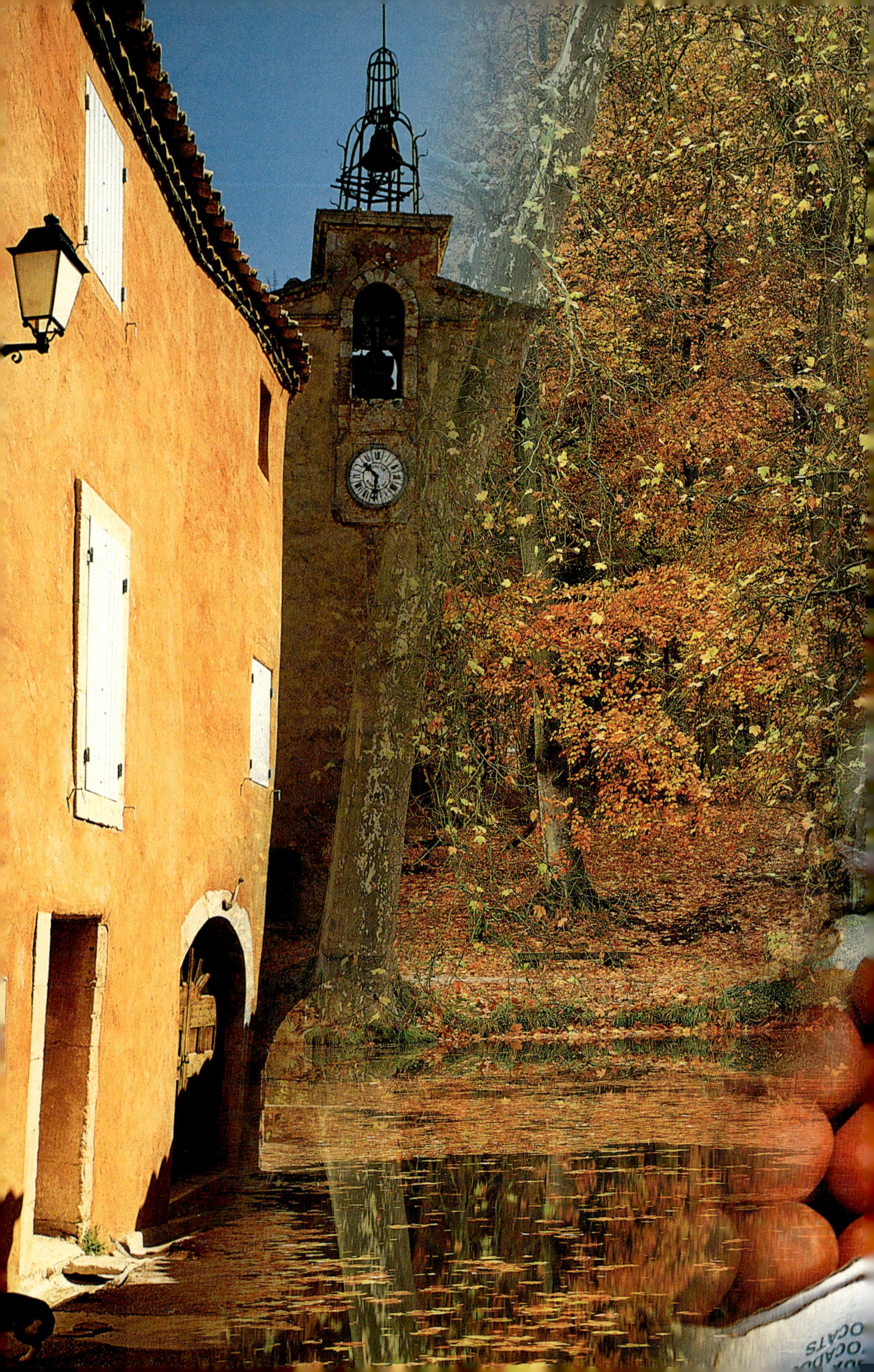

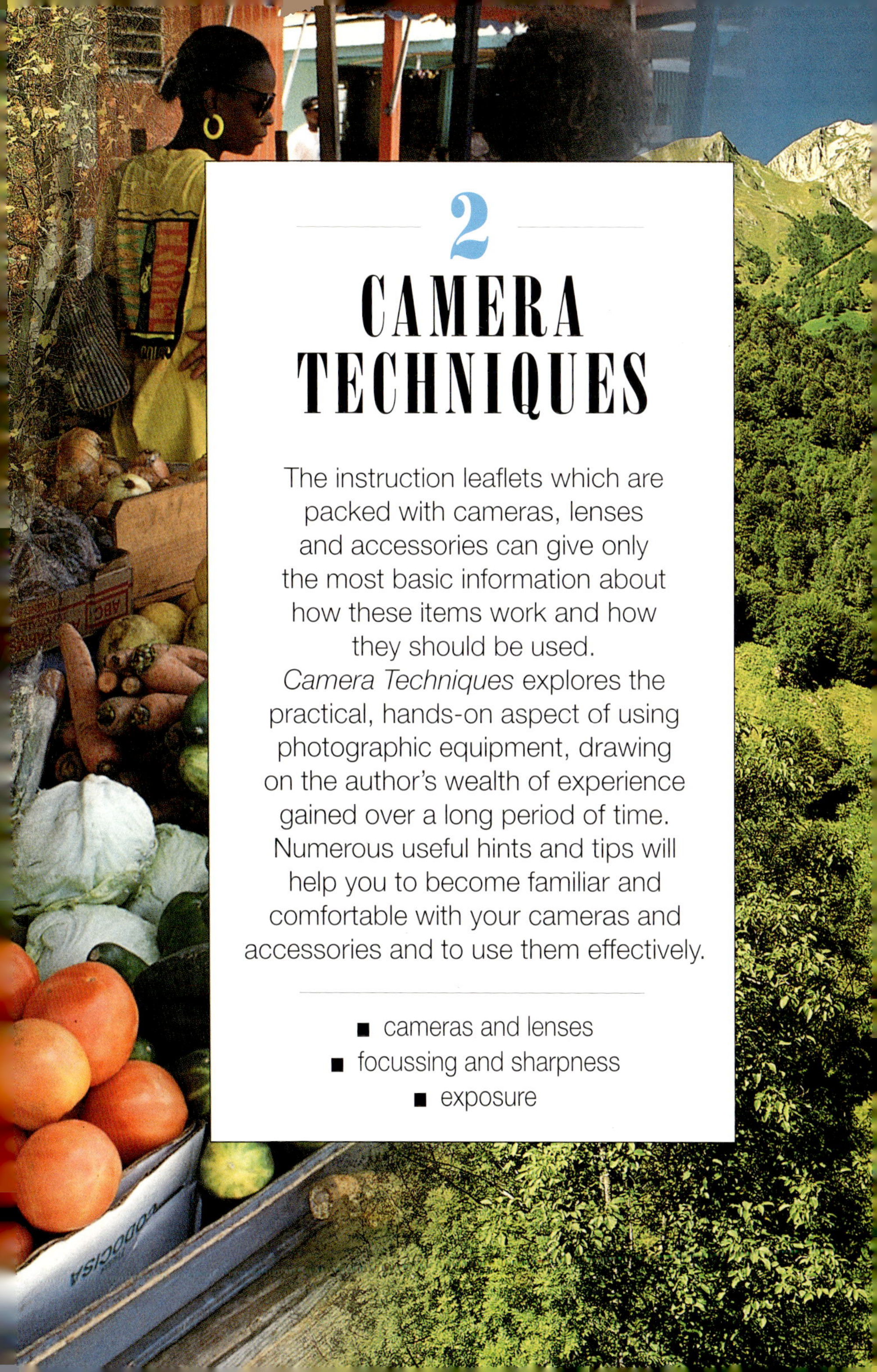

2

CAMERA TECHNIQUES

The instruction leaflets which are packed with cameras, lenses and accessories can give only the most basic information about how these items work and how they should be used. *Camera Techniques* explores the practical, hands-on aspect of using photographic equipment, drawing on the author's wealth of experience gained over a long period of time. Numerous useful hints and tips will help you to become familiar and comfortable with your cameras and accessories and to use them effectively.

- cameras and lenses
- focussing and sharpness
- exposure

2 Cameras and Lenses

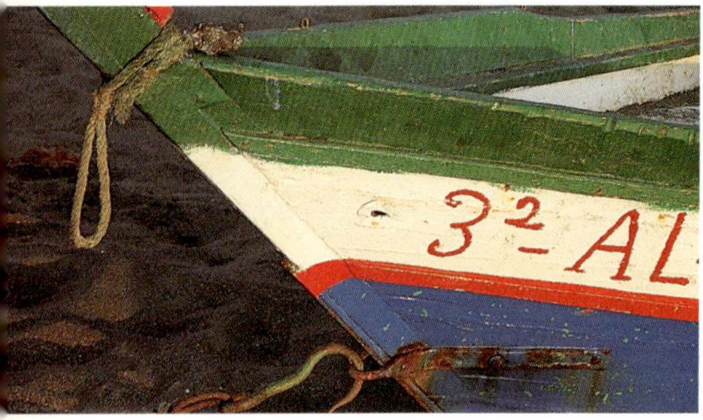

2.01 ● With compact cameras there is usually a wide safety margin in the viewfinder and this is why, when you see the final photograph, the subject is often smaller than expected. To overcome this, it is often best to move closer to your subject so that it fills the frame right to the edge. ▲

2.02 ● To ensure that the film in manually-wound cameras is loaded properly, check that the film-rewind knob rotates as you wind on to the first frame. The frame indicator will usually advance each time the winder is moved, even if the film is not being wound on.

2.03 ●● You can guarantee the maximum degree of sharpness when using a tripod-mounted SLR camera with slower shutter speeds only by using a mirror lock. The vibrations caused by the mirror flipping up can produce a noticeable loss of definition, especially when lenses of more than double the standard focal length are fitted to the camera. ▼

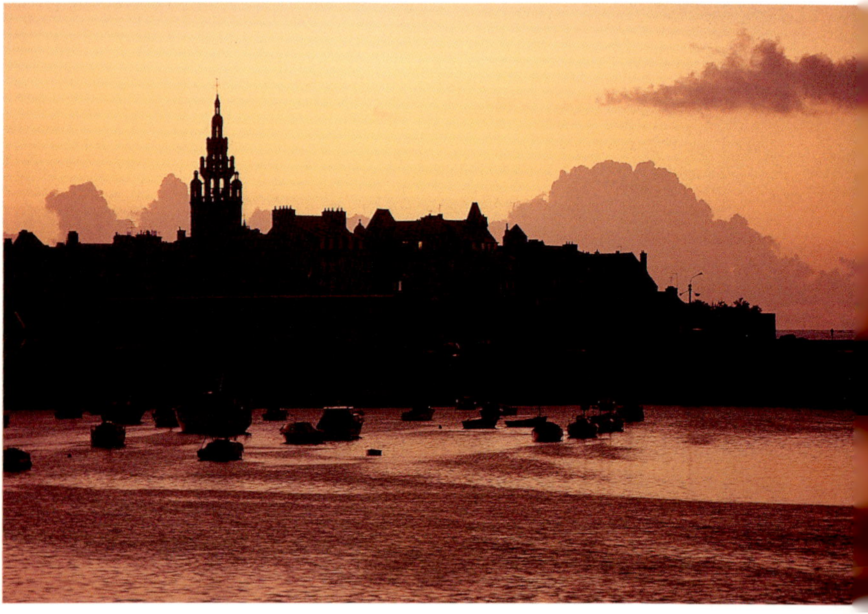

2.04 ● Acquire a professional photographer's almost instinctive way of using a camera by establishing a standard working procedure in which you follow the same steps each time you take a photograph. This can be designed to suit individual preferences and cameras, but a good sequence is as follows:

① Frame and focus the image.

② Set the exposure.

③ Fit filters, if needed.

④ Change lens and alter framing, if necessary.

⑤ Select the best viewpoint.

⑥ Modify the exposure, if necessary.

⑦ If the picture won't improve by waiting – shoot!

2.05 ● When unloading a used film from a 35mm camera, make sure you wind back all the film into the cassette. This will avoid the risk of mistaking it for an unused roll and exposing the film twice.

PRACTICAL HINT

□ To establish the difference between the area of a subject shown in the viewfinder and that actually recorded on the film, remove the film, open the camera back and, with the shutter held open on the time setting, place a piece of tracing paper in the film plane. Although the image you see will be reversed left to right and upside down, you can make a direct comparison between the two views.

2.06 ●● Always use a cable release with a tripod-mounted camera set for slower shutter speeds. The delayed release facility on many cameras provides a useful alternative, and a radio or an infrared (IR) remote release is an even better option to ensure that the camera is not jarred when the shutter is tripped.

2.07 ●● To change to a different type of film before you have finished exposing the one in the camera, follow these steps:

① Make a note of the frame number, then wind the film back, stopping as soon as it is free from the take-up spool.

② Write the frame number which had been reached in marking pen on the film leader.

③ When you want to continue shooting with this film, reload it as usual.

④ Check that the lens cap is in position, then fire and wind on until you reach one frame further (for a safety margin) – and you're ready to go.

2.08 ● The maximum safe shutter speed for hand-holding a camera should be a fraction of the focal length of the lens being used, ie. with a 250mm lens the maximum safe shutter speed is 1/250 sec; with a 35mm lens the maximum safe shutter speed is 1/30 sec. This applies to photographers who have a good grip and a steady hand; others should consider halving or quartering these shutter speeds.

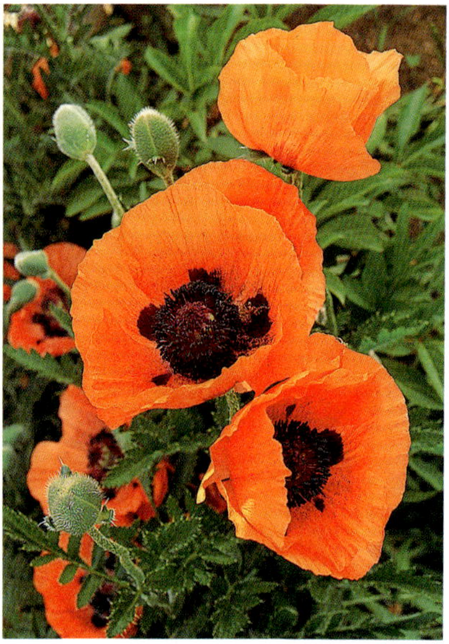

2.09 ● When shooting in bright daylight, especially when using roll film, you should always try to find a darker area in which to change films to prevent the risk of fogging. As a last resort, turn your back to the sun and use the shade of your body.

2.10 ● Changing partly used 35mm films can be difficult, as many cameras with autowinders automatically take all the film back into the cassette. You can usually prevent this by opening the camera back as soon as you hear the film release from the take-up spool. If this method fails, you can buy a film leader retriever from a good photographic store, which will recover the film leader from its cassette.

2.11 ●● Taking close-up pictures with a viewfinder can be tricky because of the parallax error. This is the difference in viewpoint between the taking lens and the viewfinder lens, which results in an area of the subject slightly different from that seen in the viewfinder appearing on the film. If you use a tripod, you can overcome this difficulty by measuring the distance between the viewfinder and the taking lens, and making marks which represent this distance on the tripod's centre column. You can then frame your shot keeping the higher mark on the centre column level with the tripod top. Move the camera up by the marked distance, to align with the lower mark, and you are ready to make the exposure. ◀ ▲

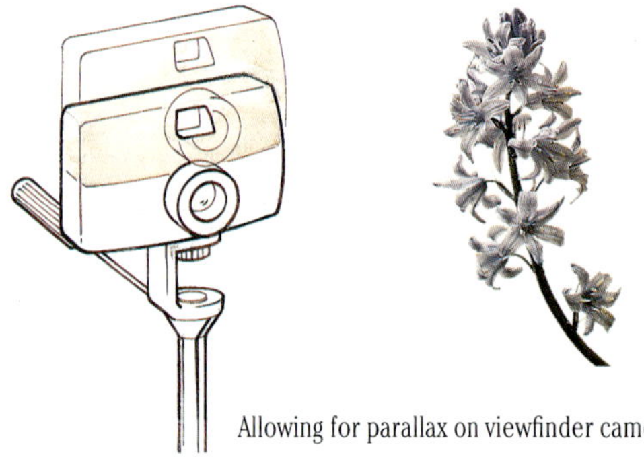

Allowing for parallax on viewfinder cameras

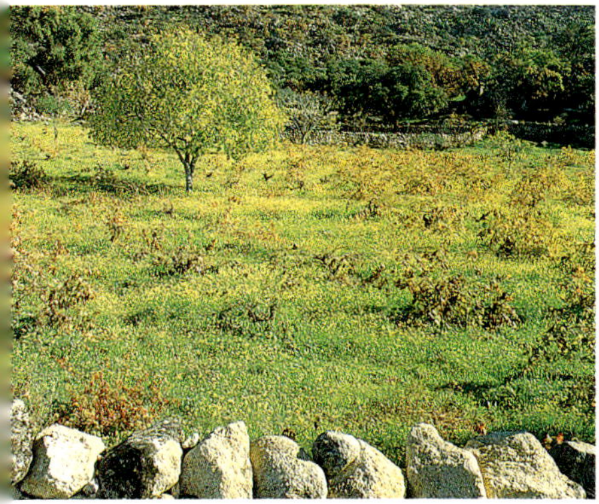

2.12 ●● You can ensure that you have maximum depth of field from foreground to distance by selecting the smallest aperture and focussing on the hyperfocal distance. This is indicated by the depth-of-field scale marked on the focussing mounts of most camera lenses. By setting the focus so the infinity mark is aligned with the aperture you are using, the lens will be focussed at the optimum point. The same depth-of-field scale will also show the nearest distance at which details will be sharp. ▲

2.13 ● The depth of field, when viewed in the stopped-down mode, it is likely to be less in the photograph than appears on the screen, but take into account the fact that the depth-of-field scale marked on the lens mount is relative to the size of the image. A photograph may appear to have sufficient depth of field when enlarged to 10 x 8in (25 x 20cm), but will lack sharpness in a 16 x 20in (40 x 50cm) print.

2.14 ● Action or sports subjects present a special problem in terms of focussing and sharpness of shots. Movement can be frozen by the use of fast shutter speeds and panning techniques, but it can be difficult to obtain precise focus on a rapidly moving subject, even with the new generation of autofocus lenses. Always try to anticipate the subject's direction of movement and focus on a predetermined spot, shooting the picture the instant the subject arrives there. You will find this easier to achieve if you use 'peak-of-the-action' moments when the subject's movements are either at their slowest or most dramatic, for example a horse jumping a fence, a formula-one car cornering, or a sprinter leaving the starting block or breasting the tape.

2.15 ● Remember when you calculate depth of field that it extends further behind the subject than in front of it, in the proportion of about one-third to two-thirds. At closer focussing distances this proportion diminishes, while for subjects very close to the camera it is about equal.

2.16 ● In the majority of photographs, the main area of interest is recorded sharply, but you can obtain interesting and atmospheric effects by using selective focus; only one specific area of the scene is brought into focus, leaving the

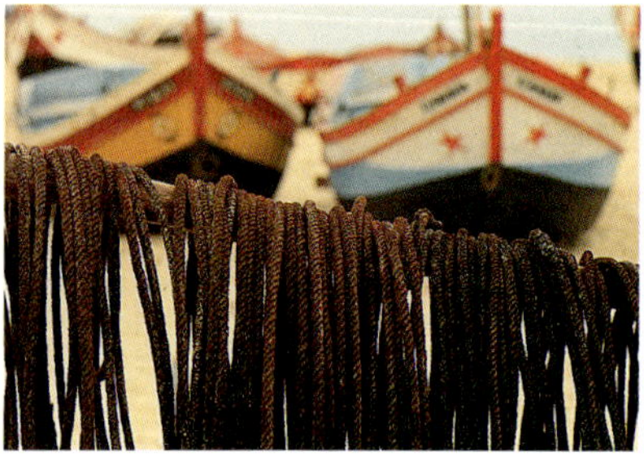

TECHNICAL TIP

- It is important that the unfocussed areas are very positively blurred and not just slightly out of focus, so you should use the widest possible aperture and, preferably, a long-focus lens.

remainder of the image blurred. A sharply focussed foreground with an out-of-focus background is often used in subjects like outdoor portraits, but a blurred foreground can add both atmosphere and interest to a sharply focussed distant view or building, for example. Conversely, it can be equally effective to focus on foreground subjects and allow distant details to remain out of focus. ▲▼

2.17 ●● If your camera does not have a depth-of-field preview setting it is often possible manually to stop down the lens to its preset aperture by unlocking and partly unscrewing it from the camera body.

2.18 ●● Some autofocus cameras have a focus-trap setting in which you can focus on a predetermined spot and press the shutter release; the camera will not allow the exposure to be made until the subject moves into sharp focus, when it trips automatically.

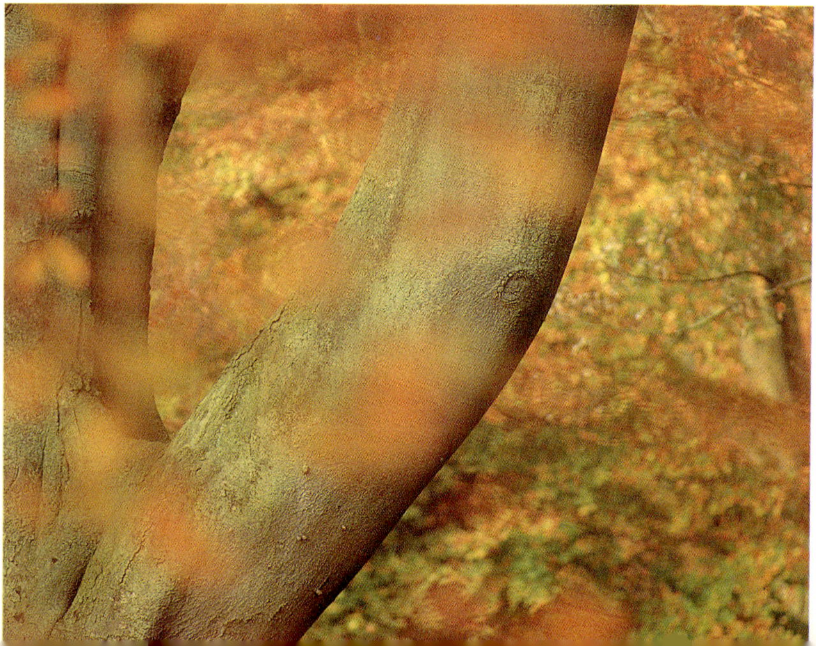

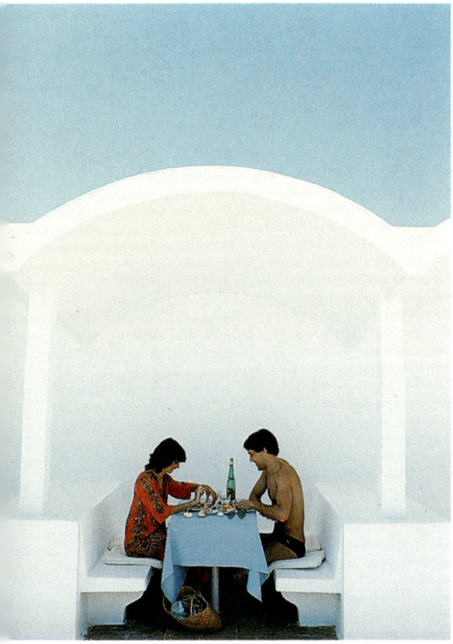

2.19 ● Many of today's cameras have a choice of metering modes which, if used wrongly, can often lead to disappointing results. For general use, the centre-weighted or matrix setting will give the optimum exposure for subjects of normal tone and contrast. The spot-metering mode should be used with caution as it measures only from the precise area indicated by a circle on the viewing screen and will ignore other tones. The averaging mode should not be used for subjects where there is a marked difference in brightness between the centre and borders of the frame unless an allowance is made.

2.20 ●● When you calculate exposures for a subject which has an abnormal tonal range or is predominantly light or dark, take a substitute reading from an object or area which approximates to the mid tone on the Kodak grey scale. Grass is one such useful substitute, or you can cut a piece of 18% Grey Card to the largest size which will fit in your camera bag. Make sure that, whatever you use as a substitute, it is illuminated in exactly the same way as the subject you intend to photograph. ◀ ▼

2.21 ●● In difficult lighting situations, or with subjects of abnormal tone, it can be useful to take a substitute exposure reading in the manner indicated above.

2.22 ● With an automatic camera you can change the film speed setting if you want to give extra or less exposure. ISO 100 film set to ISO 200 will give one stop less exposure, and if you set to ISO 50, it will give one stop more. Do remember, however, to return the setting to normal after taking the picture.

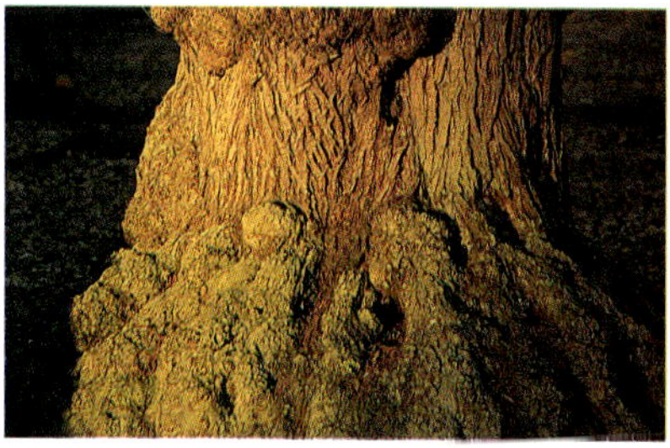

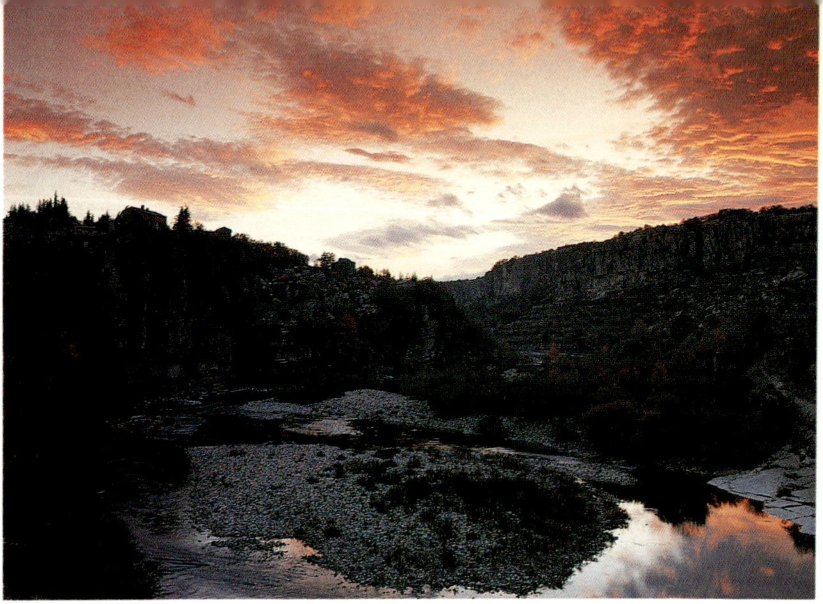

2.23 ● To photograph a bright sunset, take an exposure reading by aiming your camera at about 45 degrees towards the area of sky above the sunset. Make sure that the sun itself and the very brightest part of the sky is excluded. This will prevent it from recording too dark in tone and colour. ▲

2.24 ● It is always worth bracketing sunset pictures fairly widely, a stop or more lighter and darker in half-stop or one-third of a stop increments, especially when using transparency film. The colour quality of a sunset can vary considerably according to the exposure and will often produce quite different, but equally acceptable, results over a wide range of settings. ▼

2.25 ● If you are using a camera manually, there is a quick and easy way of bracketing exposures which avoids using a wider aperture and restricting depth of field. First, make one exposure at the correct setting, make

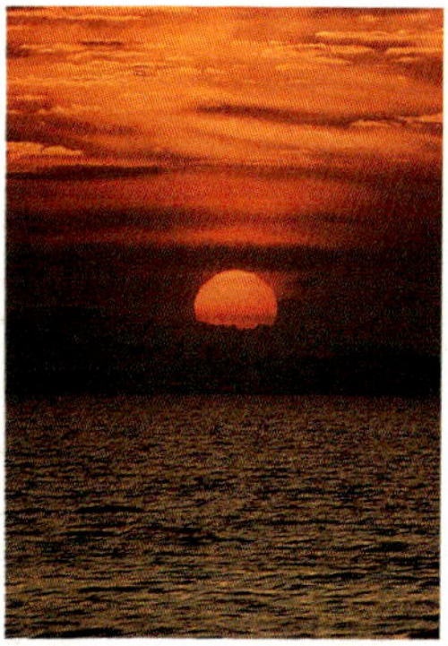

another at a half-stop smaller aperture, then alter the shutter speed to the next slowest setting (from 1/60 sec to 1/30 sec, for instance). For a wider bracket, stop down one whole stop after making the correct exposure, and then set the shutter to the next-but-one slower exposure (from 1/60 sec to 1/15 sec, for example) to give one stop extra.

2.26 ● When taking photographs of fairly distant subjects in mist or fog, give more exposure than is indicated by an averaging meter reading. In most circumstances an extra stop will suffice, but a more certain method is to take a substitute reading from a mid-toned object in the foreground. ▶

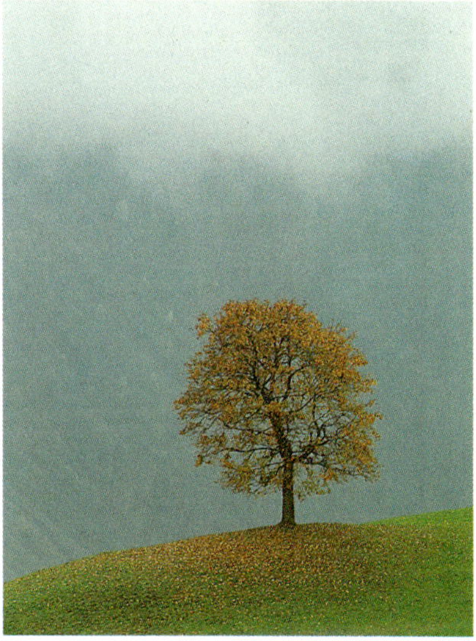

One stop more exposure than the indicated reading was given for this misty landscape.

2.27 ●● Use TTL metering with caution if you shoot black-and-white film with a deep coloured filter (such as red or blue), as these can cause the meter to give a misleading reading. It is safer to take the exposure reading without the filter, then simply increase the exposure by the stated filter factor. X2 filters require a one stop increase, X4 require two stops and X8 need three stops extra exposure.

2.28 ● It is easy to misjudge the potential contrast of a scene; the camera may record shadow areas as dark tones devoid of detail when, visually, they appear much lighter and open. A useful technique is to view such scenes through half-closed eyes, and this gives a far more accurate impression of the depth of any areas of shadow. An alternative method is to use the depth-of-field preview button, which is present on many SLR cameras, to view the subject at a small aperture, such as f11 or f16.

TECHNICAL TIP

- Many cameras have a spot-reading mode and this can be used to take a localised reading from a small section of the subject which has a more normal tonal range. Alternatively, you can extend a zoom lens to its narrowest field of view to take a selective reading from a more representative area of a scene, then pull back to recompose your picture.

2.29 Many modern cameras have built-in exposure systems which will produce a satisfactory exposure in average conditions. Most disappointing pictures occur when the photographer fails to notice that the conditions are not average and neglects to make a simple adjustment to the exposure setting. Four situations are most commonly the cause of such problems, and these are easily identified and corrected:

① A subject with more than about 20 per cent of very dark tones, or shadows, will need less exposure than indicated – as a rule of thumb half a stop less for each extra one-fifth proportion of dark tones. ▼

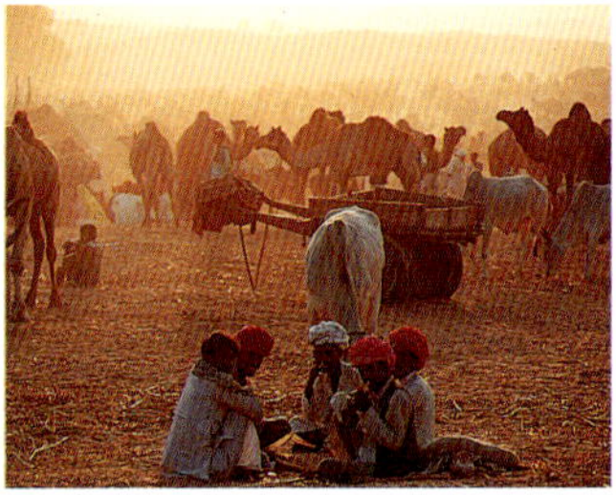

④ A strongly side-lit subject will need less exposure than indicated, between half a stop and one and a half stops less, depending upon the angle of the light and the amount of shadow created. ▼

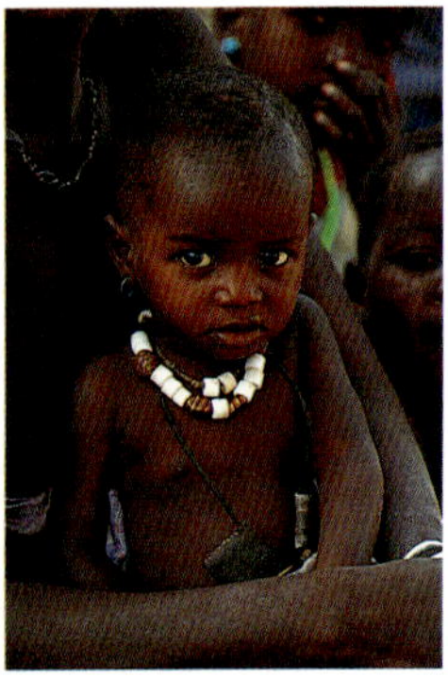

③ A strongly back-lit subject or a subject that includes bright light sources, will need more exposure than indicated – between one and two stops extra, depending upon the extent and brightness of the highlights created. ▲

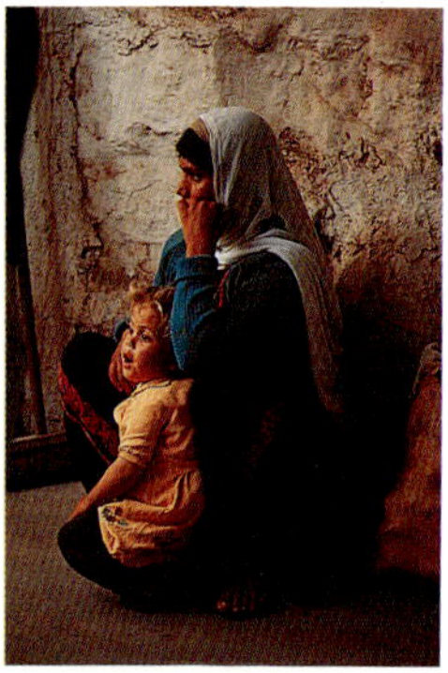

② A subject with more than about 20 per cent of very light tones will need more exposure than indicated – half a stop more for each extra one-fifth proportion of light tones. ▶

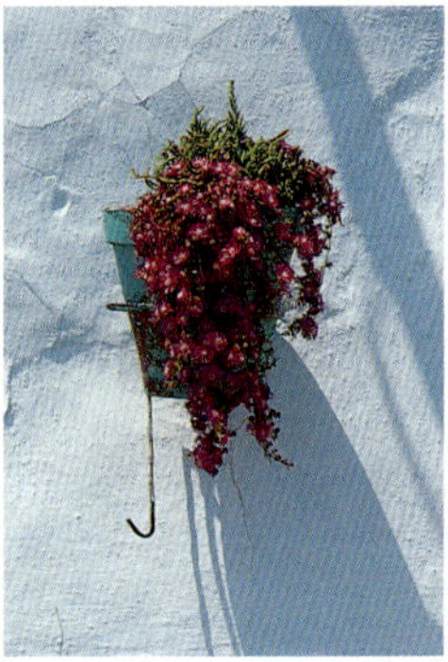

The effects occurring as a result of these situations can be exaggerated, compounding the problems, for example a back-lit bride in a white wedding dress, so make the appropriate allowance for such factors.

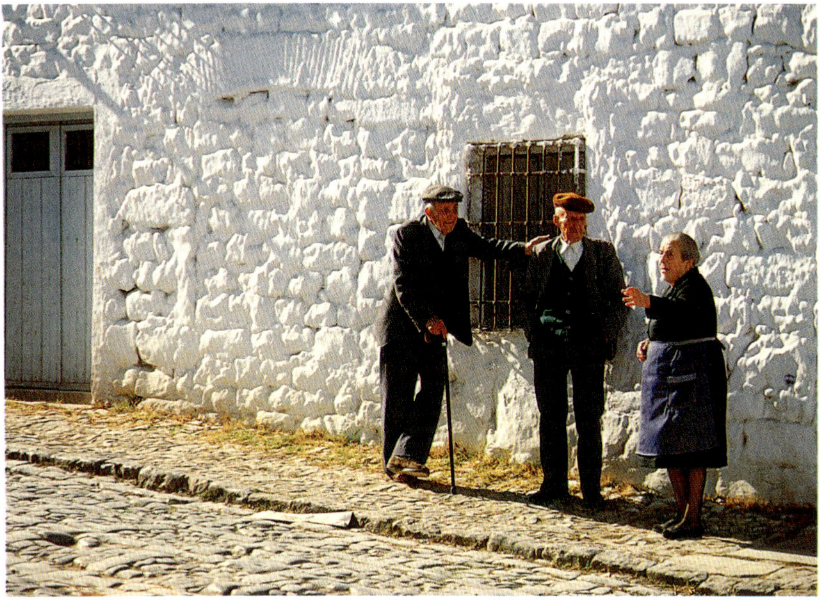

One and a half stops over the indicated reading were given to allow for the large area of sunlit white wall.

2.30 ● When judging the brightness of the tones in a subject to calculate exposure, you must also consider the colours. Bright colours, like yellow, can have an effect similar to a highlight on the exposure reading, and when there is a large expanse, like a field of sunflowers or rape or a wall, for instance, you should give more exposure to avoid underexposure.

PRACTICAL HINT

- ☐ When clip testing remember to shoot all the frames at the same exposure, keeping the light level constant. As a reminder, mark the change in film speed clearly on the cassette or film tongue with a marking pen, and indicate legibly on the packet in which you send the films to the lab by how much you want the film pushed or pulled.

2.31 ●● When taking photographs of an important or unrepeatable subject on colour transparency film, shoot a few frames at the end of the roll (or at the beginning of a 35mm cassette) which can be cut off and processed first. The remainder of the roll can be adjusted for any exposure errors by up to one stop darker and two stops or more lighter when it is processed. This is known as clip testing, one of the services offered by professional processing laboratories.

2.32 ●● You can learn a great deal about how your exposure meter works, and how to interpret its readings and use it to the best advantage by planning out a straightforward experiment:

① Set up a small still-life arrangement of objects of average tone and colour (a basket of vegetables or fruit would be ideal).

② Place it on a mid-toned background and light it fairly softly from a diffused source, at an angle of about 45 degrees to the camera.

③ Frame the image so that the subject occupies one-third of the viewfinder and take an exposure reading.

④ Now take readings with the still-life placed on a white background, a black background and from view points which allow the background to occupy both more and less of the image area.

By giving the subject the same exposure, regardless of these changes, the variations in the readings you obtain will show just how your particular metering system responds, and will help you to understand how you should modify its readings in different situations. ▶

2.33 ● When bracketing exposures for negative films, you need to vary the exposures in one-stop increments only, for all but the most exacting work. With colour transparency film, however, variations of one-third of a stop are far more satisfactory.

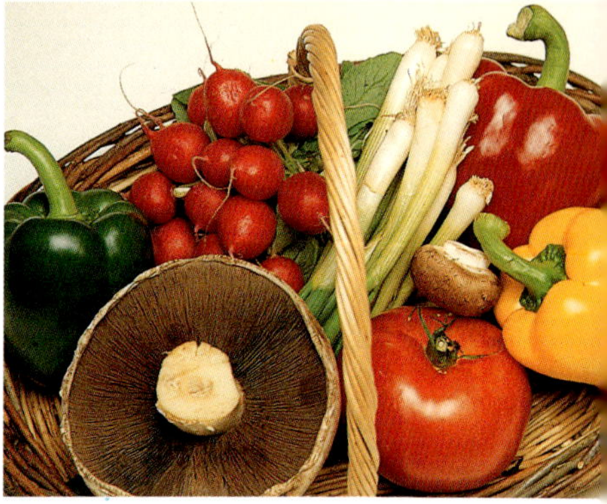

With the basket of vegetables almost filling the frame, the indicated exposure gave a correctly exposed transparency.

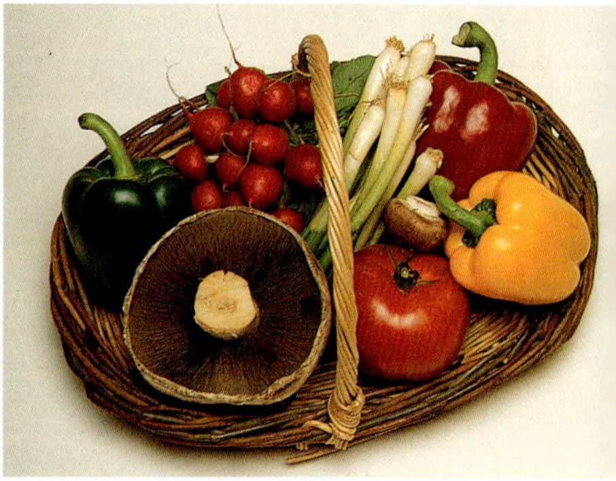

The additional area of white background caused the subject to be underexposed by half a stop.

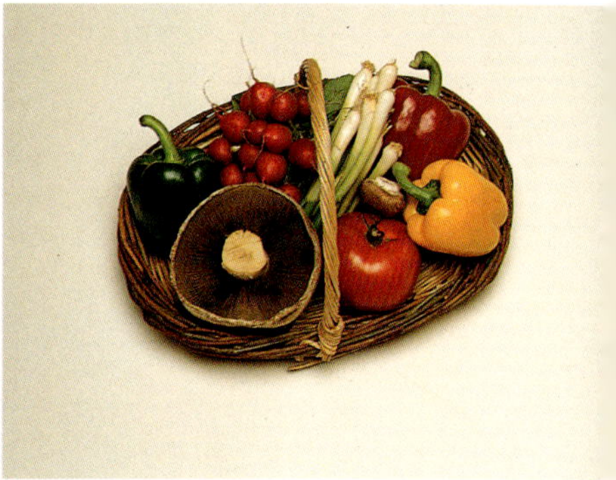

The large area of white background indicated an exposure which resulted in the vegetables being underexposed by one stop.

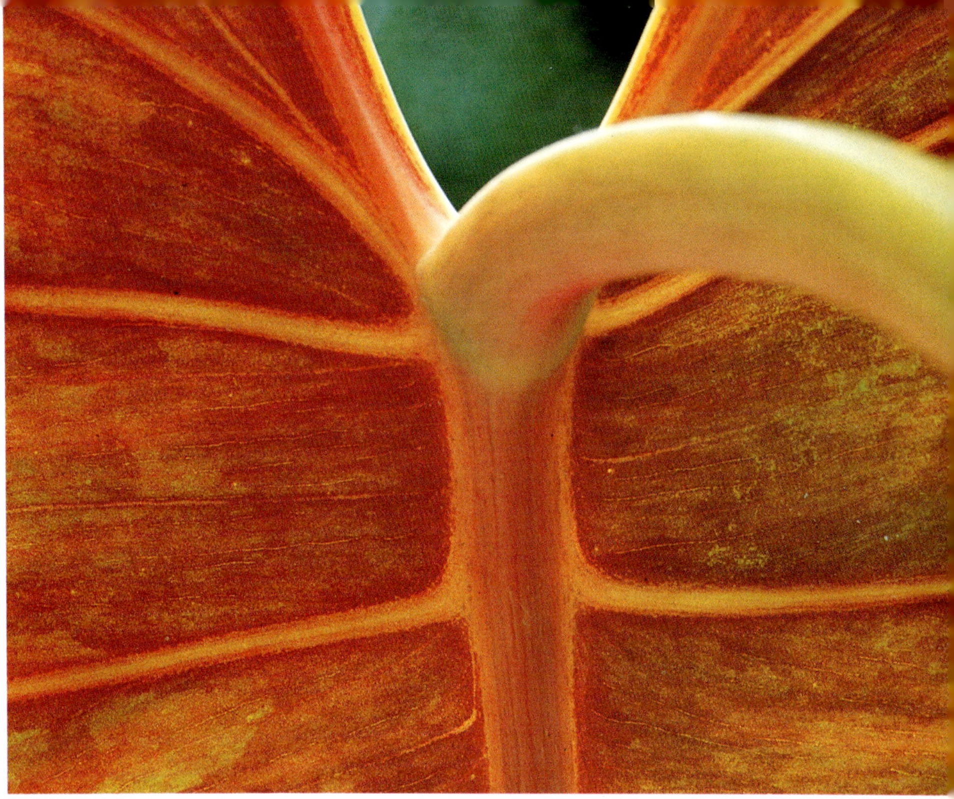

2.34 ●●● For close-up photography with an SLR camera, it is important to appreciate that extension tubes and bellows units require additional exposure, because they extend the lens further from the film plane and reduce the brightness of the image. TTL metering will measure this difference and indicate the correct exposure, but in situations where a separate meter is used, (for example with flash or an incident light reading), you should make an allowance for the measurement given.

A simple way, using a calculator, to work out the necessary increase is to use the following formula:
The exposure needed is equal to the actual exposure reading, multiplied by a factor obtained by squaring the result of dividing the total amount the lens is extended by the focal length of the lens.

For example, if you obtain an exposure reading of 1 sec using a 50mm lens which has been extended to 80mm gives the formula:
1×80÷50 squared = 2.56 sec. ▲

TECHNICAL TIP

- Colour negative film has a much wider exposure tolerance than transparency film. An error of one stop either way will have a minimal effect, whereas just half a stop over or underexposure will make a considerable difference to the image quality of transparency film.

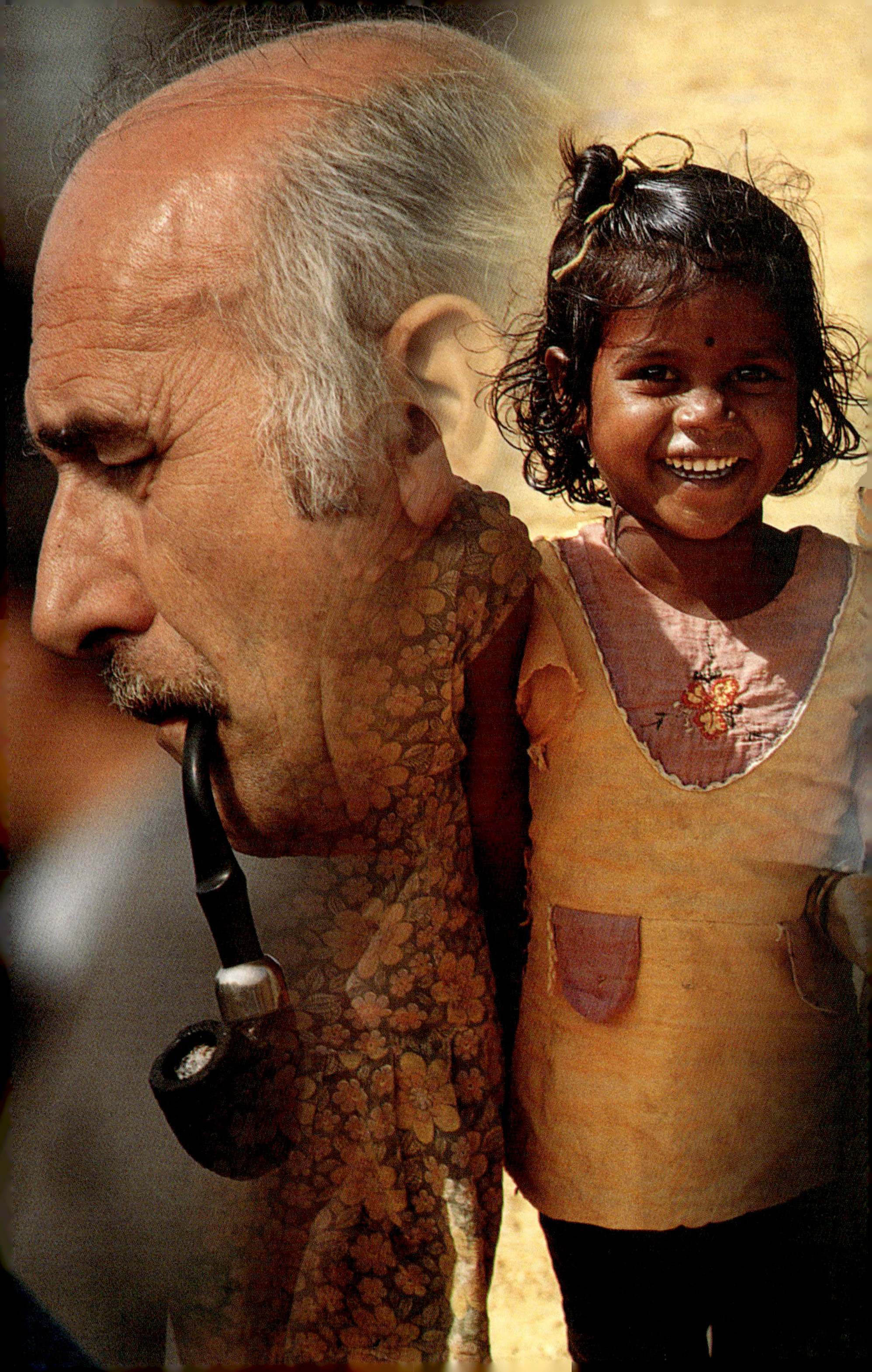

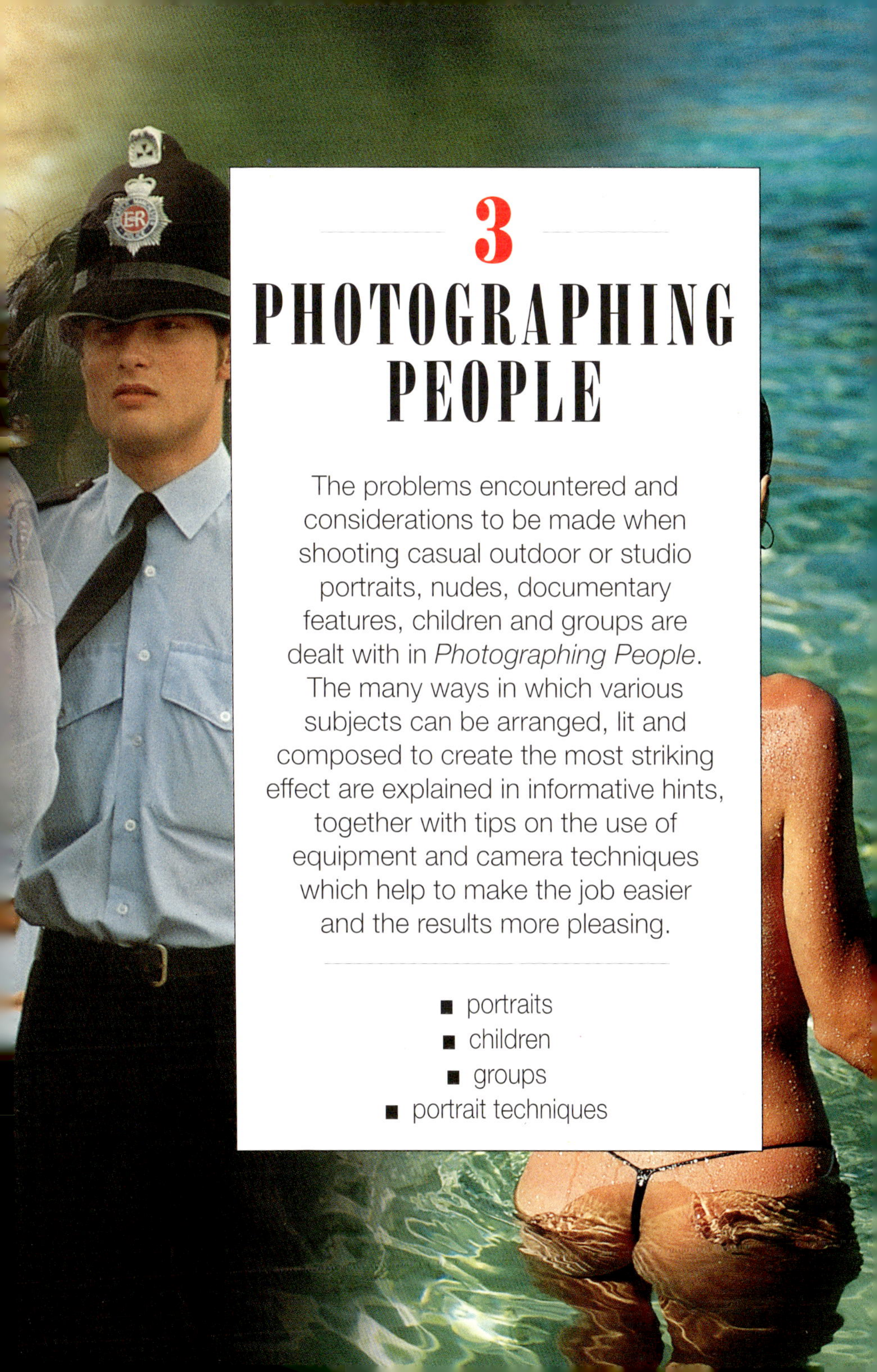

3

PHOTOGRAPHING PEOPLE

The problems encountered and considerations to be made when shooting casual outdoor or studio portraits, nudes, documentary features, children and groups are dealt with in *Photographing People*. The many ways in which various subjects can be arranged, lit and composed to create the most striking effect are explained in informative hints, together with tips on the use of equipment and camera techniques which help to make the job easier and the results more pleasing.

- portraits
- children
- groups
- portrait techniques

3 Portraits

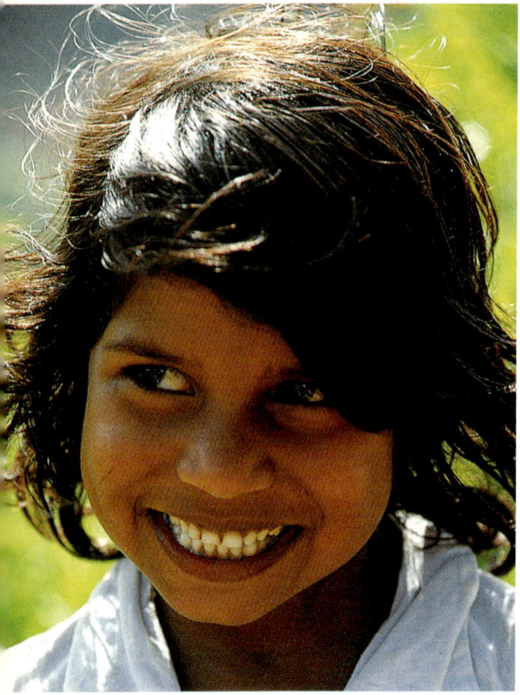

3.01 Before starting a portrait session it is essential to have a clear idea of what you want to achieve. Decide where you want to take the pictures, choose your background, the way in which you want the model to sit and pose and, if it is a studio shot, the type of lighting arrangement you want to employ. Set up and arrange these things before the model arrives, and have your camera loaded and ready for use. Always try to have a back-up plan of alternative ideas if the first scheme turns out to be unsuitable, or if the image style changes as the session progresses.

3.02 A fussy and intrusive background often detracts from outdoor portraits. If possible, find an area of fairly plain tone or colour against which your subject will stand out clearly. A light wall is a good choice, for example, for someone wearing dark clothes, or an area of deep shadow behind a light-toned subject.

3.03 When taking close-up, full-face portraits, always focus on your model's eyes; when you want to shoot the face in three-quarter view or in profile, focus on the mouth. Remember that the depth of field becomes extremely shallow when the camera is quite close to the subject, or when a long-focus lens is used, so select a small aperture to get both the model's mouth and ear in sharp focus. ◀

3.04 To ensure a comfortable and relaxed pose for your model when you are shooting head-and-shoulder portraits, place a low-backed chair where you want to photograph the model, so that the seat faces away from the camera. Ask the model to sit astride or side-saddle, using the chair back as a prop for arms or elbows. Alternatively, position a box, or pile of books, about 30cm high, in front of your seated model and ask him or her to place one foot on it. The raised knee provides a convenient and comfortable arm or elbow support for your model. ▶

3.05 If your model becomes too rigid and unexpressive during a portrait shoot, ask him or her to turn, or look away from the camera at something else for a short while and then to swing back spontaneously towards the camera and look into the lens. Some of the best shots are taken by catching this moment.

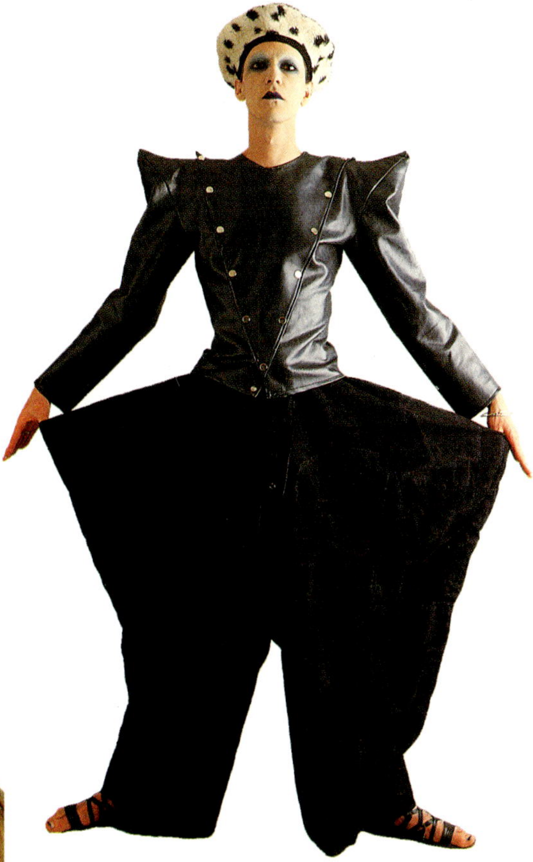

3.06 For a full-length photograph of a person, kneel down so the camera is approximately level with your subject's waist. This will be more flattering and prevent the appearance of foreshortened legs. Unless you want a deliberately exaggerated effect, avoid using a viewpoint closer than 2 metres, preferably even further away. ▶

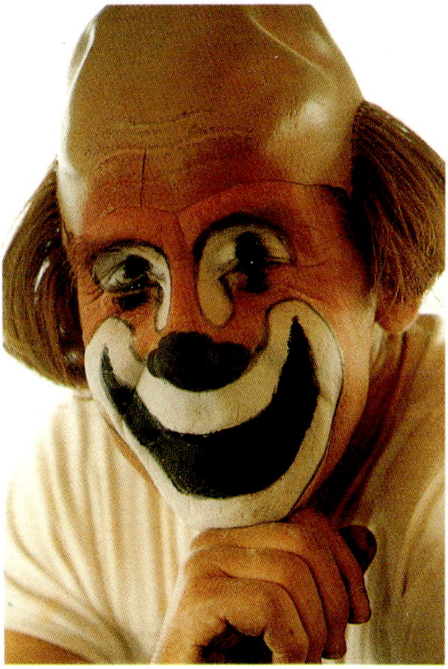

PRACTICAL HINT

- Creating good and original poses for portrait and figure shots can present a problem even for more experienced photographers. Study the work of top-class celebrity and fashion photographers which is displayed in glossy magazines. Although the images produced by photographers like Annie Liebowitz would not always be entirely appropriate, they can be an invaluable source of inspiration and ideas.

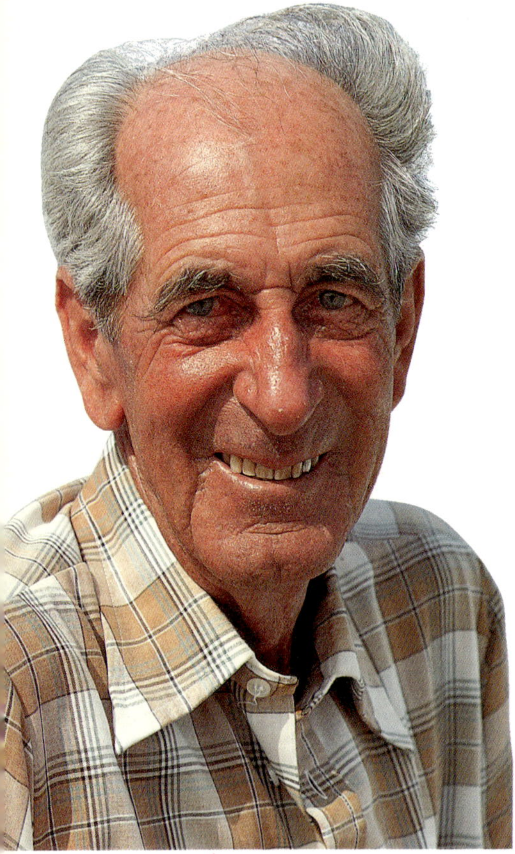

3.07 ● If you can, try to keep up a constant patter when taking photographs of people: even short periods of silence can cause the subject to become self-conscious and awkward. It is also important to make positive and encouraging remarks throughout the shoot, constantly reassuring your subjects that they are looking good and telling them when you are pleased with a shot. ▲

3.08 ●● Outdoor portraits can be given a more formal and studio-like quality by the simple expedient of using an artificial background, such as a roll of cartridge paper or fabric. You can buy collapsible background panels (those made by Lastolite, for example) in a wide range of colours and textures from professional photographic suppliers, which are ideal for this purpose. ▼

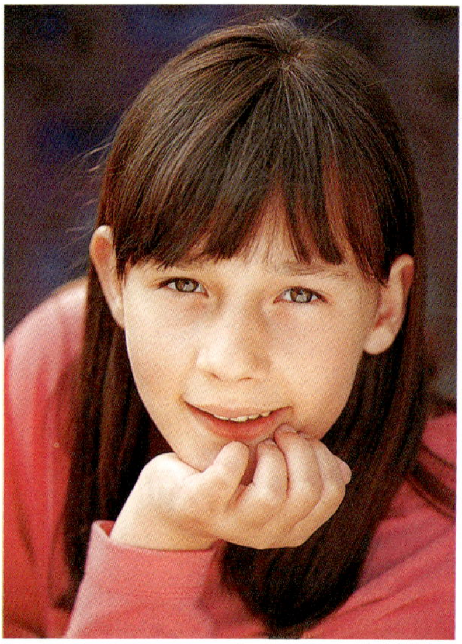

3.09 ●● To support a roll of background paper effectively when shooting portraits in the home, thread a piece of strong cord through the cardboard core on which the paper is wound. Tie it in a loop, leaving about 1 metre of slack, then suspend the roll by the cord from a couple of hooks on the wall or hanging from a picture rail. ▶

TECHNICAL TIP

- Where the surroundings are unavoidably fussy, such as in a garden or park, place your model as far away as possible from the background and select a wide aperture. The background details will be thrown well out of focus, creating a smooth homogeneous tone. This technique will be even more effective if you use a long-focus lens.

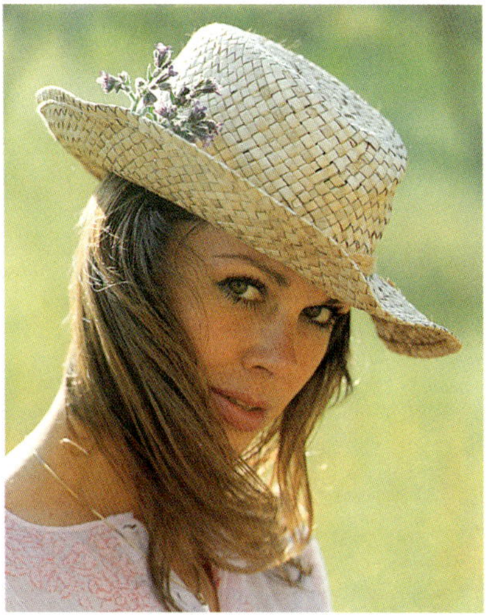

Placing your model a long way from any distant detail makes the background unobtrusive.

3.10 Although many photographers prefer the freedom that is allowed by a hand-held camera, a tripod can be an invaluable accessory for portrait photography. This is because you are not obliged to have your eye permanently glued to the viewfinder eyepiece. Hence you can take your pictures while continuing to maintain direct eye contact with your subject, which can be very helpful in creating a good rapport with your subject. It is also more likely to provoke responsive and lively expressions from your model.

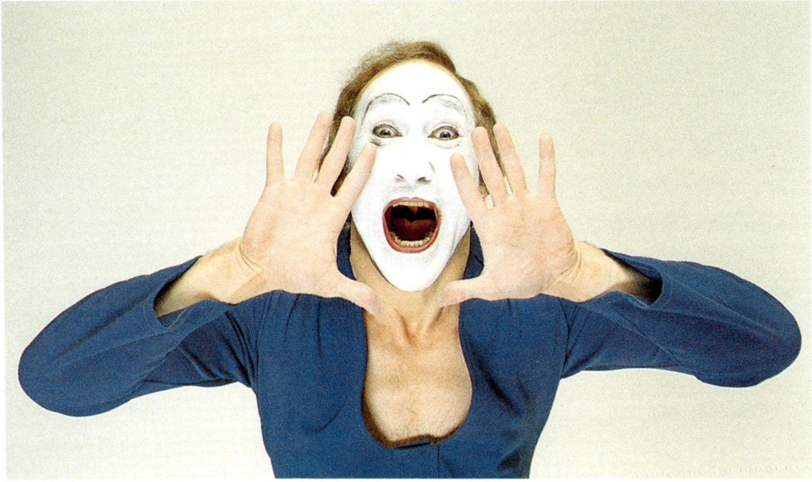

3.11 The effect of perspective can have a subtle but quite marked influence on the way a person's features are recorded in a photograph. Avoid a viewpoint closer than about 2 metres when shooting portraits, unless you wish to create a deliberately distorted, and invariably unflattering, effect. For large head shots you must use a long-focus lens so the frame can be filled without having to move the camera closer to the model. ▼

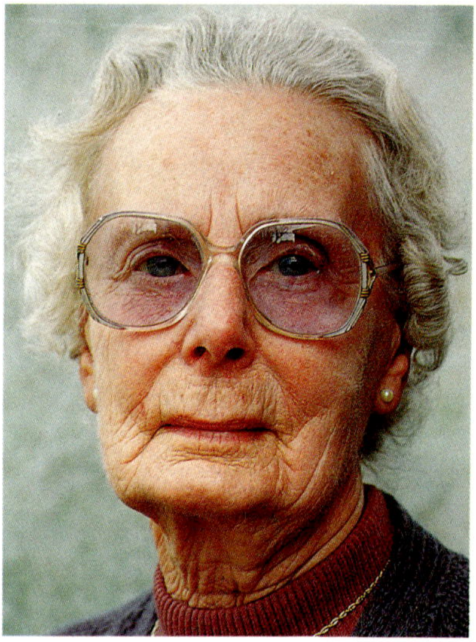

With the camera at 5 feet away the perspective has a much more natural appearance.

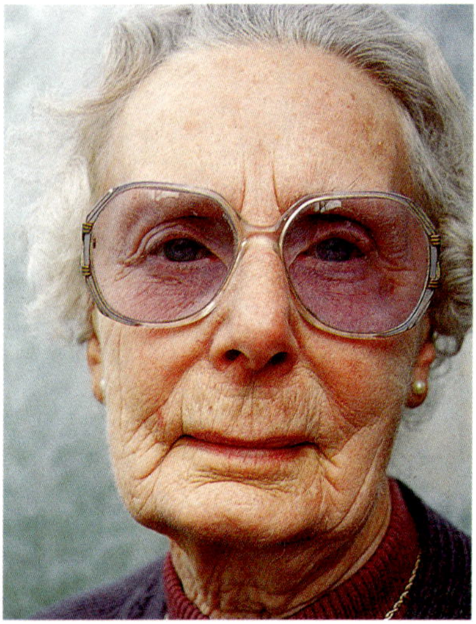

In this shot taken from about 2 feet from the model's face, her features appear very distorted.

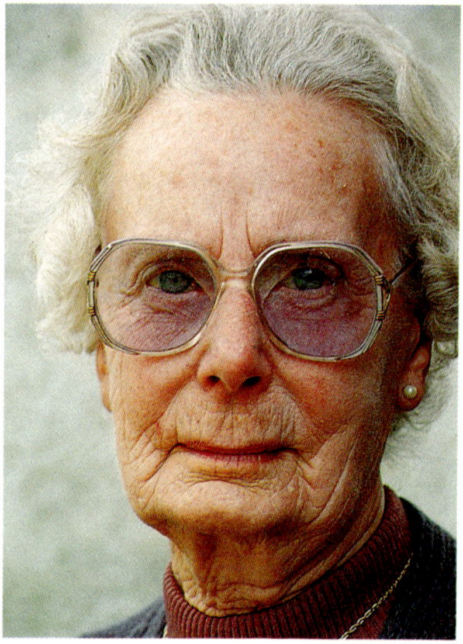

From a distance of 8 feet the model's features appear in their true perspective.

PRACTICAL HINT

- With 35mm cameras a 75–150mm zoom is ideal for portraits because you can alter the framing to allow both head-to-waist shots and close-up heads to be taken from the same camera position.

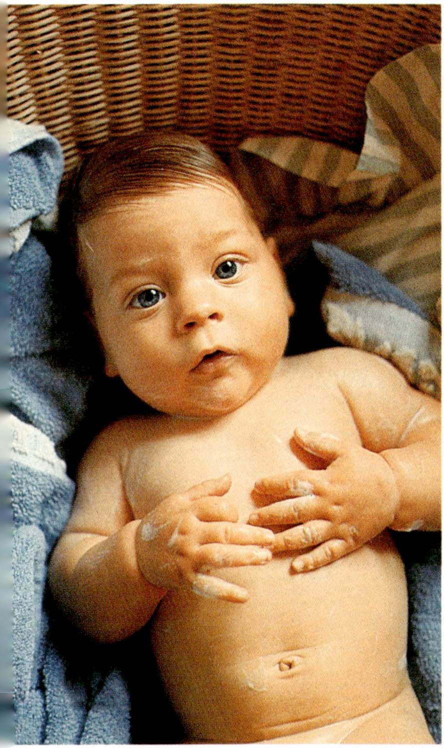

3.13 ●● A Polaroid camera can be a useful tool when shooting portraits of a child who is less than enthusiastic about having a photograph taken. The subject's interest is invariably aroused if he or she is able to see an instant picture and can keep the print, resulting in a much more co-operative situation.

3.14 ● For photographs of young children and toddlers, try to shoot from their level. A 'normal' camera viewpoint will give a distorted and less intimate impression of young subjects. When taking more formal pictures of children in the home or studio, raise them on a chair or platform: when shooting casual pictures, in the garden for instance, use a low camera viewpoint. A camera with a waist-level viewfinder can make this much easier. ▼

3.12 ● When photographing a young child, have another person present who knows the child well. He or she can help to keep your subject amused while you make your preparations and can also help to encourage interesting and spontaneous expressions during the shoot. Although you can also do this to some extent, the child will be looking towards the camera, so it is often useful to place your assistant in a position which encourages the child to look off camera, creating a different head angle. ▲

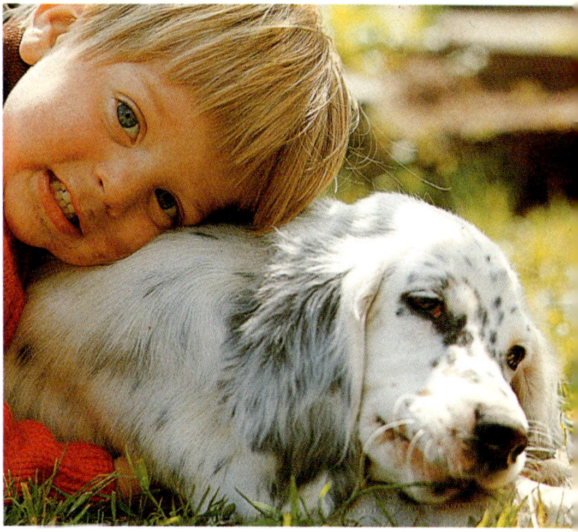

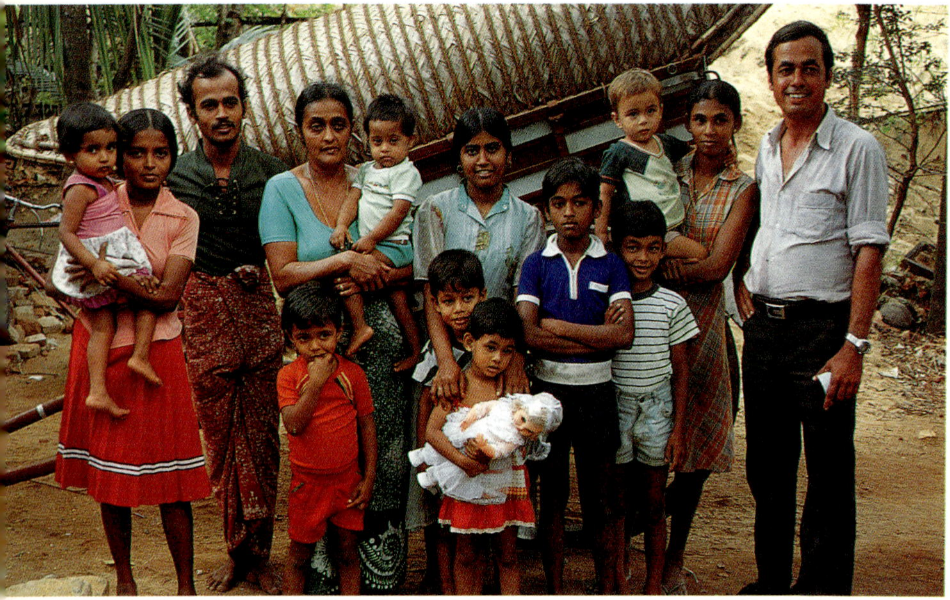

3.15 If you use a wide-angle lens to photograph a group of people, it is particularly important to try to keep the camera level and avoid placing people's heads near the corners of the frame; this can cause noticeable, and very ugly, distortion. It will also help to avoid undue distortion if you shoot from lower-than-eye-level, aiming the camera at a point located somewhere between the subjects' shoulders and waists.

3.16 Arrange subjects for a group photograph in a slightly convex curve, so that those at the ends are standing slightly forwards of the people in the centre. If a large group is arranged in a straight line, people at the ends will appear to be smaller than those in the centre, especially if you need to use a wide-angle lens.

3.17 The soft, diffused lighting, which is characteristic of an overcast or hazy day, is best for photographing a large group of people. This is because the area occupied by each individual face will be very small and the shadows created by direct sunlight will tend to obscure features and expressions. On a sunny day, try to arrange the group in an area of open shade. If this is not possible, use fill-in flash to add detail to the shadow areas and reduce the contrast of the image. ▲ ▶

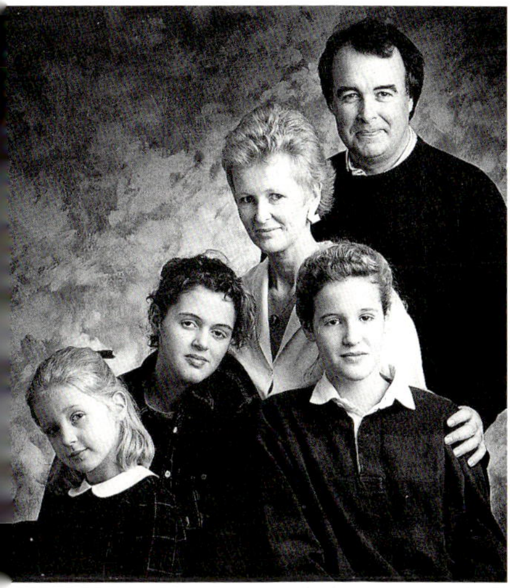

3.19 ●● When arranging a group of people for a portrait, begin with just one and add others, rearranging them progressively to build up a balanced and harmonious composition. Find ways to place people's heads at different levels to add interest and movement to the arrangement. With a group photographed full-length, make use of the varying heights of individuals and ask people to kneel. For closer shots combine people seated at varied levels with standing and kneeling figures to create a variety of interesting arrangements. ◀

3.18 ● Carry a whistle when photographing a large group of people (at a wedding, for instance). When you are ready to take the shot, a short blast on the whistle will help to ensure that everyone is looking at the camera.

PRACTICAL HINT

- To arrange small groups of people in the studio, use a cluster of boxes, crates or stools of varying heights, covered with a draped fabric chosen to tone with the background.

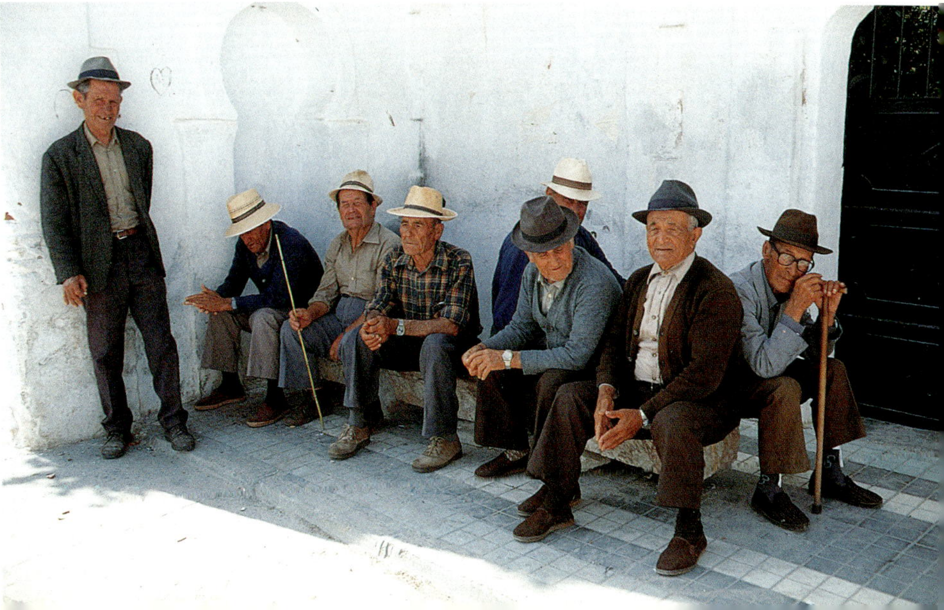

3.20 ●● Modern camera lenses can be extremely unforgiving and unflattering for portrait photography and various techniques like soft focus and canvas bonding have been developed to alleviate this problem. One method which has a purer photographic quality and which can also add an element of mood and atmosphere, is to make use of the film's grain structure. Choose a very fast film and frame the image so that it can be enlarged to a considerable degree; the resulting print will have a very pleasing crystalline granularity which can both flatter the model and create an image of striking quality.

This technique can work equally well in both black-and-white and colour photography. I recommend Kodak's 2475 Recording film for its very attractive, gritty grain structure in black-and-white photography, and you will find that Scotch Chrome ISO 800/3200 is a good choice for most colour work. ▼

3.21 ●● Make any skin blemishes your model may have less noticeable when shooting black-and-white portraits by using a red filter. The model's lips will appear lighter in tone, however, so portraits usually can be improved if the model wears a dark, or blue-toned, shade of lipstick.

PRACTICAL HINT

- A zoom lens can be very useful for pictures where a high degree of enlargement is required, because you can frame the picture with the zoom fully extended and then pull back to its widest setting to make the exposures.

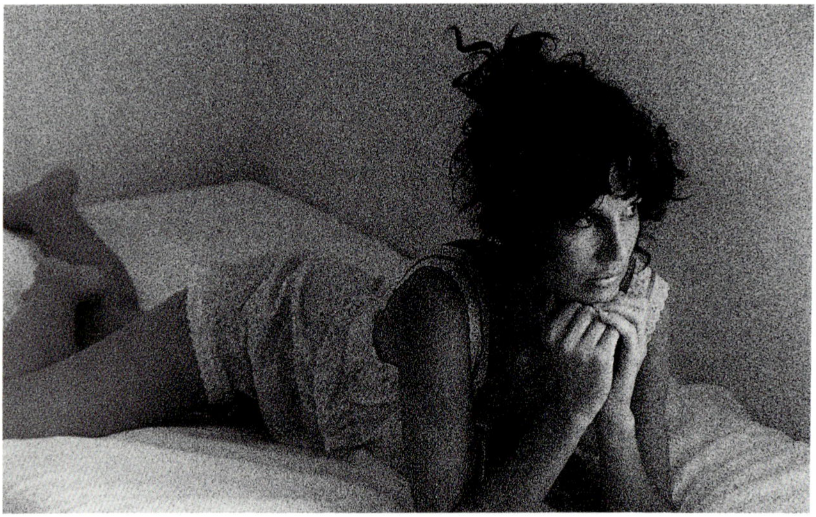

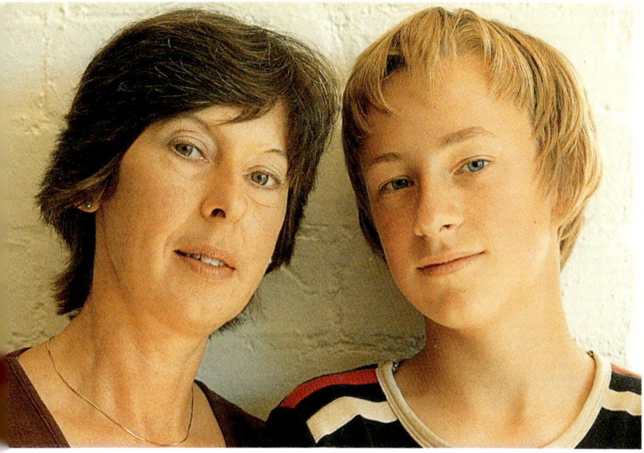

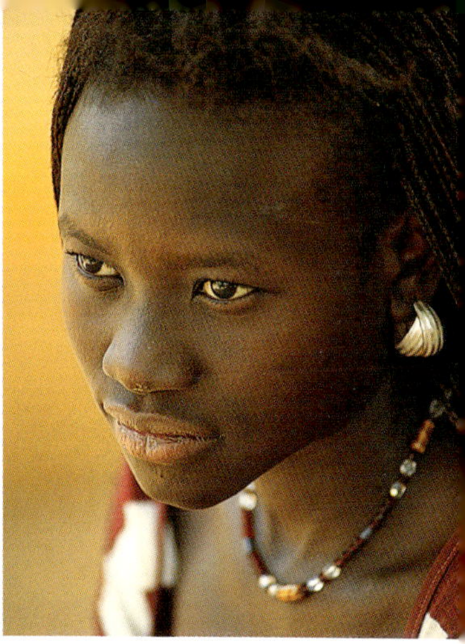

3.22 ●● Today's cameras are valued for their fine lenses and their sharp definition, but portraits do not require this high degree of sharpness, especially where a more romantic and atmospheric image is wanted. A variety of manufactured devices is available, for example the Zeiss Softar which reduces the definition of lenses and creates images with less detail, to give a more flattering rendition of skin tones. Such devices are very effective, but simple home-made gadgets can give equally good results for little or no cost:

- Cut a small hole in the centre of a piece of fine-mesh nylon, or crumpled cellophane and use an elastic band to hold it over the lens.
- Stretch strips of sellotape over the end of a lens hood, again leaving a hole in the centre to allow a core of sharpness to remain.
- Smear a film of clear petroleum jelly on to a piece of glass or a filter mounted on the lens. This method is particularly effective and has the advantage that you can tease the jelly around with your finger tip to vary the effect, or place it more thickly over areas where detail needs to be lost.

TECHNICAL TIP

- The smaller the hole left in the centre of a home-made diffuser, the larger the lens aperture and the longer the focal length of the lens used, will each make the image more diffused. These methods all tend to reduce image contrast, so unless a very subtle effect is required, they are best suited to colourful or strongly lit subjects.

3.23 ● The exposure for portraits of people with a dark skin needs to be rather less than indicated by a close-up averaging reading, and rather more for people with a pale skin. The amount varies according to the actual skin colour, but as a general rule try a stop extra for a pale skin and a stop less for a dark skin. Use a substitute or incident light reading for a more precise method of calculation. ▲

3.24 ● When shooting candid pictures in an alien environment, allow some time for people to become accustomed to your presence before starting the shoot. Avoid the use of an ostentatious camera bag and keep a low profile by changing films and lenses in a quiet corner, out of sight.

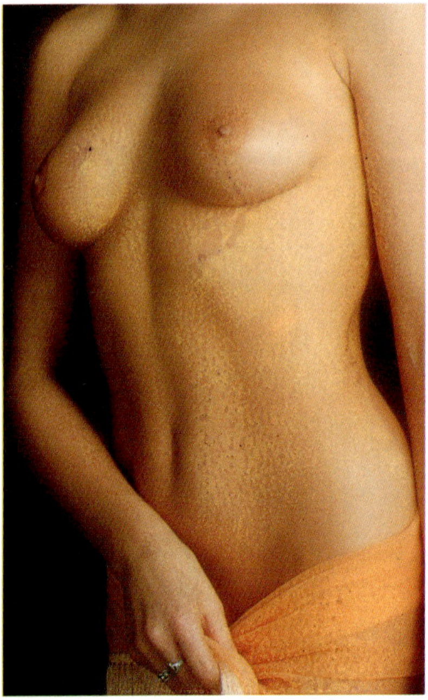

3.25 ● For nude photography, the model must remove all items of tight clothing at least an hour before the shoot is due to begin, to allow time for marks caused by waistbands, belts and shoulder straps to fade completely. Such marks are invariably more pronounced on film than they appear to the eye. ▲

3.26 ●● To adopt a more distant viewpoint so that subjects are unaware that they are being photographed, some photographers choose to use a long-focus lens, although a wide-angle lens gives better results in some circumstances. With a long-focus lens it is usually obvious at whom the camera is aimed, but it is also possible to take pictures from very close quarters using a wide-angle lens in a way which gives the subject the impression that they are not being specifically targetted. ▶

PRACTICAL HINT

- ☐ Most people see themselves mainly in mirrors, so a photograph is often more pleasing and familiar to them if you revese it during printing; they will see it as a mirror image with their features reversed left to right.

3.27 ● If you are shooting portraits for the subject's own use, look for ways in which they can be flattered to give less prominence to the least attractive features. A model with a double chin or a plump face will look more attractive when photographed from a higher viewpoint where a three-quarter face pose is adopted: a large nose will be less prominent if the pose is full-face. Thinning hair, or a bald head, will be less noticeable by using a lower camera angle; avoid top lighting or use a flag to mask the light from the top of the model's head and

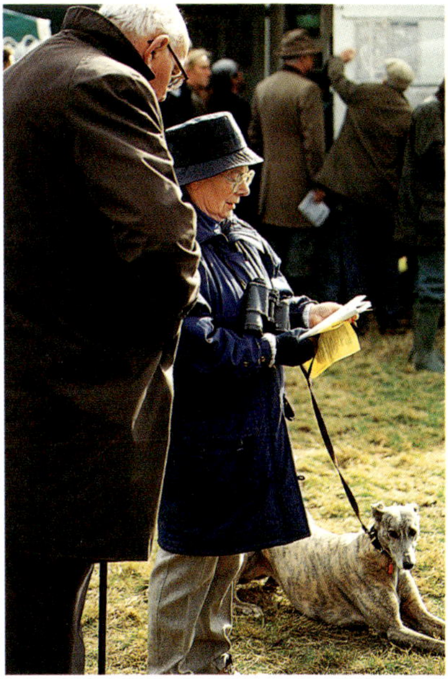

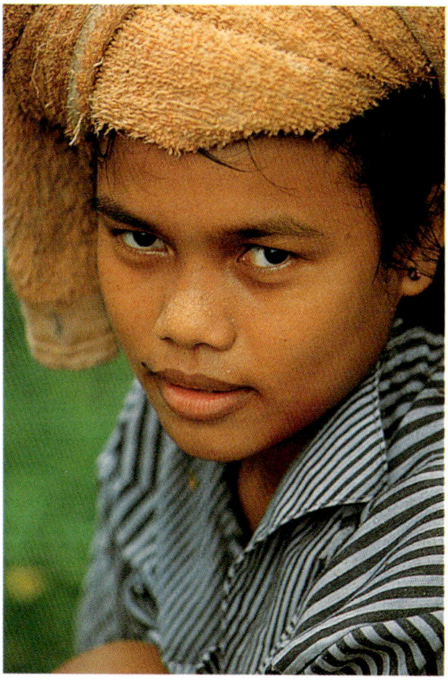

a background tone which minimises the contrast. Few people have entirely symmetrical faces and one side is usually more photogenic than the other: identify this and you will be able to choose the best pose and establish the most effective type of lighting for your shot. Always avoid front-on, wide smiles of models with uneven teeth.

Don't shrink from suggesting some make-up to cover skin blemishes, even for a male portrait, and when featuring the model's hands in a portrait look out for bad manicures, nicotine stains, cuts and bruises. All the above flaws are often much more noticeable on film than in real life. ▶

3.28 ●● To enhance the effect of weathered skin when shooting 'character' portraits in black-and-white, use a strong blue or green filter. You can achieve a similar effect by using orthochromatic film.

3.29 ● While very pleasing portraits can be taken with the subject looking away from the camera, such as in profile shots, there is no doubt that eye contact between model and lens can create a very powerful effect and tends to give a picture a more intimate and personal quality. Many professional portrait photographers have found that pictures with the subject looking into the camera are more popular with their clients than portraits where the model is looking away. ▲

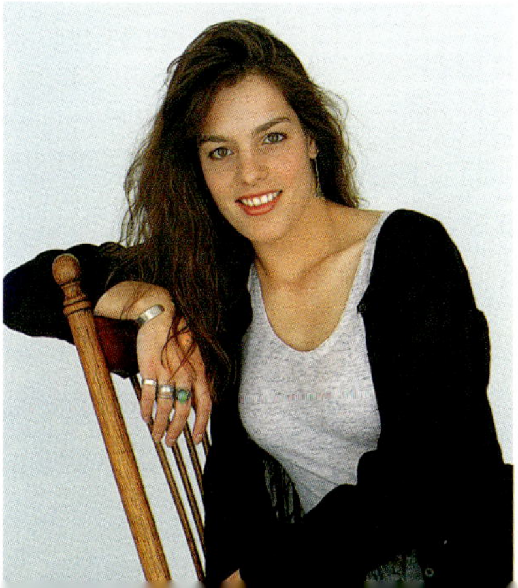

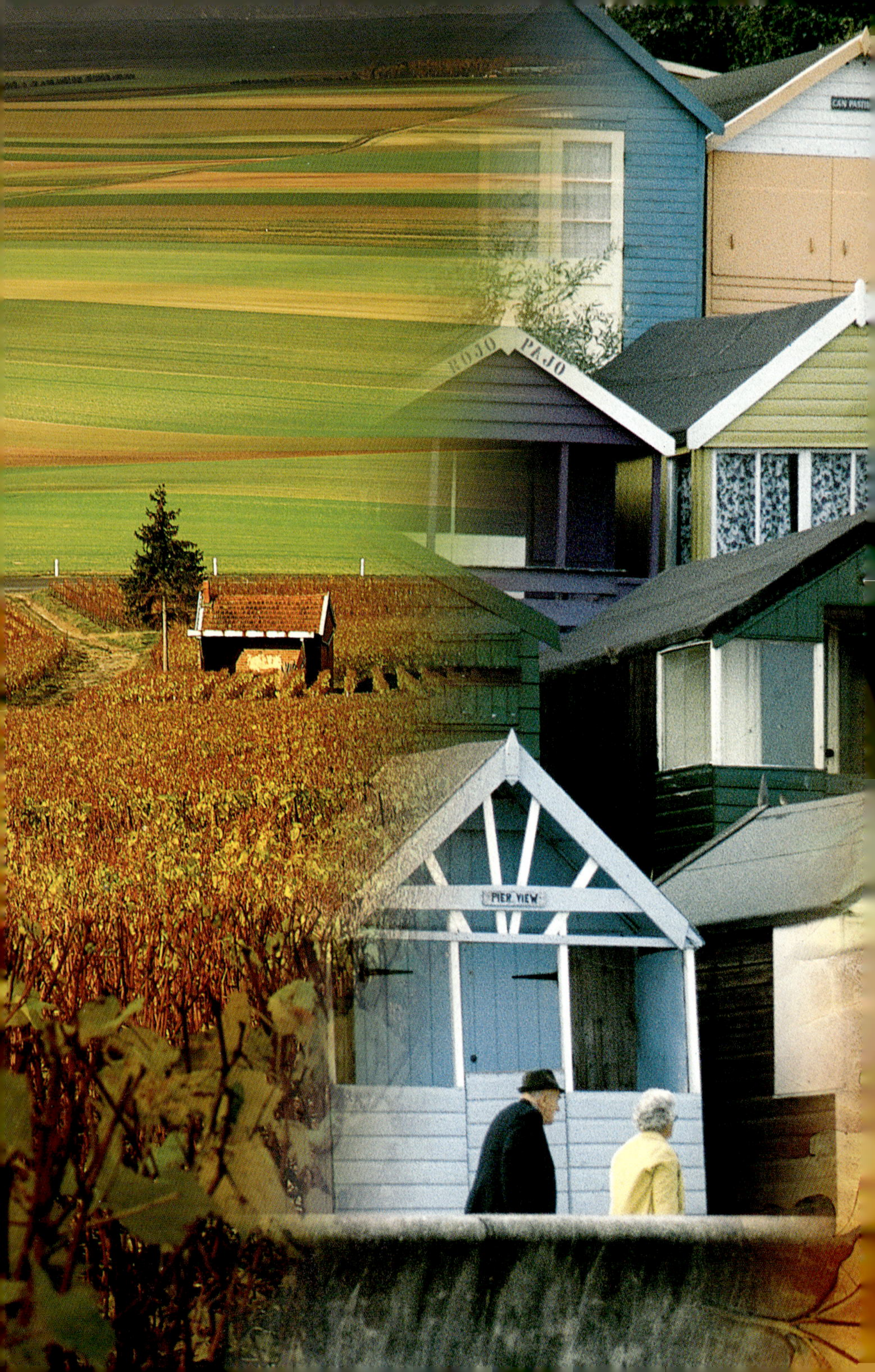
ROJO PAJO
PIER VIEW

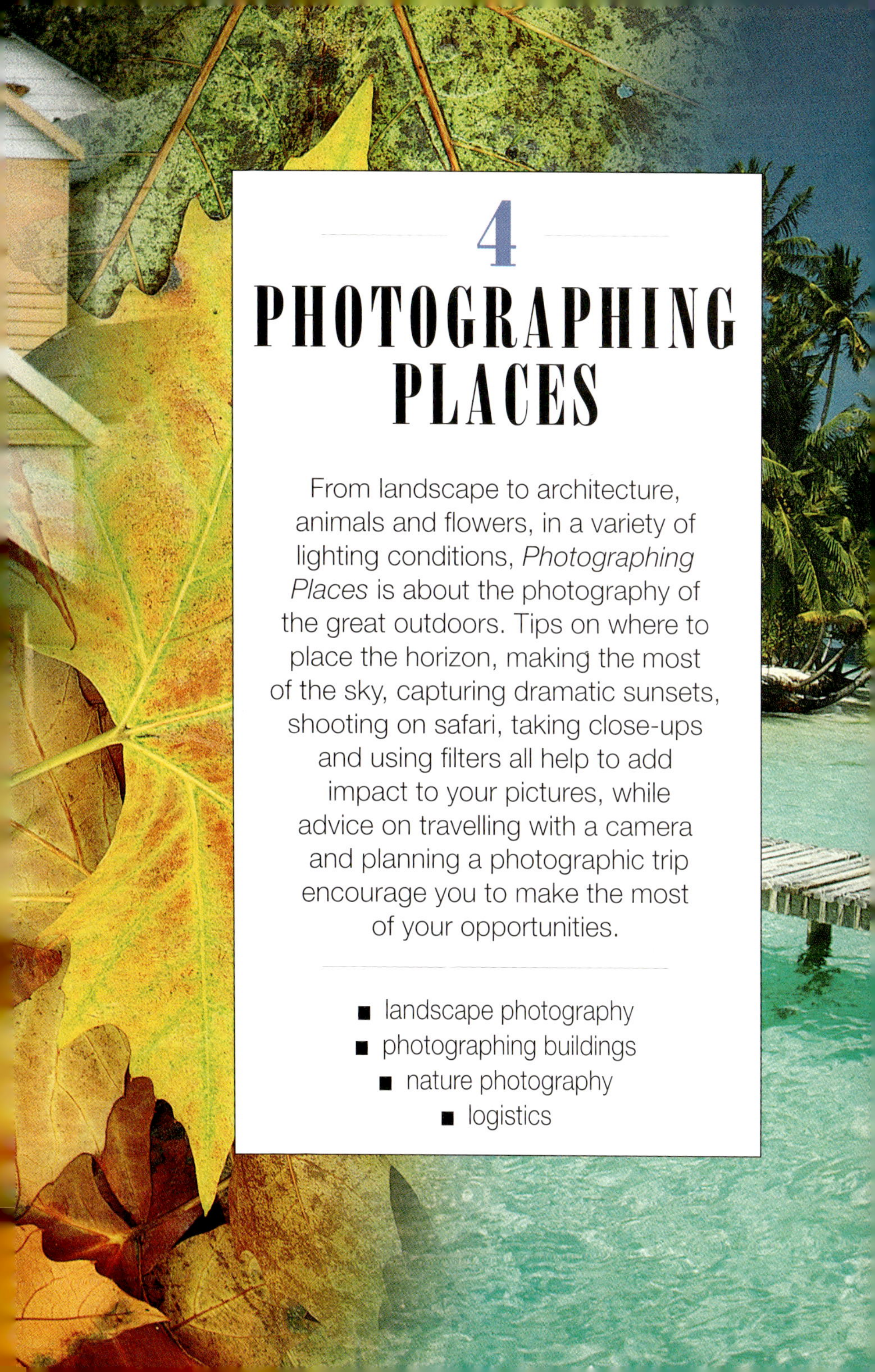

4

PHOTOGRAPHING PLACES

From landscape to architecture, animals and flowers, in a variety of lighting conditions, *Photographing Places* is about the photography of the great outdoors. Tips on where to place the horizon, making the most of the sky, capturing dramatic sunsets, shooting on safari, taking close-ups and using filters all help to add impact to your pictures, while advice on travelling with a camera and planning a photographic trip encourage you to make the most of your opportunities.

- landscape photography
- photographing buildings
- nature photography
- logistics

4 Landscape Photography

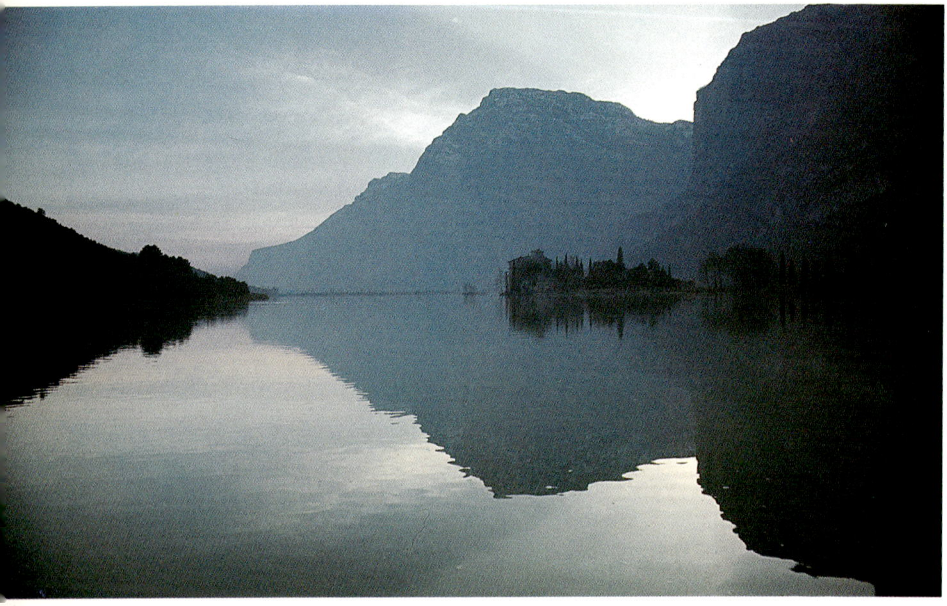

4.01 Judging where to place the horizon can be one of the most important decisions a photographer has to make when taking landscape photographs. If you use a camera's viewfinder casually, like a gunsight, invariably the horizon will run through the centre of the image – and this is seldom the best place for it. As a general rule, when the sky is uninteresting or featureless, or when you wish to give most emphasis to foreground details, place the horizon line near the top of the frame. ▲

4.02 If you are photographing a view on a dull day, include close-up foreground details which have a darker tone or are colourful, for example a wall or wildflowers. This will add contrast and depth to the picture. ▼

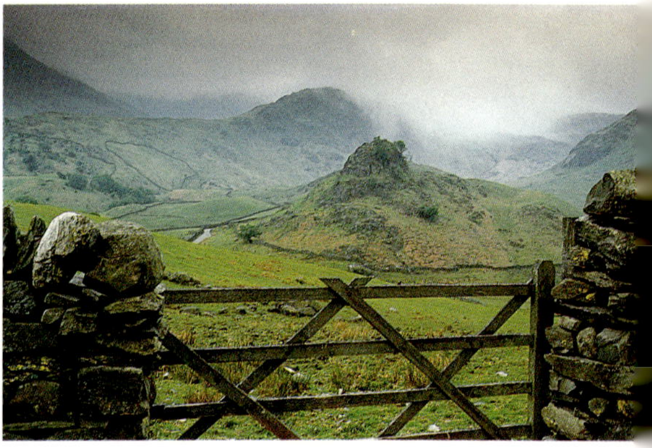

4.03 ●● Give photographs of moving water, like a waterfall or fast-flowing river, a powerful and atmospheric quality by using a slow shutter speed. You will need a tripod, as the most striking effects are obtained with shutter speeds of 1 sec or less. If the light is very bright and it is not possible to use such slow speeds, even with the lens stopped right down, use a neutral density filter or a polarising filter to reduce the brightness of the image. ▶

4.04 ● The 'rules' of composition dictate that the horizon should divide the picture into a proportion of one-third to two-thirds and this will provide a pleasing balance in most circumstances. In practice, however, you must judge the position of the horizon in relation to other elements of the composition, and use this as a means of balancing objects and details which project above and below the line it creates. ▼

4.05 ● When the sky has dramatic clouds and creates rich tones it can be more effective to place the horizon nearer to the bottom edge of the picture.

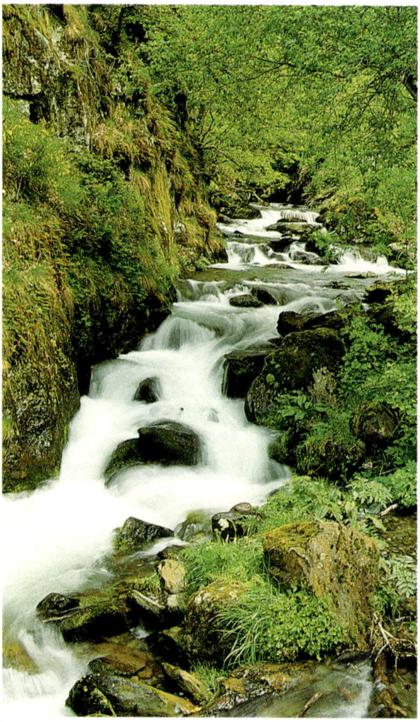

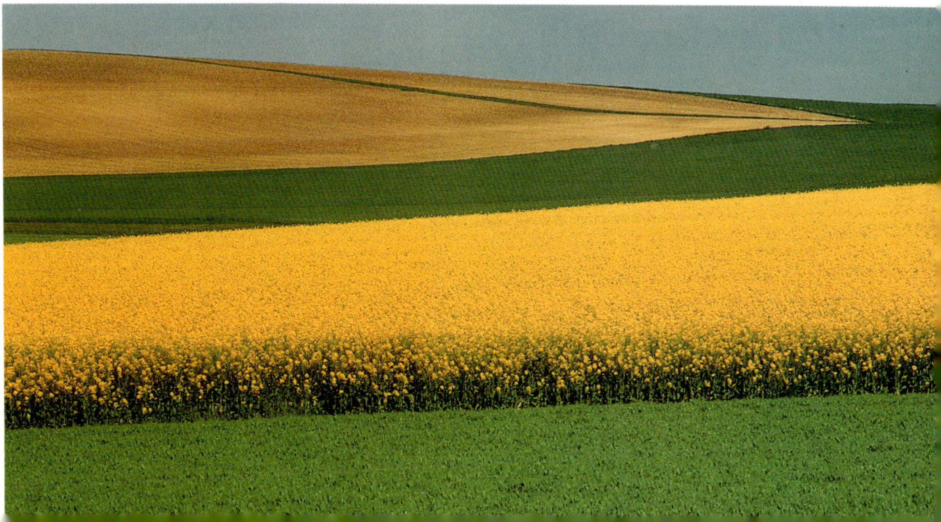

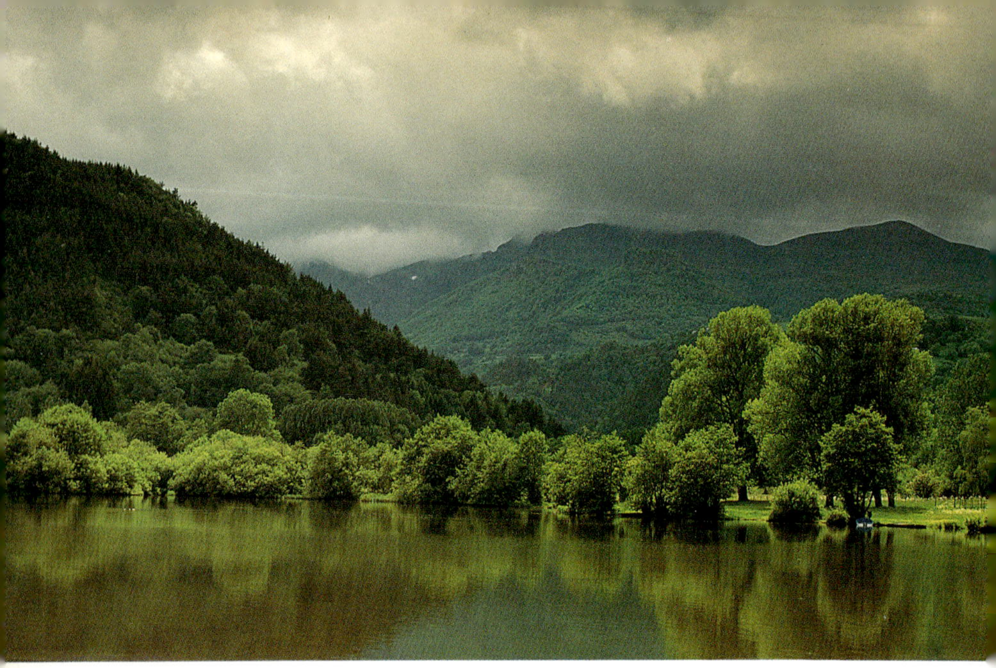

4.06 ● You will find that a wide-angle lens will increase the contrast and colour saturation of pictures taken on a dull day, whereas a long-focus lens will tend to reduce them.

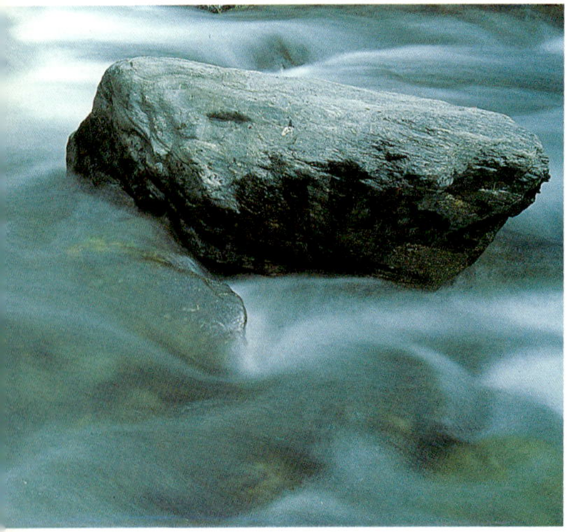

A series of consecutive exposures results in the smoky effect of the moving water.

4.07 ●● When taking landscape photographs on overcast days use a neutral graduated filter to prevent the sky from becoming too pale or bleached out. This filter will also help to avoid the risk of underexposing the foreground where it will create more contrast and detail. ▲

TECHNICAL TIP

□ To photograph moving water, creating a subtly different effect, use a sequence of faster shutter speeds with the camera's multiple exposure setting on the same frame of film. Take your exposure reading in the normal way, let's say that it is 1/60 sec at f16. Instead, make a series of 8 exposures at 1/500 sec, or 16 at 1/1000 sec, over a period of a minute or two on the same frame of film; you will achieve an effect similar to that of a single exposure of several seconds. It is, of course, vital not to move the camera or tripod until the sequence is complete.

4.08 ● With the exception of deliberately contrived pictures, there is a cardinal rule about horizons – they must be level. This is not as easy to ensure as it might appear, especially when using wide-angle lenses. There are, however, a number of ways to avoid the problem of sloping horizons. You can mount a spirit level on the camera, but you must use a tripod. For hand-held cameras, a focussing screen with a grid can be a solution. With or without a tripod, move the camera down momentarily so the horizon runs along the top edge of the frame, check that they are parallel then move the camera back to the desired position to shoot. ▶

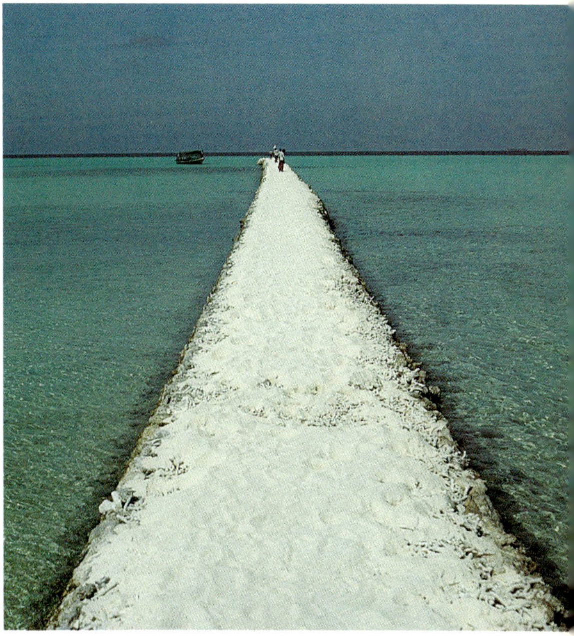

4.09 ●● If you wish to shoot landscape photographs in dull light, or perhaps at sunrise or sunset, a flash gun can be an effective way to illuminate foreground details. Simply calculate the aperture necessary for the flash exposure and then select the shutter speed needed to give the correct exposure to capture the colours of the sunset. ▶

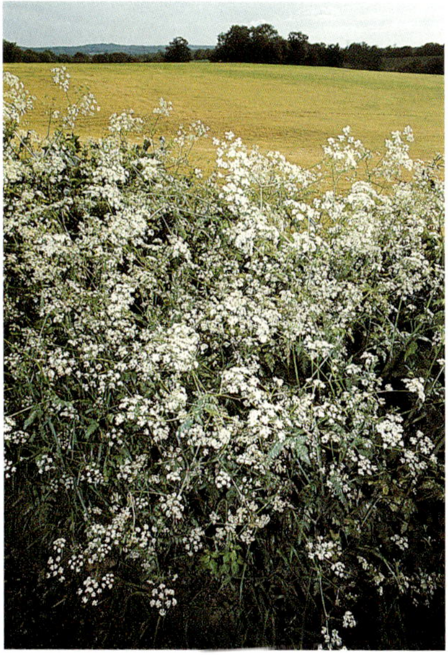

TECHNICAL TIP

- ☐ For a dramatic or abstract effect, try using a coloured filter over the flash. If you hold the flash to one side of the camera, more depth and texture will be created.

4.10 ● Find something to create foreground interest when you are photographing sunsets, but remember that the exposure needed to create a good range on tones and colours in the sky will result in foreground details being underexposed. An object with an intriguing shape, a bare-branched tree for instance, is especially useful for this purpose as it makes an equally attractive silhouette. Alternatively, look for very light or reflective foregrounds, such as wet sand on a beach, as this will echo the colours of the sky and prevent the foreground from becoming too dark. ▼ ▶

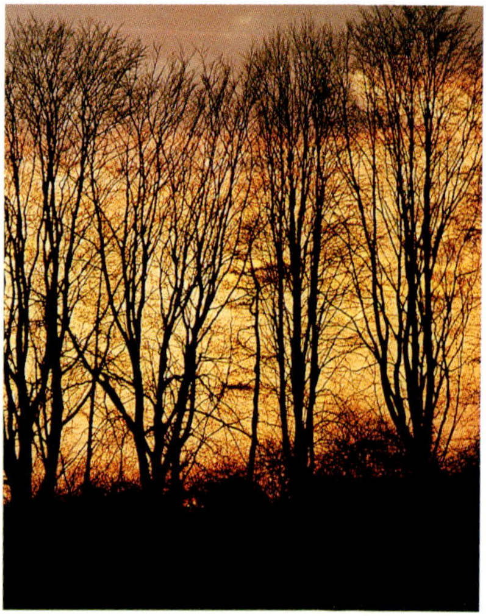

Silhouetted trees add interest to this sunset shot.

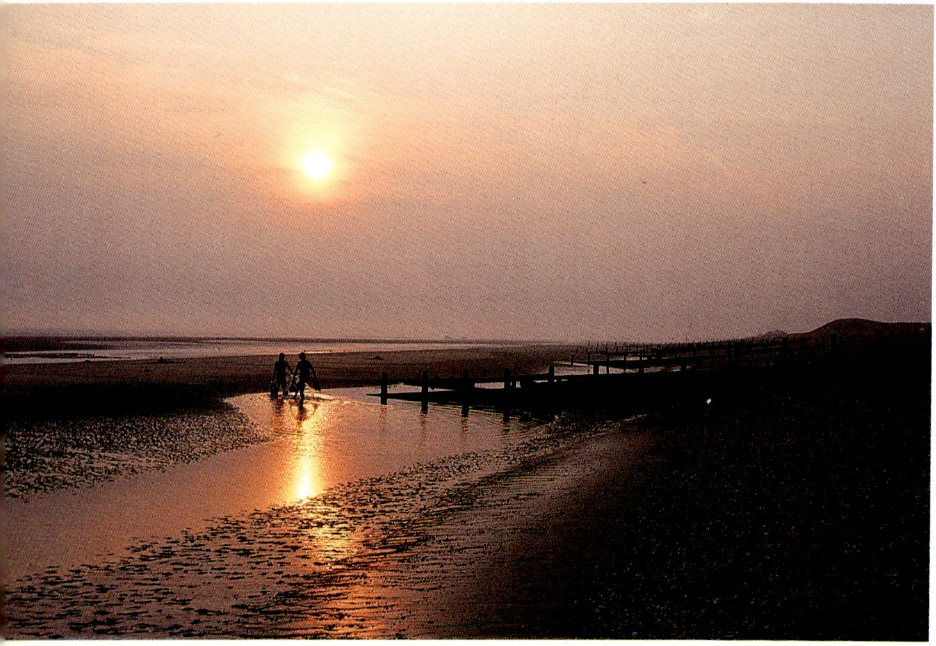

Reflections from the sky in the wet sand have added both tone and colour to the foreground of this shot.

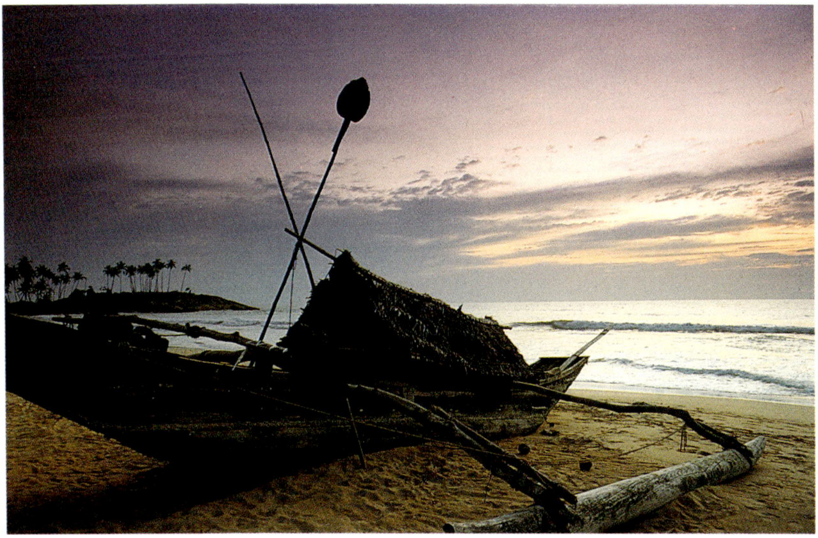

A neutral graduated filter holds the tone and colour in the sky while giving extra exposure to retain detail.

TECHNICAL TIP

- Even with a light, reflective foreground the sky area will be much brighter than the rest of the scene, so use a graduated filter to record more detail and colour in this area. Use a neutral, or grey graduated filter as the results with a coloured version invariably look artificial.

4.12 • Some of the most striking colours are created after the sun has set, and it is often worth waiting a while to see what develops. On summer evenings, when the cloud conditions are right, vivid hues can form in the sky for up to an hour after sunset.

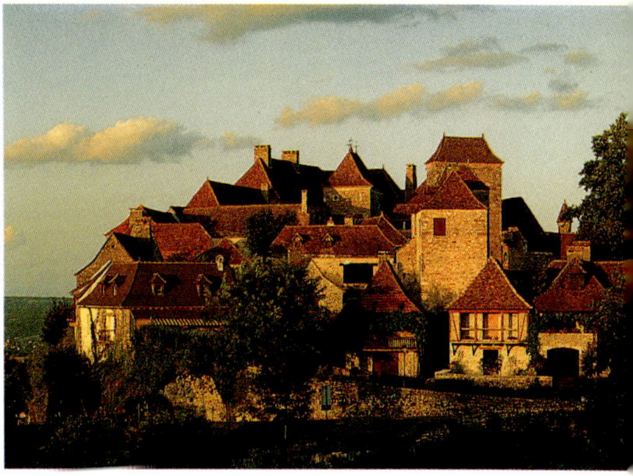

4.11 • Although the potential of sunrise and sunset pictures is usually focussed on the colours in the sky, it also pays to look behind you at the scene it is illuminating. The warm mellow light at this time of day can transform details which may pass unnoticed at other times, and the extremely low angle of that light can reveal striking textures in the landscape. ▶

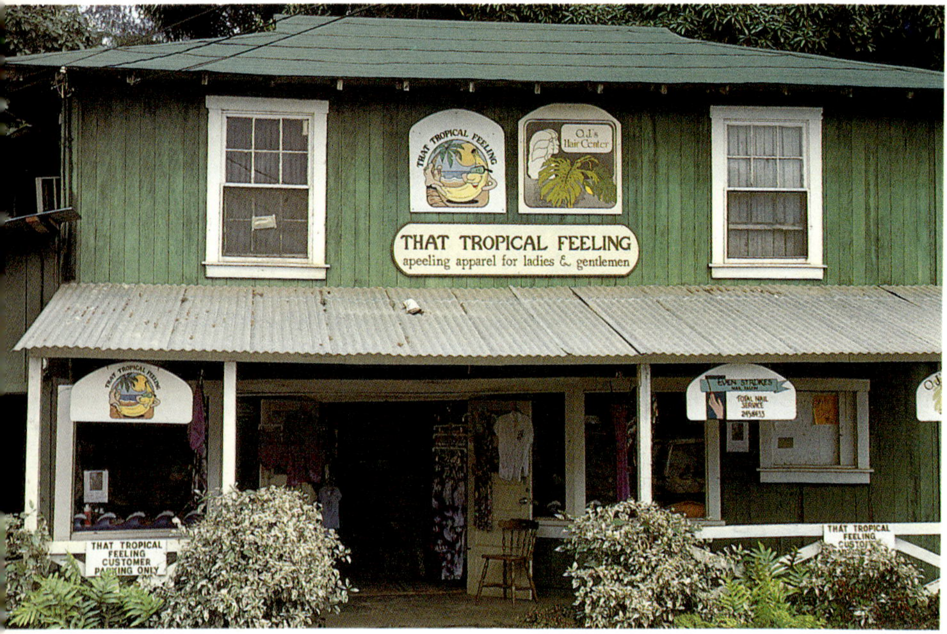

4.13 ● Use a slow film instead of a fast film when taking pictures of subjects like views or buildings on dull days, as slow films tend to have more contrast and greater colour saturation. With low contrast subjects like views or buildings, the grainier results of faster films will become much more apparent. ▲

4.14 ●● A red or orange filter used with black-and-white photography will make blue skies appear darker and will enhance the appearance of white clouds. Unfortunately, these filters will also tend to make green foliage darker, but you can avoid this difficulty by using a graduated red or orange filter positioned so that it affects only the sky area of a scene, leaving the foreground unfiltered.

4.15 ●● Add a warm filter, such as an 81B or C when taking views or seascapes with a polarising filter, to counteract the effect of the more pronounced blues created in the sky and water.

4.16 ●● If you use a polarising filter to make a blue sky a darker and richer colour, remember that it can create an uneven tone when fitted to a wide-angle lens. Instead, use a blue or neutral density graduated filter. These filters can also be used when the area of sky included in the frame is unaffected by a polarising filter. ▶

4.17 ●●● Infrared film can create particularly striking effects when used for landscape photography. This film is available in both colour and black-and-white emulsions; the latter is produced in 120mm and 35mm formats. The black-and-white emulsion gives the best results when used in conjunction with a deep red filter, recording blue skies as near black and green foliage as almost white. The colour version should be used with a Wratten 12 filter, but I have found that the Cokin tobacco filter often gives interesting effects.

Results with both types of film are unpredictable, so bracket your exposures by at least one stop around the suggested ratings. Infrared film is especially vulnerable to fogging; ideally, you should try to load and unload it in a darkroom or very subdued light. ▶

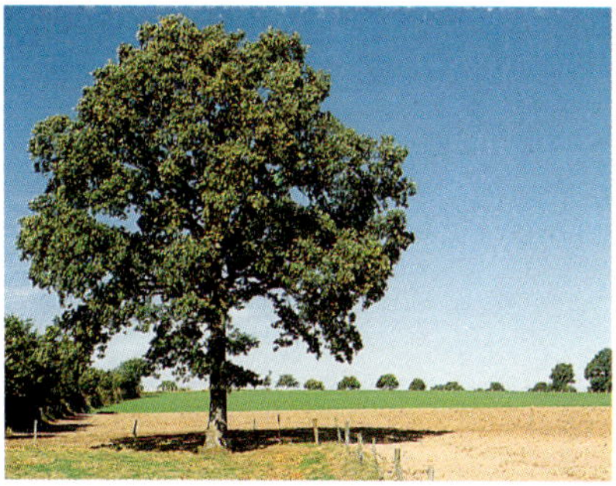

This was shot with normal transparency film.

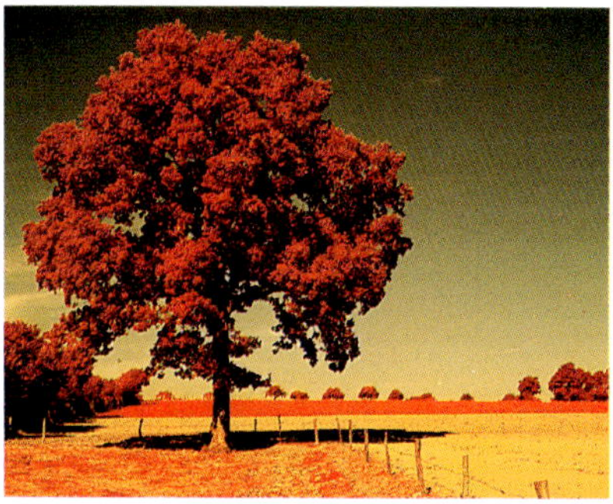

Kodak's Infrared transparency film with a Cokin tobacco filter was used to create this effect.

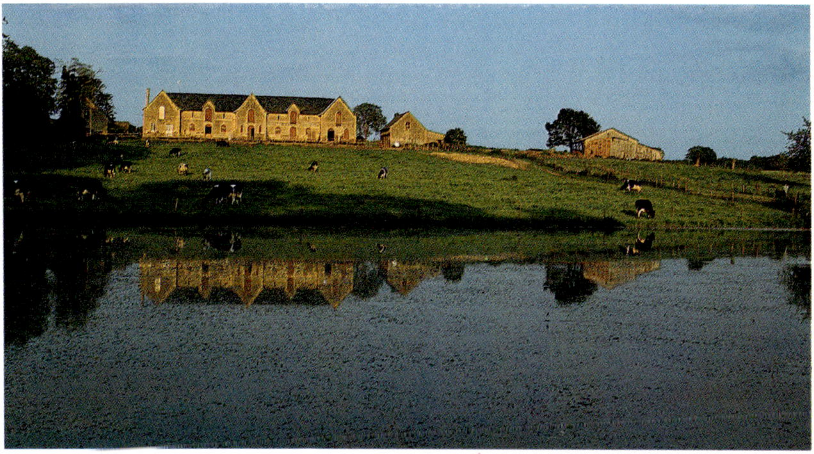

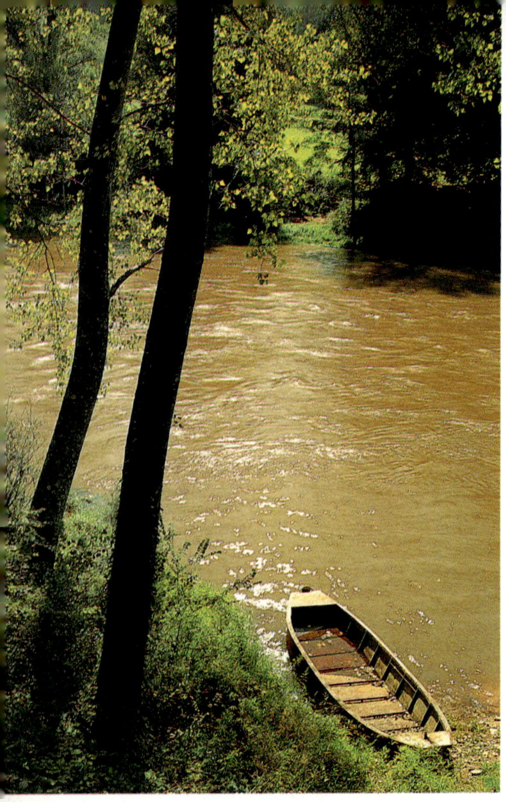

4.18 ●● A polarising filter is useful for reducing the strength of highlights when photographing scenes which include the sparkle of backlit water; these scenes can easily become bleached-out and devoid of detail. ◀

4.19 ● If you are photographing landscapes on a grey or overcast day, you can improve the quality of your pictures by tilting the camera downwards, therefore including just a small amount of sky, or no sky at all. Cutting out the sky of a dull or softly lit landscape has the effect of increasing the contrast of the image. This increase helps to enhance the amount of colour saturation you have in the shot.

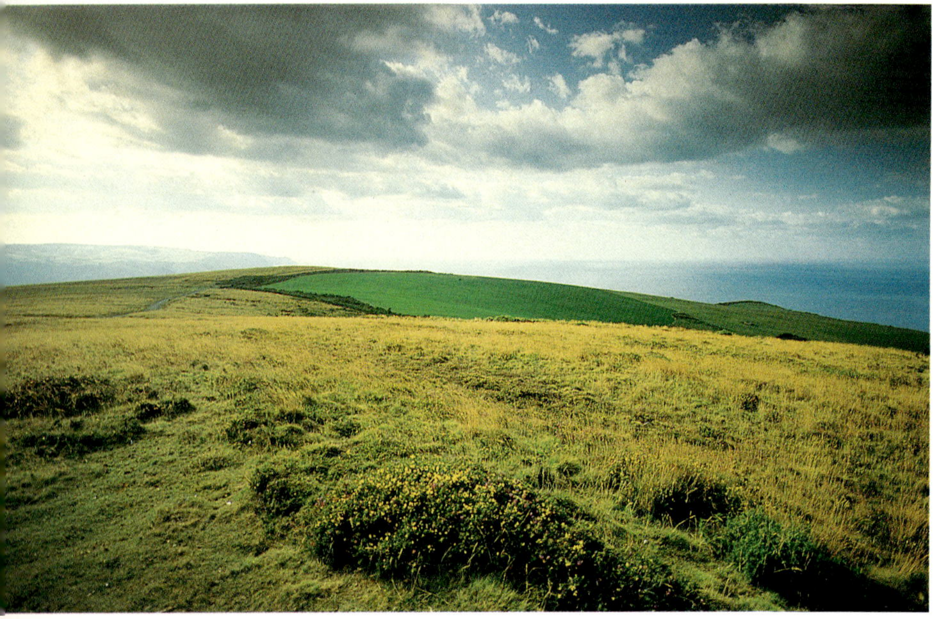

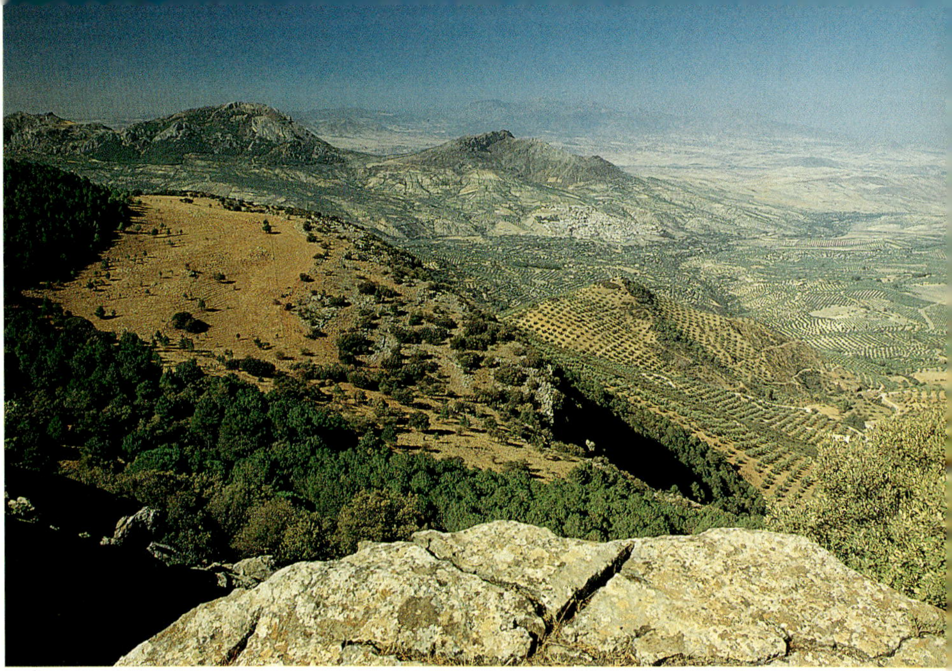

4.20 ● A long-focus lens will tend to accentuate the effects of mist or haze, but a wide-angle lens will help to give images of greater clarity. ▲ ▶

4.21 ●● When shooting distant scenes in colour, haze can often be penetrated to give greater image clarity by using a polarising filter. An ultraviolet (UV), skylight or a filter in the 81A to 81EF range will also help.

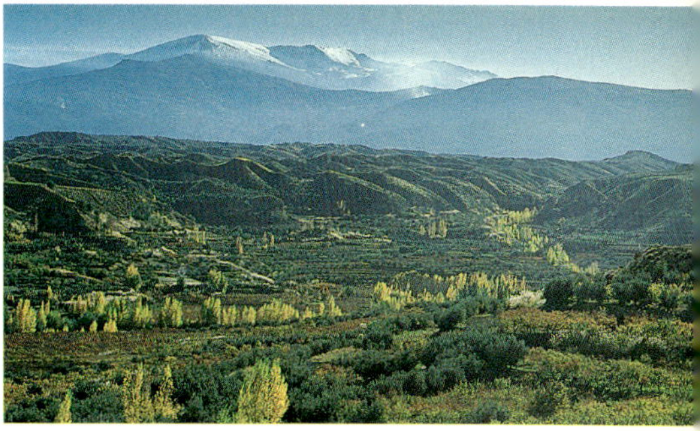

Combining a polarising filter and Wratten 81EF helped to give greater clarity in the distant detail.

4.22 ●● Landscape photographs taken into the light can result in the sky being washed out. To overcome this, combine polarising and graduated neutral density filters. ◀

4.23 ●● While graduated filters are most commonly used to alter the tone or colour of the sky area in landscape photography; they are also useful when used 'upside down' to make the foreground darker in order to enhance the impression of depth in a picture. Use them at any angle to help reduce the brightness range of a subject where an excessively light area creates a fairly straight-edged shape near one side of an image, such as a diagonal view along a street, where the pavement is sunlit but the houses are in shadow.

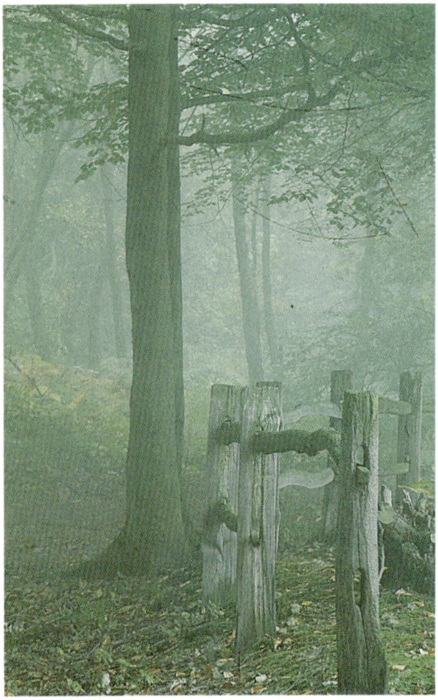

4.24 ● For distant photographs in mist or fog, give more exposure than is indicated by an averaging meter reading. In most circumstances an extra stop will suffice, but a more certain method is to take a substitute reading from a mid-toned object in the foreground. ◀

4.25 ●● The rich colours of spring and autumn woodland scenes are often most successfully captured on dull or overcast days when the light is soft and diffused and there are no dense shadows and bright highlights to dilute the colour. A polarising filter will usually enhance the colour saturation and a warm-up filter like an 81B or C will make greens and browns even richer. ▼ ▶

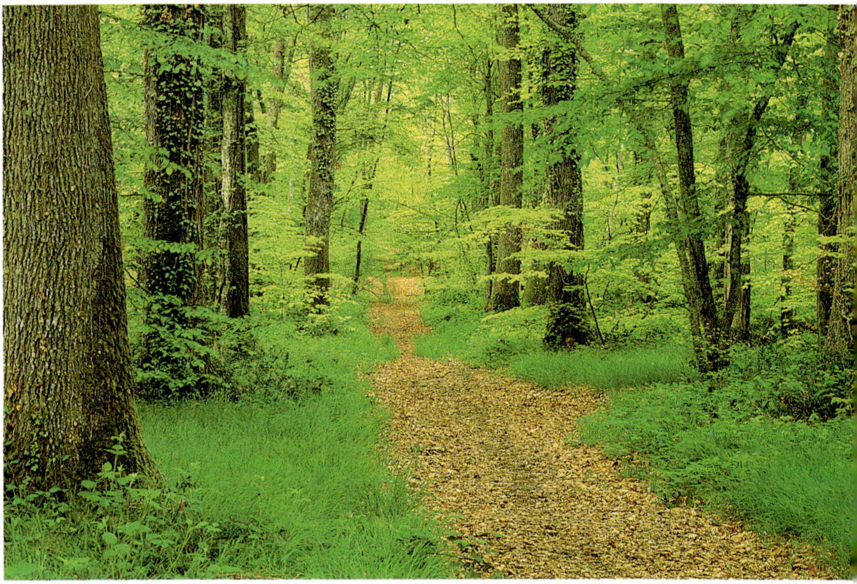

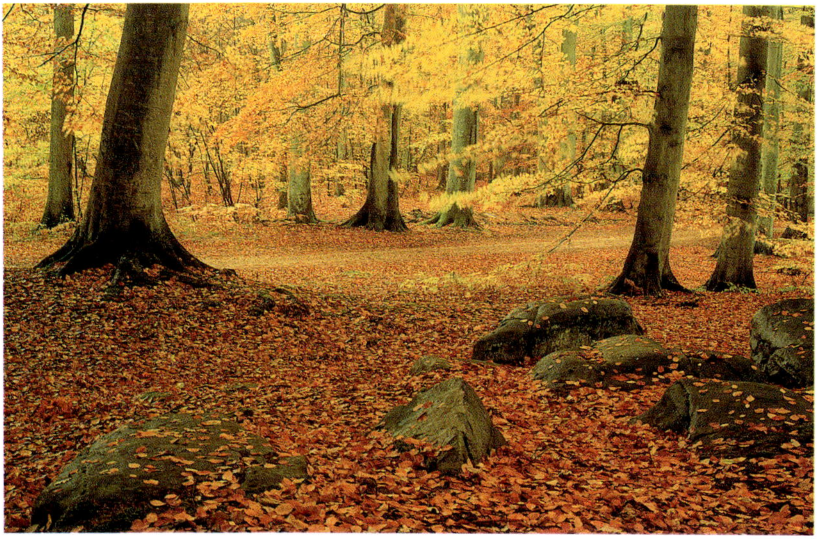

This viewpoint was chosen because it minimised the amount of daylight visible between the trees.

PRACTICAL HINT

- Heighten the effect of colour and concentrate the composition of woodland shots by choosing a viewpoint and framing the image in such a way that the minimum amount of daylight can be seen between or above the trees. When the trees are in foliage, most woods are very dark compared to the light outside the wood; the exposure needed to record the interior of the wood will cause the exterior to be very overexposed. If significant areas of daylight are included in the image, they will appear bleached-out and distracting.

4.26 ●● Use a blue filter, like an 82A, when taking black-and-white photographs on a misty day to enhance the effect. Conversely, a red or orange filter will help to penetrate the mist and give greater clarity. You can obtain a similar effect by using orthochromatic film, which is insensitive to red. ▼

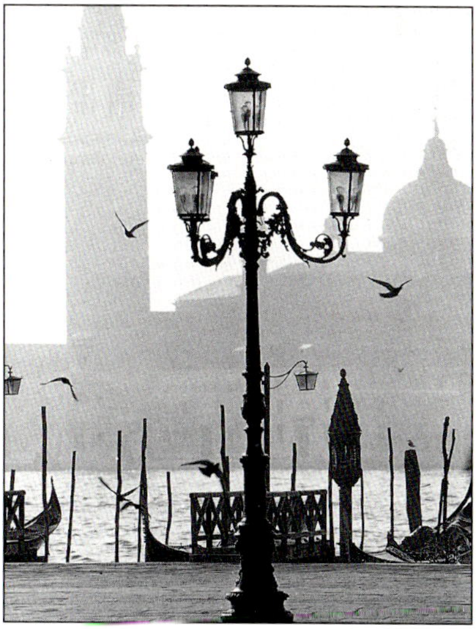

4 Photographing Buildings

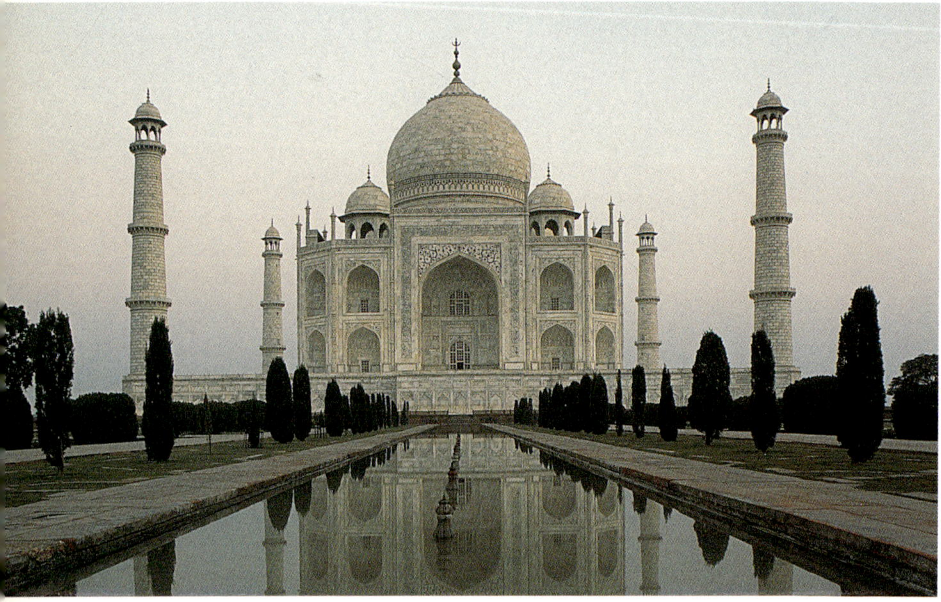

4.27 ●

When you want to take photographs of a place which is popular with tourists and it is difficult to avoid crowds, aim to shoot before 9.00 am as holidaymakers tend not to be early risers. A Sunday morning is also a good time. ▲

TECHNICAL TIP

- As an alternative to time-lapse exposures, give a long exposure of several minutes or more, long enough, in fact, to ensure that no one person has remained stationary for more than about one-tenth of the exposure time. Use a neutral density filter, obtainable in a range of strengths, when the light level will not allow such a long exposure at the smallest aperture.

4.28 ●●●

To photograph a building on a busy street where crowds or traffic will spoil the shot, use time-lapse exposures which will prevent moving objects or people recording on the film. The technique involves making a number of exposures on the same frame of film using the camera's double-exposure device. Take an exposure reading in the normal way, let's say it is 1/60 sec at f16, and then make 16 exposures at 1/1000 sec (or 8 of 1/500 sec) without winding on the film. The more exposures you make the less likelihood there is of ghost images recording when people, or vehicles, are moving slowly, or remain stationary for a period.

4.29 If you need to tilt your camera upwards, to include the top of a building for instance, do it in a positive way to make a feature of the converging verticals which will result. The effect can be even more striking if you use a wide-angle lens, but do not include the base of the structure since this will simply make it look as if it is toppling over. ▶

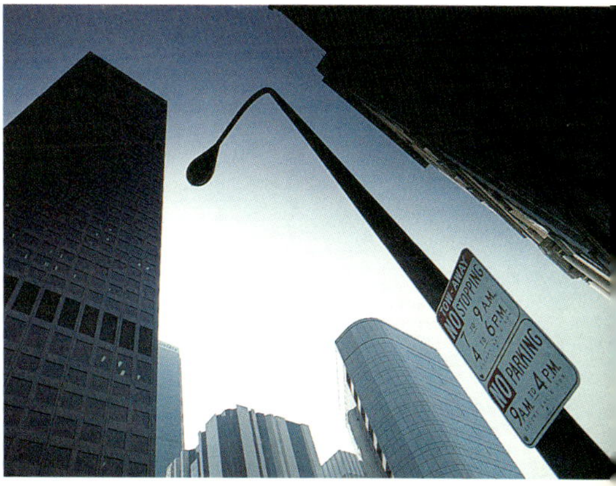

4.30 Parked cars and traffic are an unwelcome distraction in photographs of buildings in an urban environment. To overcome this in locations where there is street lighting and illumination, shoot at dusk or after dark when such details are usually lost in shadow. ▼

PRACTICAL HINT

- A natural frame at the top and sides of the image, for example an archway or the branches of a tree, will enhance the effect of converging verticals.

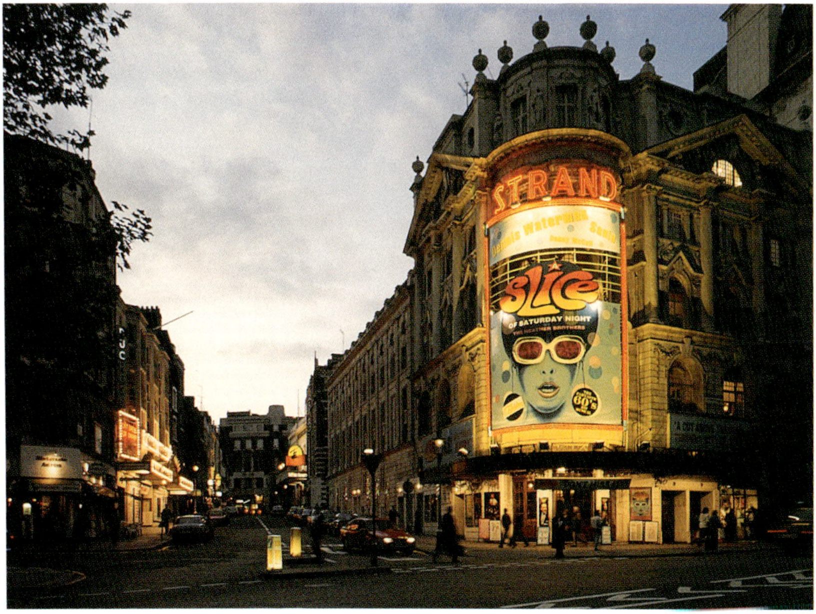

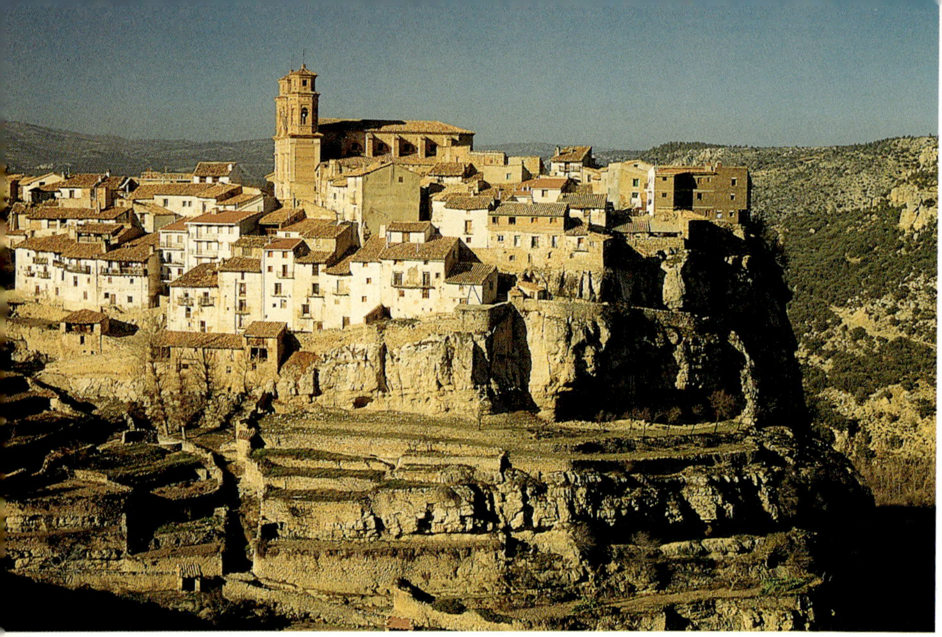

4.31 Finding a suitable viewpoint when photographing a building, a village or a view from a distance can sometimes be difficult. I try to stand in front of the aspect I wish to feature in my shot and study the surroundings for an identifiable spot at the correct angle. With the aid of a large scale map, a compass and a pair of binoculars, you will often find a good spot quite quickly which might otherwise take hours to discover. ▲

4.32 Photographs of illuminated buildings and street scenes at night are best shot before it becomes completely dark. If you wait for half an hour or so after sunset, there will still be enough light remaining in the sky to show the outline of the buildings, and the exposure needed to record detail in the shadows will not be so great that the lights themselves appear burned out. ▶

TECHNICAL TIP

- Daylight type film is generally best to capture a wet, night time street scene. If the lighting is very warm in colour, for instance red and orange neons in advertising signs, the effect of artificial light can be pleasing as the darker areas of the scene will have a pronounced blue cast and create a bold colour contrast.

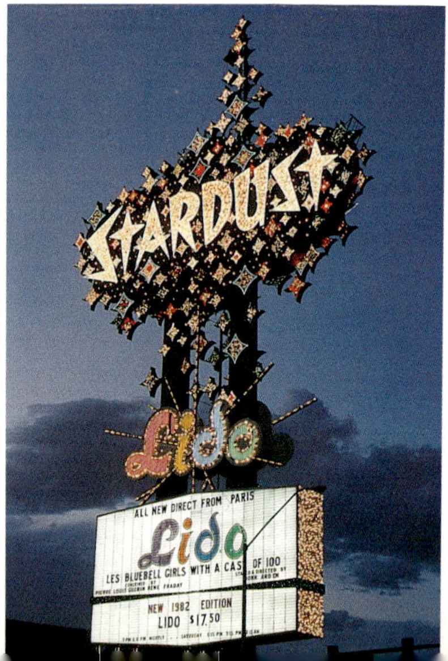

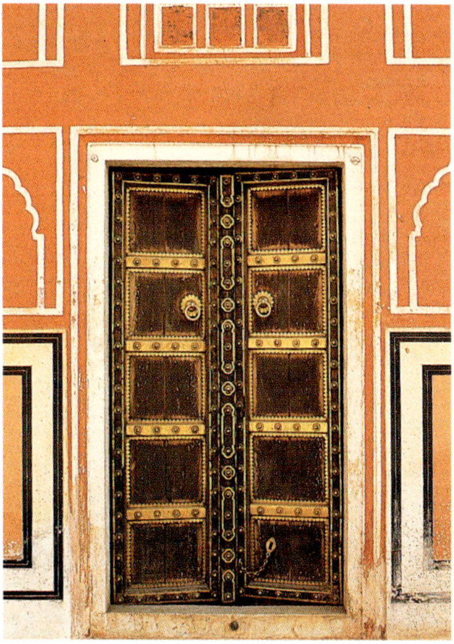

4.33 ● City street scenes at night time or at dusk are most striking after rain when the roads and pavements are wet, reflecting the colourful street lights and illuminated shop windows. Reflections add to the impact and atmosphere of a night-time shot, helping to prevent the creation of large, dark, featureless areas in the image.

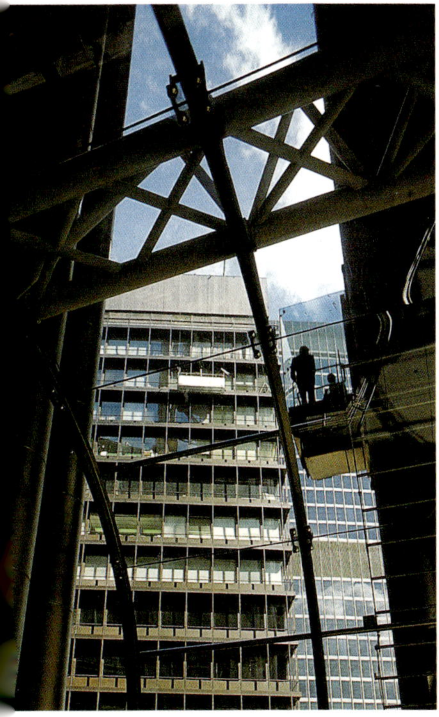

4.34 ● When shooting a building, the photographer's initial inclination is to include the complete structure in the picture. It is often more effective, however, to isolate details and emphasise the elements of texture and pattern; such pictures are frequently more satisfying and have a stronger impact and sense of design than a broader shot can create. ◀ ▼ ▲

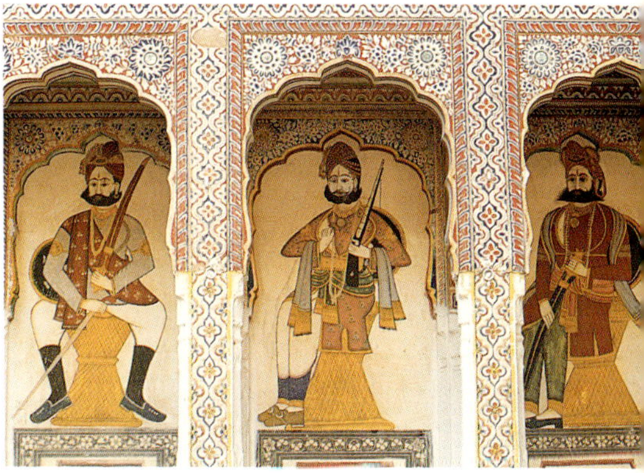

TECHNICAL TIP

- A long-focus lens allows you to isolate a small area of a building from a distant viewpoint and minimise the impression of perspective.

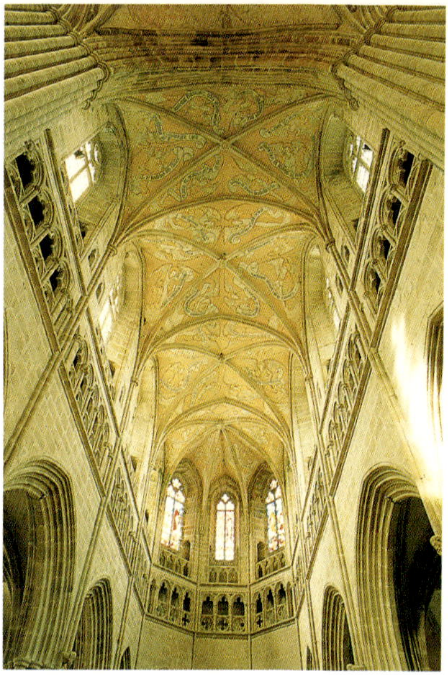

4.35 ●● An exposure meter may not give a reading if you take pictures of interiors when the light level is low. Overcome these problems by setting the camera to a ten times faster film speed, to 1000 ISO when using ISO 100 film, for example. Then give ten times the exposure indicated, 10 sec instead of 1 sec, for instance. Remember to reset the film speed dial to the correct ISO number when you have finished shooting. ▶

4.36 ● There is a tendency to produce rather cliched photographs of well-known sights or buildings, particularly when viewpoints are restricted. Try to wait for opportunities when the light or weather creates an unfamiliar quality: dusk and dawn can be especially effective in generating an unusual colour quality and shots taken in the snow, mist or rain are likely to have greater originality and will stand out from the rest. ▼

TECHNICAL TIP

- When taking a straightforward exposure reading for illuminated scenes at dusk, remember to exclude the very brightest lights as this will cause underexposure and the pictures will lack shadow detail. Take an average from the highest reading you can obtain from a small section of the scene and the lowest reading you can measure from any part of it.

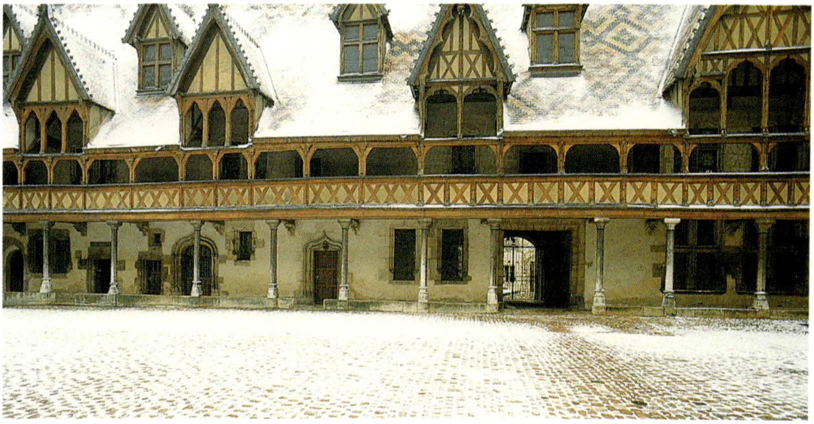

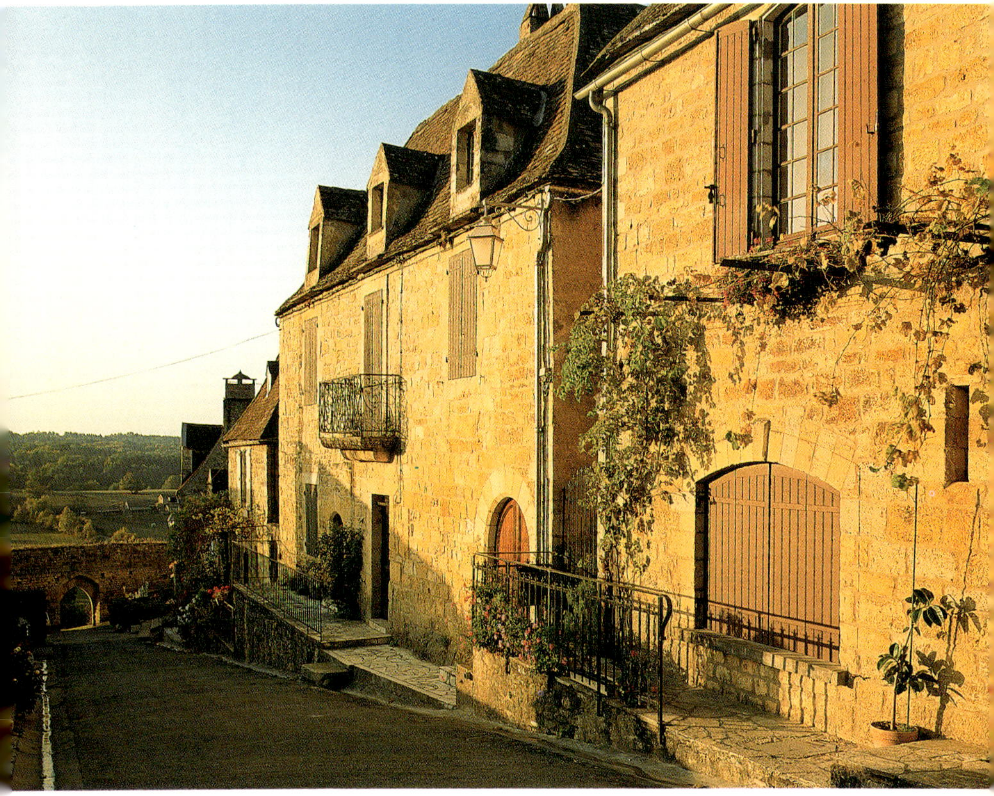

4.37 ● The texture of ancient, weathered stone and wood in old buildings and historic sites can be enhanced enormously by shooting in early morning or evening light. The lower colour temperature adds warmth to the stone and the more acute angle of the light accentuates the texture. ▲

4.38 ● Study guide books and postcards of a destination when you plan to photograph its most famous sights and buildings. These will often give you a good idea of the best times of day and the possible viewpoints of specific places, saving valuable time and effort.

TECHNICAL TIP

- When shooting sunlit buildings in black-and-white, the quality and texture of stone will be emphasised if you use an orange or red filter which creates stronger relief by making a blue sky appear as a significantly darker tone.

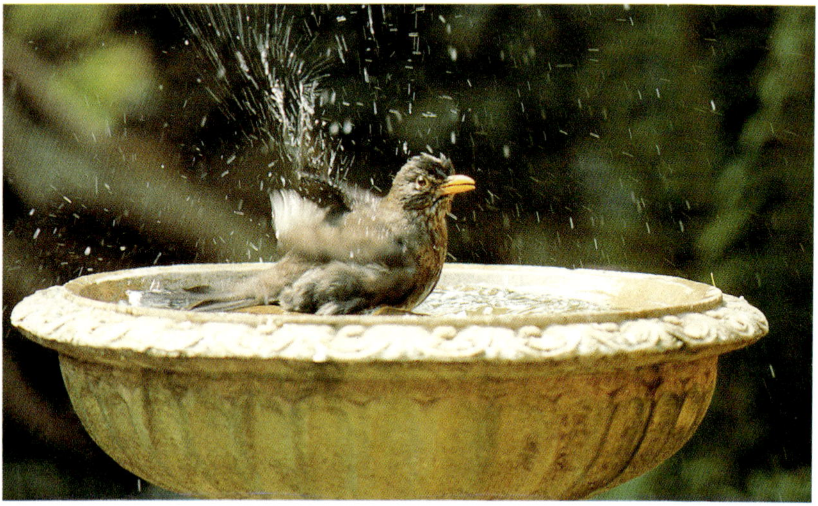

4.39 ● To photograph pets, wait until half an hour or so after they have been fed when they are a little sleepy and more compliant. If you prefer livelier pictures, shoot before the pets' usual feeding time and use favourite treats to bribe them to co-operate. ▼

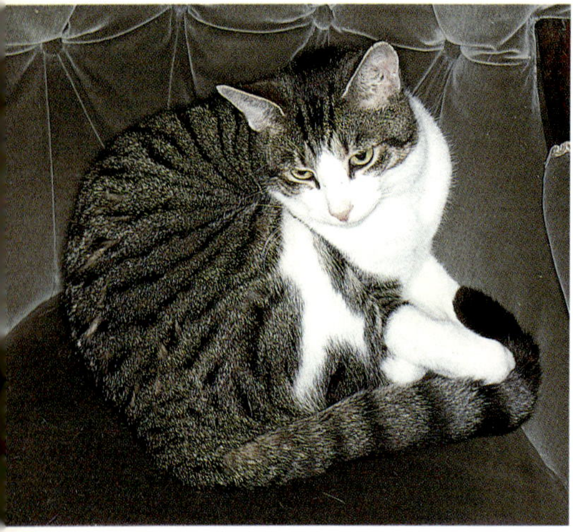

4.40 ●● Take good close-up shots of wild birds and animals like squirrels in your garden with the aid of an air release. This is a long, thin flexible tube which fits into the cable release socket of the camera, enabling the shutter to be fired by pressure on a bulb at the other end. Set up the camera behind a screen close to a bird table, or a place where the animals are habitually fed, then wait until the animals accept the screen and the subjects arrive at a prefocussed spot. ▲

4.41 ●● With autofocus, auto-exposure and autowind facilities it is, of course, possible to take a sequence of pictures without having to approach the camera. An infrared trigger is a more sophisticated and expensive type of release which is obtainable for many cameras.

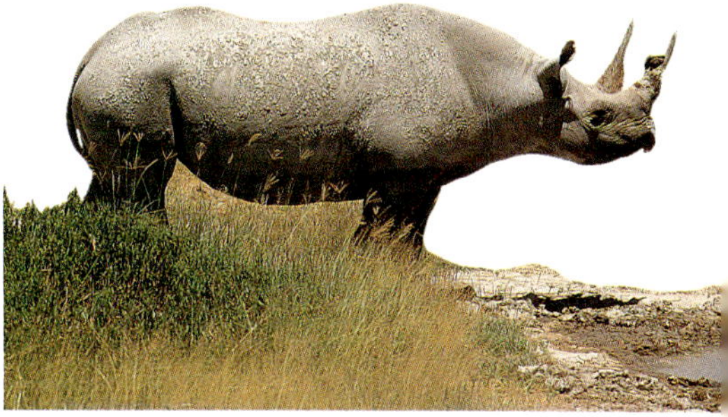

4.42 ●●● Panning is a technique which requires good co-ordination between eye and hand, and it will help to practise the skill by making dry runs with any moving subject whenever the opportunity arises. The subject generally tends to move faster than the camera; as a result, the image finishes up too close to the edge of the frame towards which it is moving. To offset this, try to keep the subject closer to the back edge of the frame in preference to the centre, as the image will look more balanced if the space in front of a moving object is greater than that behind it.

4.43 ●● When photographing animals on a safari holiday (when you are not usually allowed to leave the vehicle) ask for a window seat and try to lower your tripod (with camera attached) to the ground. This will provide a far steadier support than resting your camera on the edge of the raised-roof viewing area, as the slightest movement within the minibus or jeep can cause out-of-focus pictures when you are using a long-focus lens. If you are forced to rest the camera on part of the vehicle, use a bean bag – and ask everyone to freeze before you shoot. ▲

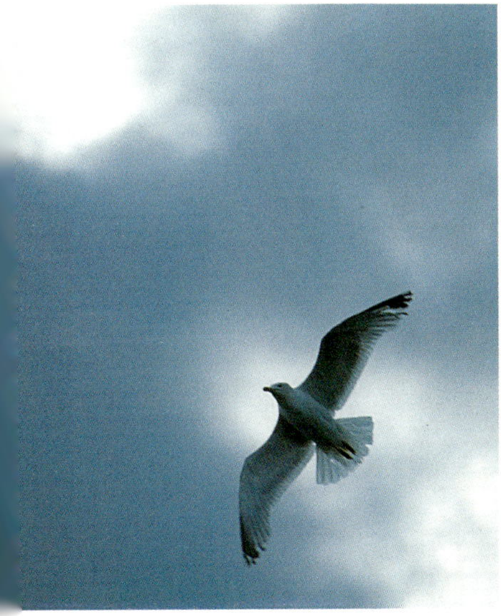

4.44 ●●● To obtain a sharp, 'frozen' image of moving animals, or birds in flight, select the fastest possible shutter speed (preferably 1/1000 sec or less) and use the panning technique described above to keep pace with the creature's movement. You will achieve reasonably sharp images, even when you have used slower shutter speeds such as 1/125 sec.

When the subject is moving across the camera's view, you will find that a faster shutter speed is needed in order to freeze the creature's movement than when the subject is moving towards the camera. ◄

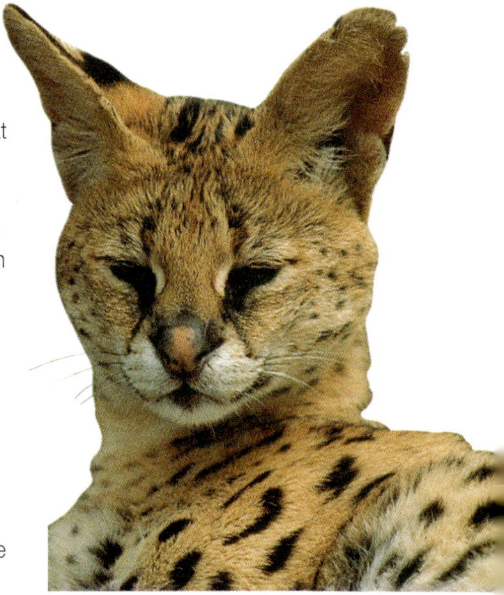

4.45 ● If you want to photograph zoo animals kept in enclosures behind wire fences, use a long-focus lens at a fairly wide aperture and place the lens as close as possible to the fence which will not be visible in the picture. It will also help to choose an area of fence which does not have bright highlights and is of a similar tone to the subject. ▶

4.46 ● Improve close-up photographs of flowers in situ by using a piece of card or fabric of a suitable colour if the natural background is too fussy or an unpleasing hue. Make sure the card is about 50cm behind the subject and keep it well out of focus.

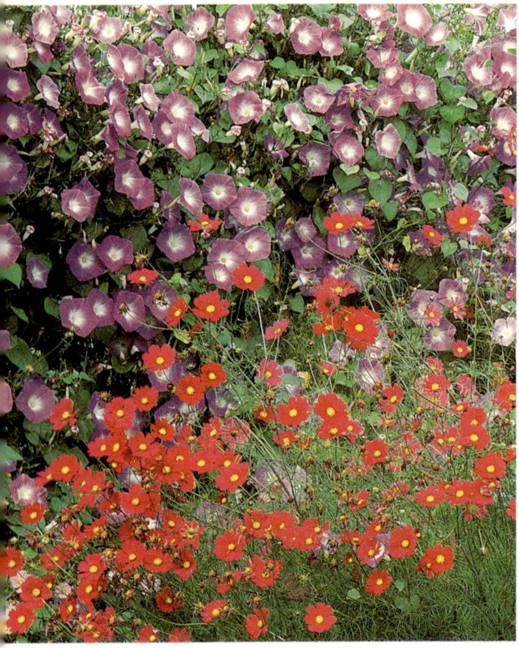

TECHNICAL TIP

- Where direct sunlight is unavoidable, shoot into the light. This type of lighting tends to create high contrast, so you will probably need to use a fill-in reflector or flash to make the shadows less dense.

4.47 ●● For close-up shots of flowers, the soft light of an overcast or hazy day is usually best; the bright highlights and dense shadows caused by direct sunlight create fussy, confusing images in which the subject's subtlety of colour and texture are lost. If your chosen subject is situated in an area of bright sunlight, you can soften the light with a diffusion screen, a large white flash or location umbrella. ◀

4.48 ● The photography of wildflowers in their natural surroundings is often hampered by even the slightest breeze, especially when you are taking close-up pictures where the smallest degree of movement of the plants will cause blur and when it is not possible to use a fast shutter speed. To overcome the effects of breezes, erect a windshield of card or rigid plastic as close to the subject as possible.

4.49 ●● Minimise individual plant movement when taking outdoor close-ups by driving splints into the ground, pushed up tight and hidden behind plant stems: flower-arranging wire is ideal.

4.50 ●● For close-up shots of plant specimens which grow too close to the ground for a table-top tripod to be used, you can make an effective camera support by fixing a ball-and-socket tripod head to a metal tent peg.

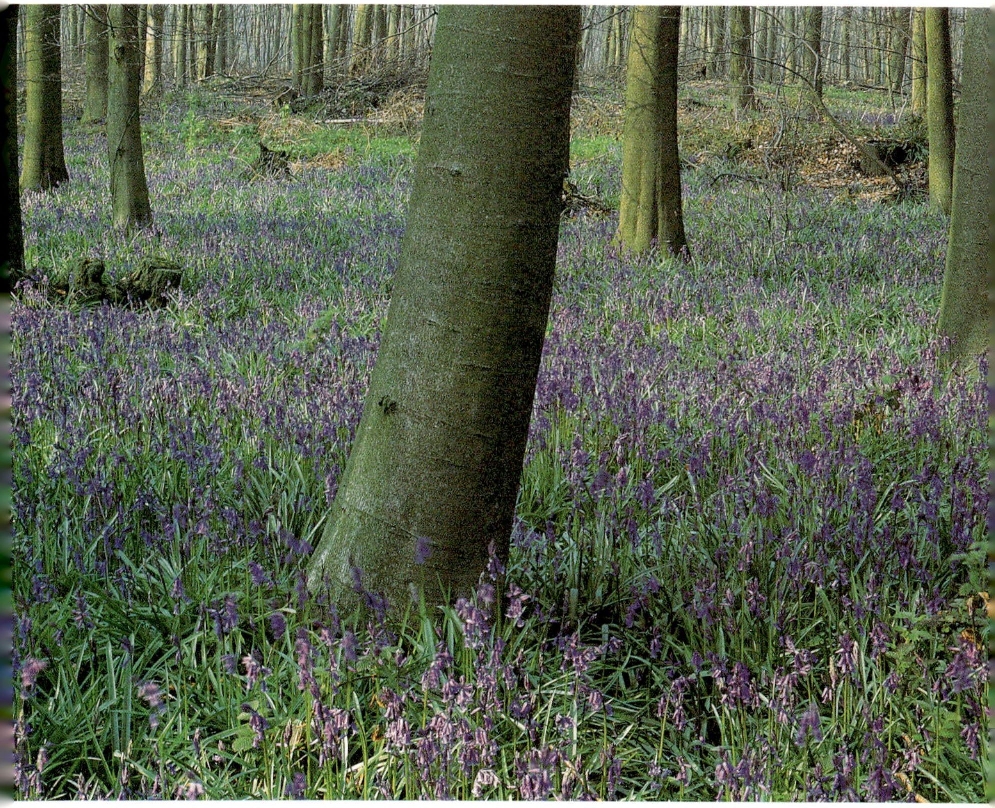

This shot needed a half-second exposure. There must be no breeze on long exposures to avoid blur.

Logistics

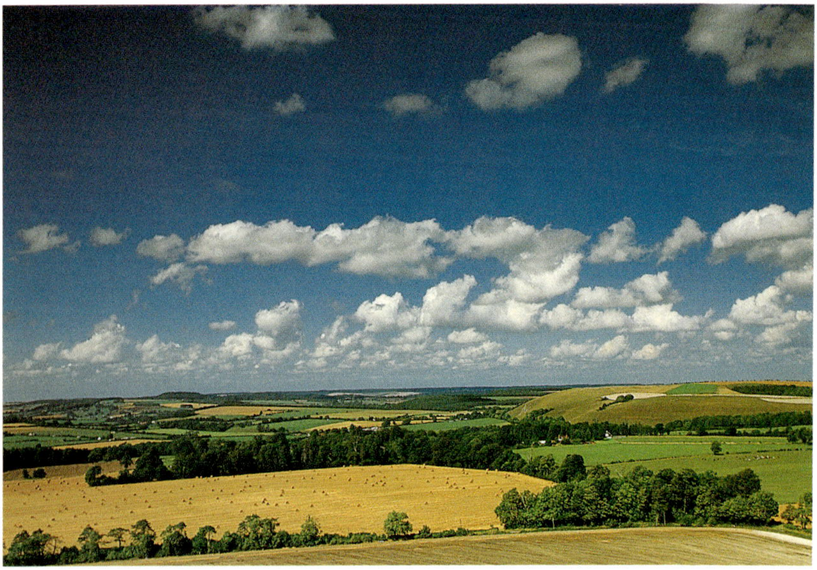

In this shot, a dramatic sky contrasts with the tranquil landscape below.

4.51 ●● A compass is a useful tool for the landscape photographer, both as an aid to map reading and to establish where the sun will rise and set. This provides invaluable information for selecting the best viewpoints and determining the best time of day to take a picture of a specific view or building. ▲

4.52 ● When travelling, a mini tape recorder is ideal and convenient for making captioning notes. It is easy to forget some of the vital details if you have to wait for a convenient moment before recording such information in a note book. A tape recorder also encourages you to describe shots more thoroughly, reducing the risk of you confusing pictures and locations after you have returned home.

4.53 ● Careful planning is essential whenever you go on a photographic shoot, especially for long trips away from home. Make lists of the places you want to visit, incorporating notes on what you feel will be the best time of day for each. With large-scale maps it is a simple matter to mark your chosen locations with a highlight pen; this saves time on the road, aids route planning, and will also help you to remember the locations of the shots taken. For extra security, mark corresponding numbers on both the map and films you shoot at each place. Highlight pens are also useful for marking locations which you chance upon and might wish to revisit, perhaps at a different time of day or on a future trip.

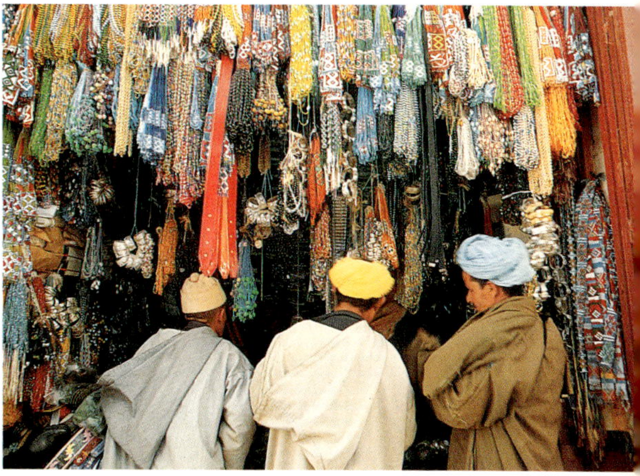

Shots like this colourful street bazaar in Morocco help to add both interest and atmosphere to a holiday record.

4.54 Good records of a holiday can be some of the most valued pieces of family memorabilia, but often they are uninteresting and incomplete collections of randomly-taken pictures. To ensure that your collection will give lasting pleasure, treat your holiday photography as a picture story in which the events unfold in an ordered and chronological way.

Use the best shots to illustrate every important aspect of the experience. Photograph new friends and characters you meet, together with local events like markets and festivals as well as atmospheric pictures of the beach, scenery and hotel. Try to vary the scale and variety of your pictures. Use different lenses to obtain both close-ups and wide views and look for ways in which you can use colours and composition to give your pictures greater variety and interest when viewed as a set. ▲

4.55 Although some of the best landscape photographs are the result of sheer good luck, it is unwise to rely upon this, and I cannot stress too highly the value of reconnaissance. The time you spend finding photogenic corners of the countryside and seeking good viewpoints is never wasted – even a short spell of good light can enable you to take a number of excellent photographs if you know precisely where to go. ▼

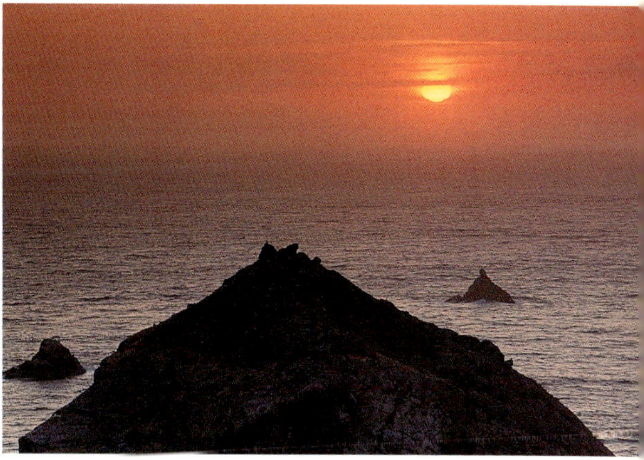

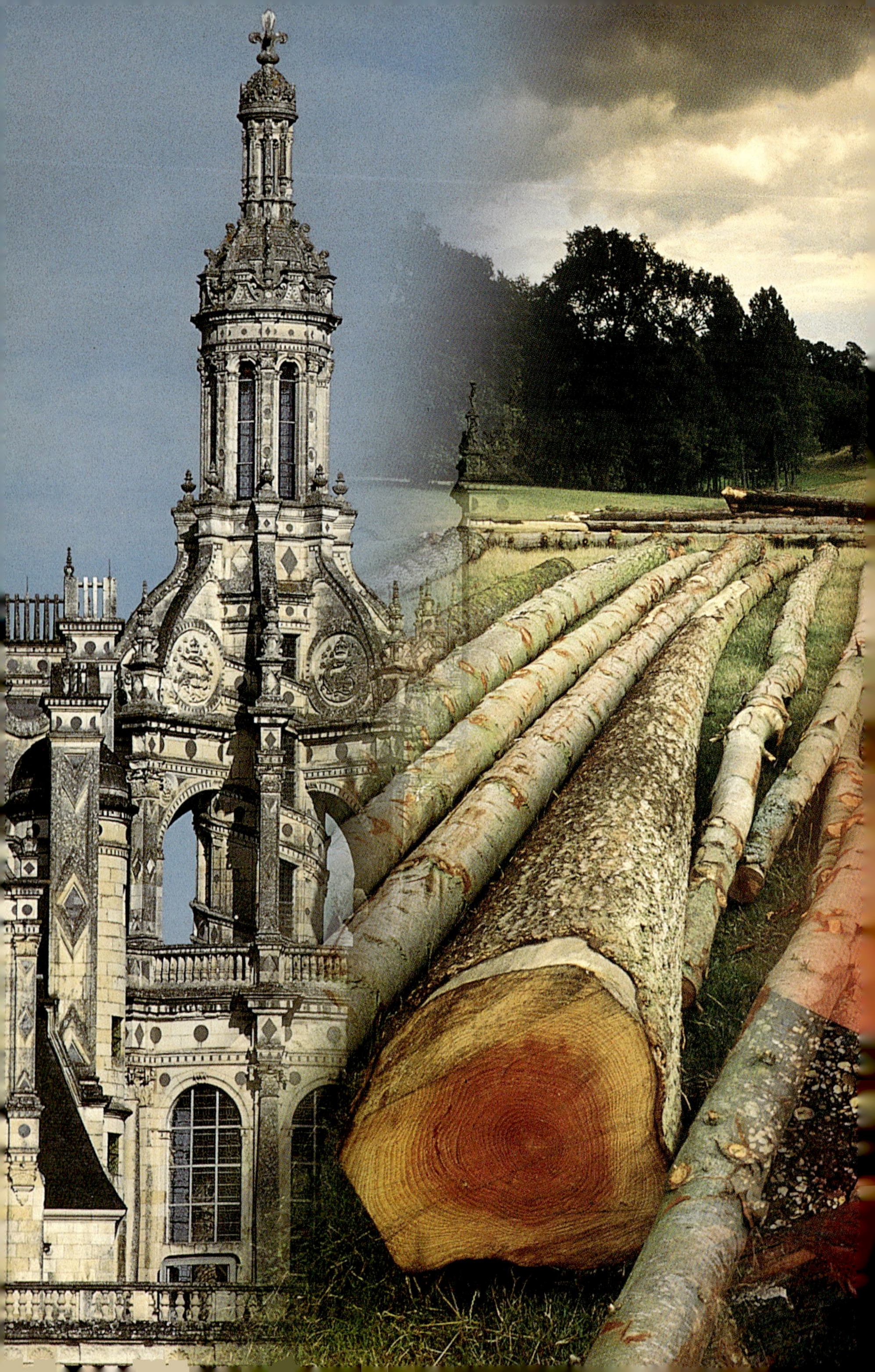

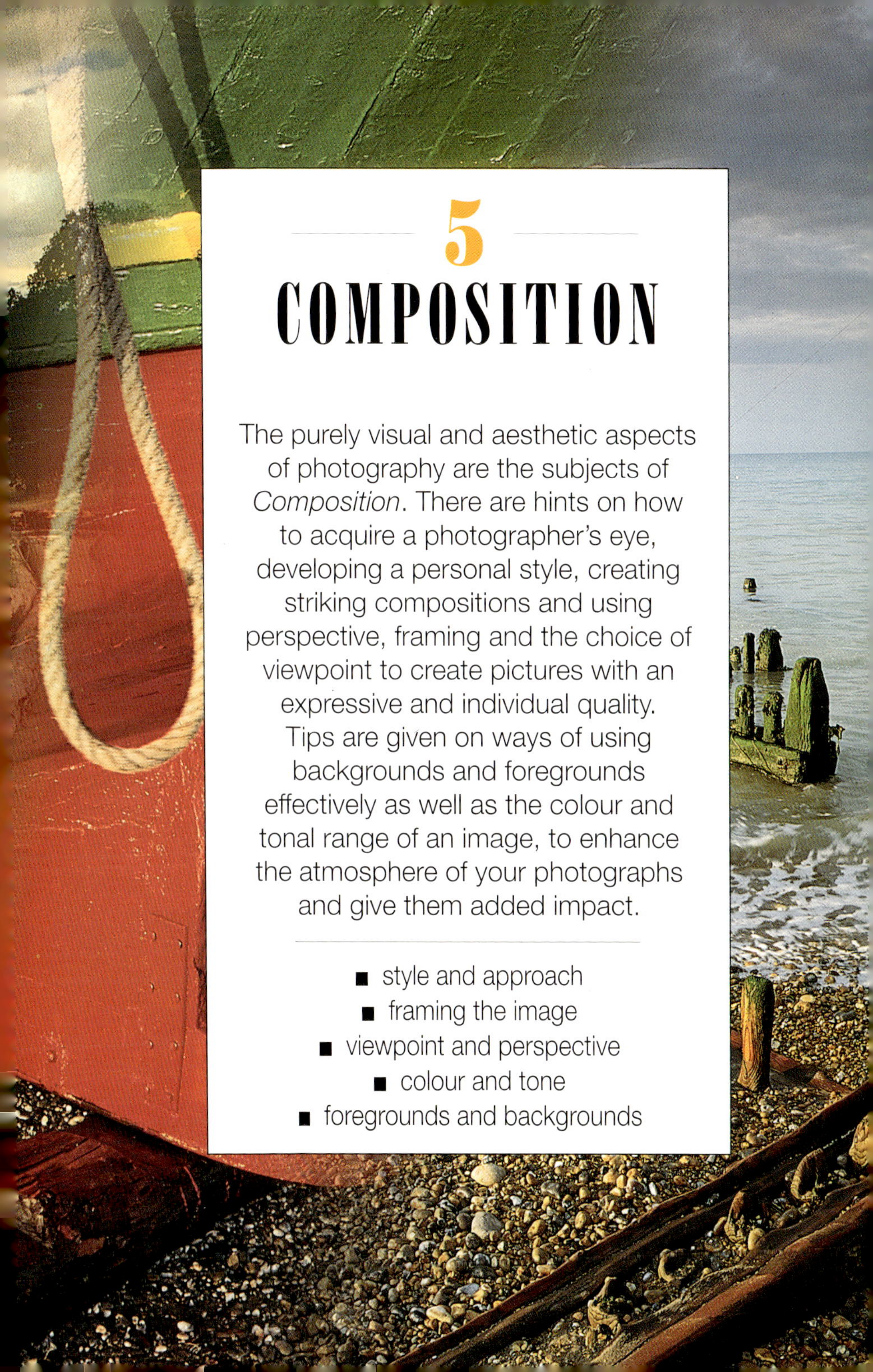

5

COMPOSITION

The purely visual and aesthetic aspects of photography are the subjects of *Composition*. There are hints on how to acquire a photographer's eye, developing a personal style, creating striking compositions and using perspective, framing and the choice of viewpoint to create pictures with an expressive and individual quality. Tips are given on ways of using backgrounds and foregrounds effectively as well as the colour and tonal range of an image, to enhance the atmosphere of your photographs and give them added impact.

- style and approach
- framing the image
- viewpoint and perspective
- colour and tone
- foregrounds and backgrounds

5 Style and Approach

5.01 • To help you to produce the sort of photographs which convey a personal and expressive quality, try to develop the habit of putting into words – in your mind will do – the feelings that you have about the subject and why it has inspired your choice of composition. For example, it may be the shape of a particular tree, the formation of clouds in the sky or the quality of early morning light in a scene. Consciously express these thoughts to yourself, and you will discover how your feelings can be best brought out and encapsulated in the images of the scene. ▼

5.02 • Whenever you produce a disappointing photograph, analyse it carefully instead of simply casting it aside. You can probably learn as much, if not more, from your failures than from your successes by becoming aware of exactly why they failed and understanding how you might avoid these faults in future.

5.03 • It is all too easy to become equipment led. Even beginners tend to have a bag full of equipment with a range of lenses, and sometimes this can hinder the essential task of actually seeing the picture. It can be very therapeutic to go out with just a

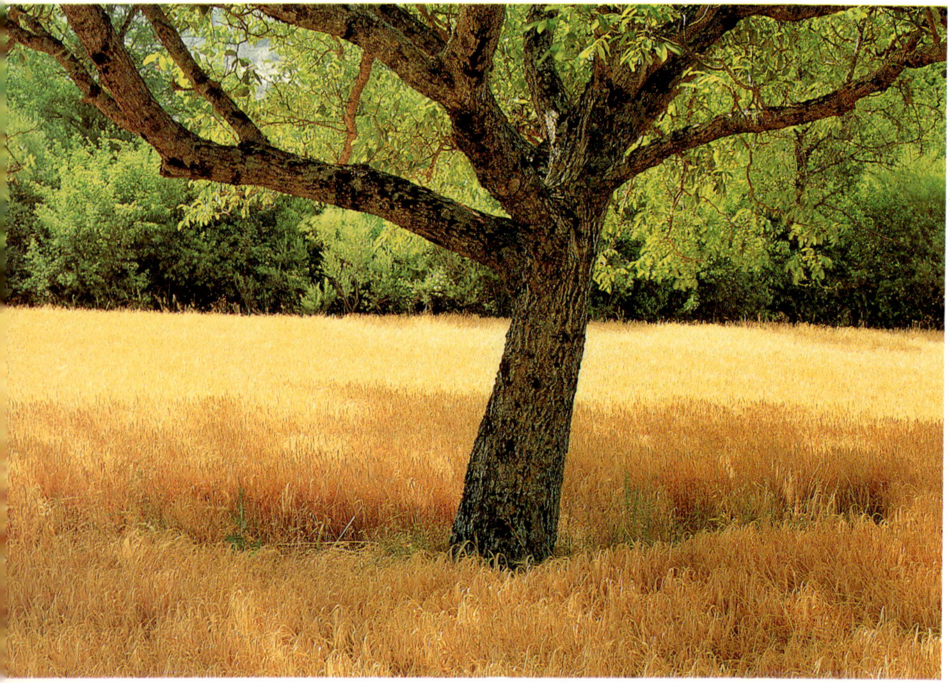

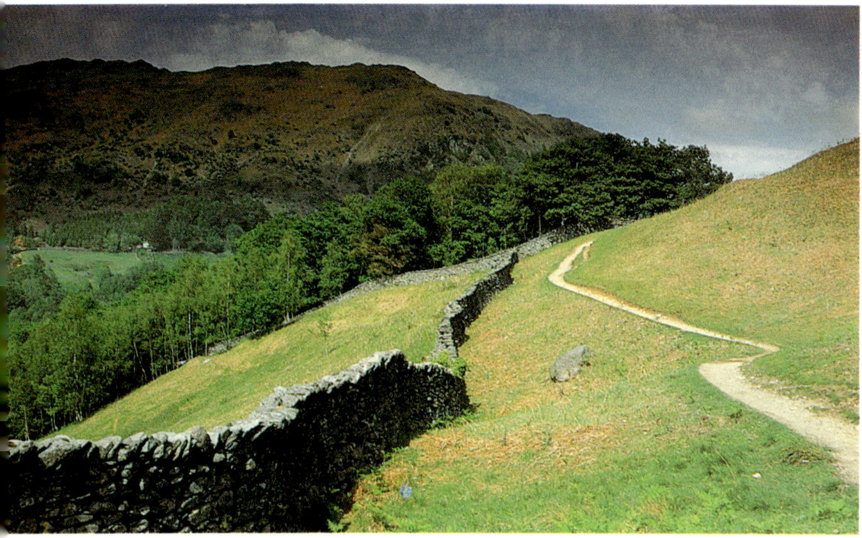

camera and standard lens; freed from the distraction of deciding which lens or accessory to use, you will be surprised just how much more observant and productive your approach can be.

5.04 Improve your photographic results by considering each picture opportunity as a potential series of photographs, rather than a single image. You do not need to make exposures of each variation, but if you explore all the possible viewpoints and the ways in which the image can be framed will ensure that you make the most of every photo opportunity that comes your way.

Good composition is made easier to understand if you make a tracing of your better shots.

5.05 You can learn a great deal about composition from your most successful photographs, and those which you particularly like in books and magazines, by placing a sheet of tracing paper over them and drawing in the main shapes and lines. Often this will reveal an underlying structure in the image, which is not always visible to the casual eye, and this will help you to see similar opportunities more easily in the future. ▲ ▼

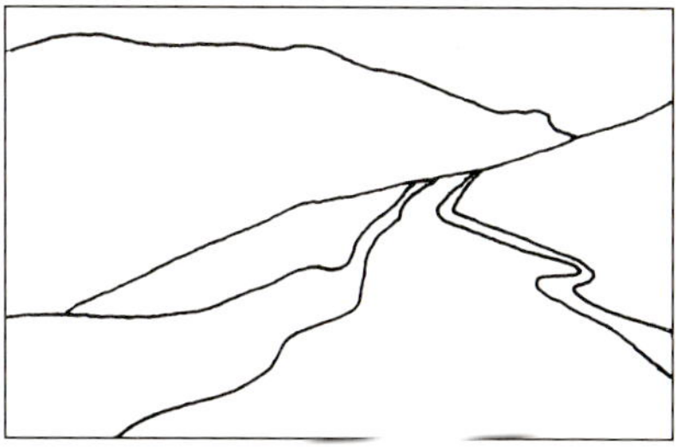

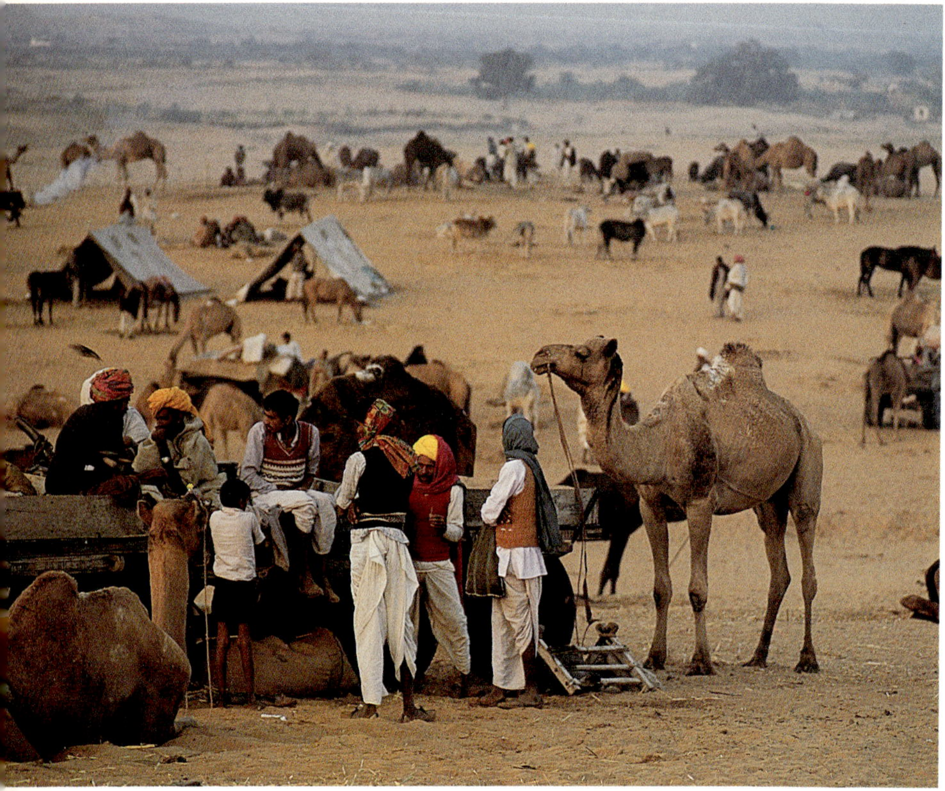

5.06 Photographers usually think in terms of the single, isolated image, but a sequence of images can be effective displayed together in some way, each contributing to an overall design. This can be in the form of a photo essay, for example, or a sequence of images where an action is depicted – like a child on a swing – or where the passage of time is portrayed – the same landscape photographed through the seasons, perhaps. Images such as these can

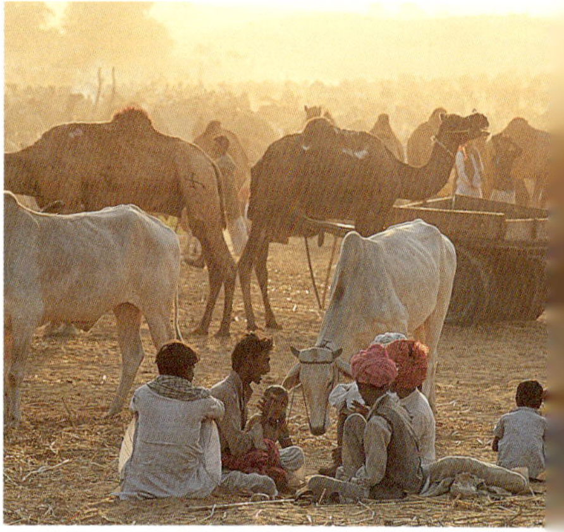

be presented as small prints on the page of a portfolio, as a group of individually framed pictures displayed on a wall, or as a collage. ◀ ▼

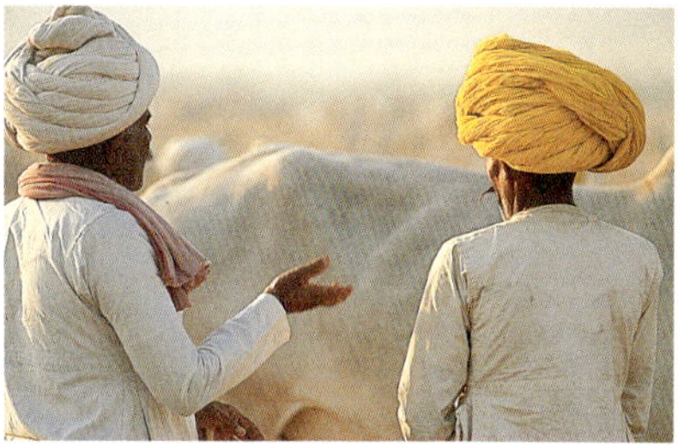

5.07 ● Many of the best photographs in glossy magazines are the products of visualisation where an art director or photographer draws a rough sketch of an image to be photographed. This sensible and productive approach can be adopted for any picture where a degree of planning is needed. It helps to focus the photographer's mind on the crucial ingredients of a shot, enabling him or her to anticipate any special props, backgrounds, equipment or techniques necessary.

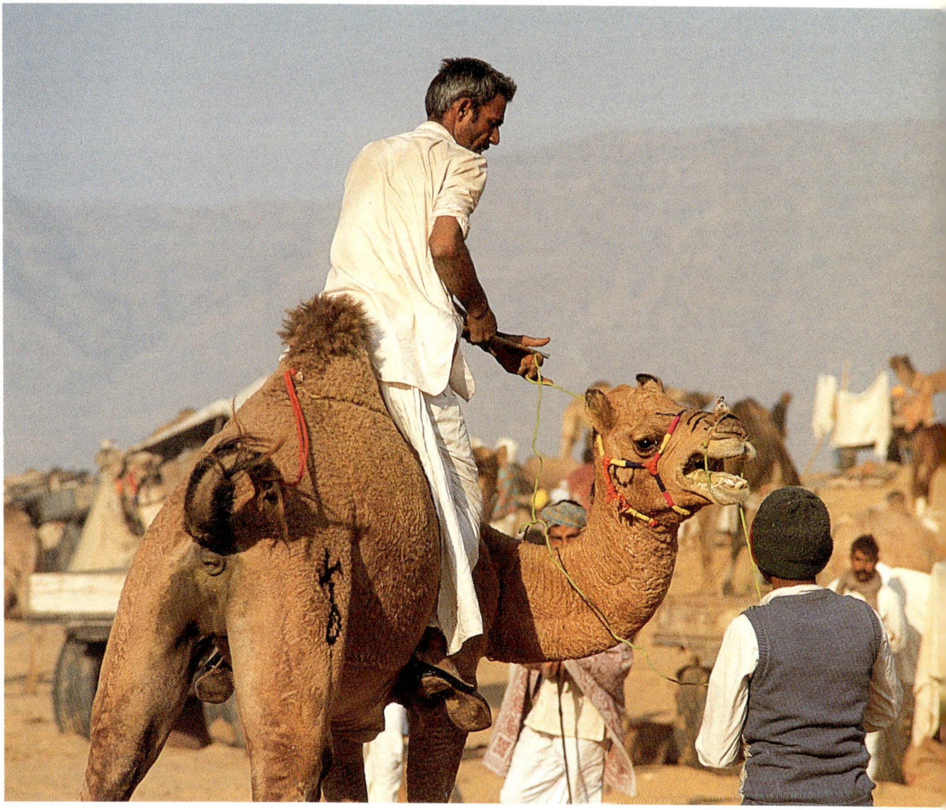

5 Framing the Image

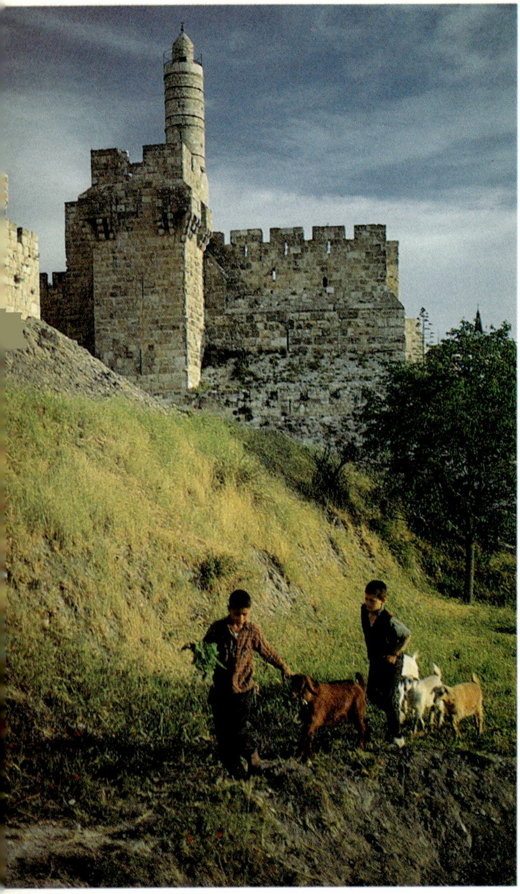

5.08 ● To judge the field of view produced by a specific lens, hold a slide mount, of the format you are using, up to your eye at a distance equal to the focal length of your lens. For example, with a 50mm lens, a 35mm slide mount should be held about 5cm away; the area seen within this mount will approximate the field of view covered by a 50mm lens.

5.09 ● Inexperienced photographers tend to focus their attention on the centre of the frame only, ignoring the surrounding details. It is a much better approach to concentrate on the borders of the viewfinder, studying each edge carefully, then move inwards to make sure that you are aware of every detail included within the frame. Only then will you be able to determine which elements of a scene are the most important and which could be excluded to improve the composition. ◀

5.10 ● Although it may seem a trifle pretentious, the film director's trick of forming a rectangle with the forefinger and thumb of each hand, held at arms' length to create a frame, can be useful in determining the best viewpoint and the most effective way to frame a shot. By concentrating the eye, it is also easier to spot any distracting elements which might spoil a shot and, in some cases, can save you the trouble of setting up your camera.

5.11 ● Ideally, there should be an identifiably dominant element in a picture. As well as objects or people, this can be something as subtle as an area of colour or a strong highlight. Once this dominant element is established, it becomes much easier to see how best to frame the image and to decide on the most effective viewpoint.

5.12 When composing shots, ensure that there is more space in front of a subject which has a sense of movement than there is behind it. Although this rule applies most readily to sport and action shots, it also works with pictures where a sense of movement is created in a static subject – the direction in which a model is looking in a portrait, for example. ▶

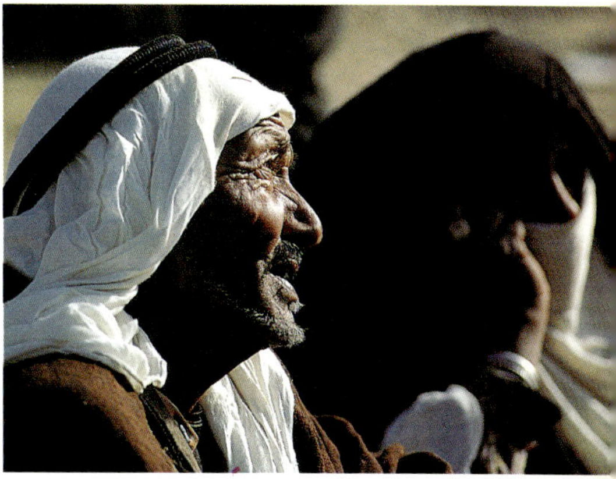

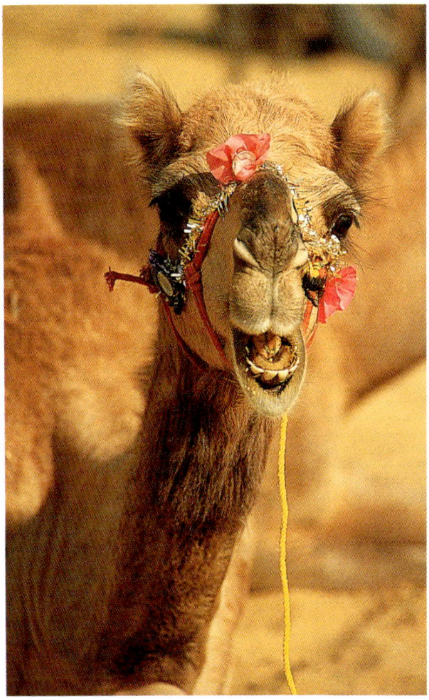

5.13 One of the most common photographic mistakes is including too much within the image. Always try to see if a closer viewpoint, or the use of a lens with a longer focal length, can improve it. ▲

5.14 It is relatively rare for the centre of the frame to be the most effective position for the image's main centre of interest. Most viewing screens have a central circle for critical focussing, and you may find that it helps to consider this a 'no-go area' for important details, unless there is a positive reason for those details to be there. ▼

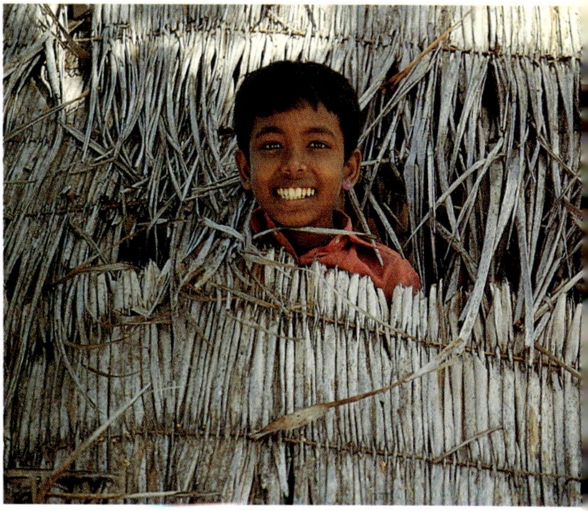

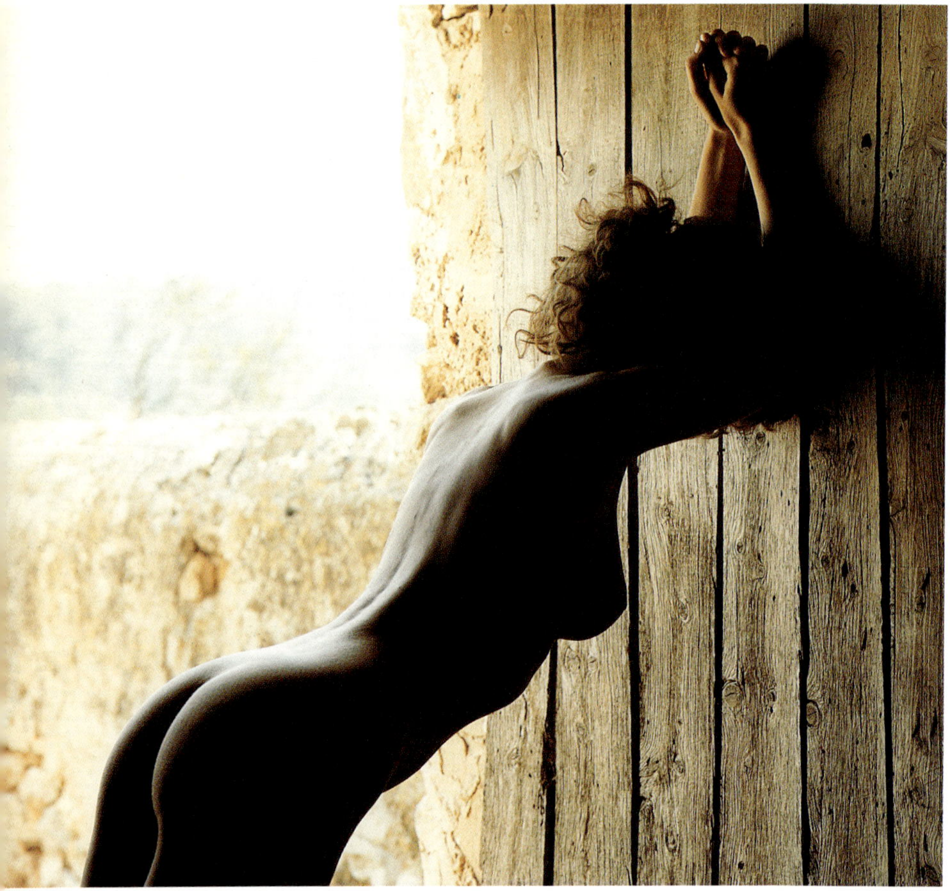

5.15 ●● One of the advantages of a square-format camera, like a Hasselblad, is that it does not have to be turned on its side to produce landscape or portrait shaped photographs; the photographer decides whether and where to crop the image after processing. The disadvantage is that there is a temptation to shoot pictures that will fit happily only into a square shape. While this will not matter necessarily for personal work, it can be a serious problem if prints are made on standard paper sizes or if the photographer is shooting with book or magazine reproduction in mind. This hazard can be avoided by drawing four lines with a thin pencil on the viewing screen outlining the A4 proportion for each shape. ▲

TECHNICAL TIP

- Using a natural frame involves shooting from a dark area towards lighter details in the distance, so there is a risk of overexposure, especially if the frame occupies a significant proportion of the image. Always take your exposure reading to exclude the darker foreground details.

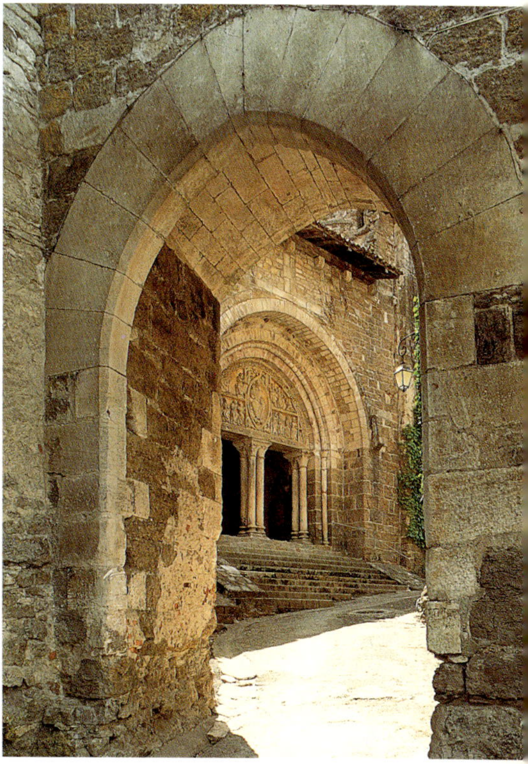

5.16 A natural frame can be an effective compositional device because it helps to contain the image and focus the viewer's attention on the main point of interest. It can also heighten the impression of depth and distance in an image. Use overhanging branches of a tree to contain only the top of the image in a landscape picture, or a window or doorway to surround the main focus of interest completely; an angular frame like this can impart a strong sense of order and cohesion. ▼ ▶

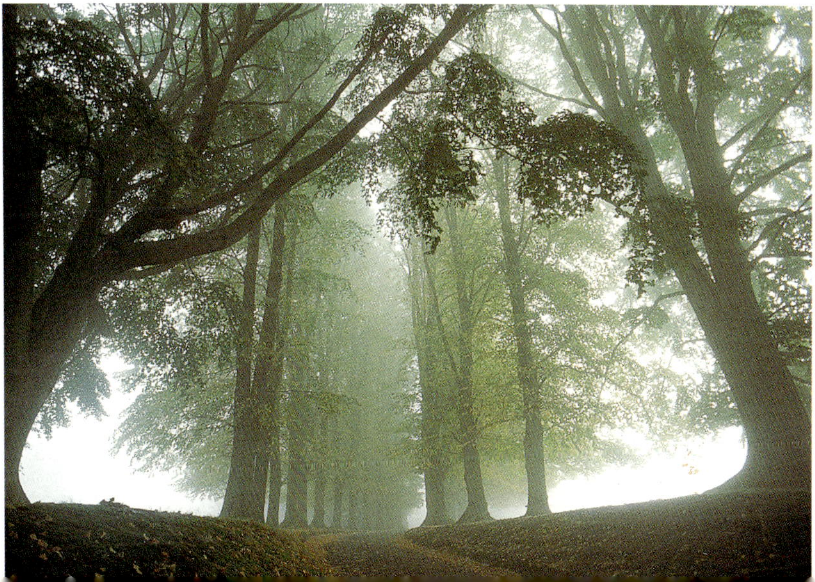

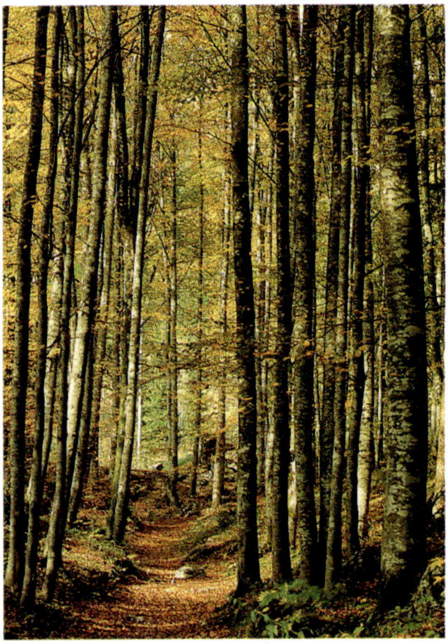

5.17 ● Most photographers find it much easier and more comfortable to hold a camera, especially a 35mm camera, in the horizontal position. Consequently, the vast majority of photographs are shot in the landscape format although, on many occasions, an upright picture would have created a better composition. To overcome this temptation, always frame the image first holding the camera vertically, so that you have to make a conscious effort to change to the landscape format. This will give you the opportunity to see if the composition is better in the vertical (portrait) format. ◀

5.18 ●● A tripod is one of the best aids to composition, as it allows you to concentrate completely on the image within the viewfinder, removing the need to hold and aim the camera steadily. If the tripod is fitted with a pan-and-tilt head, you will be able to finely adjust the lateral and vertical framing independently, making it much easier to ensure that both the horizon and any vertical lines in the image are absolutely parallel to the sides of the frame. ▼

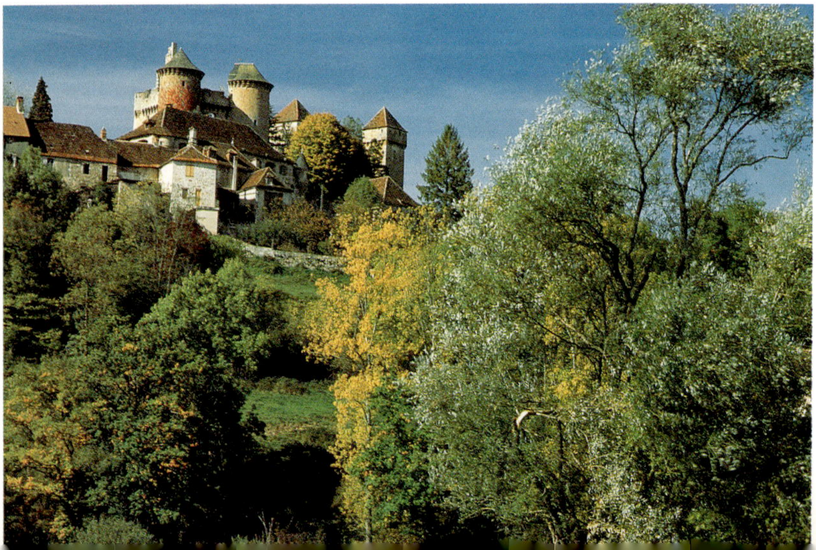

5.19 ●● Most photographs are taken from eye-level and the effect of taking shots from a higher or lower viewpoint can often be dramatic. When taking pictures of subjects quite close to the camera, try standing on a rigid camera case or box, while for more distant subjects, a lightweight aluminium step ladder such as those favoured by press photographers can make a world of difference. Similarly, lying on the ground for a worms-eye view can also produce quite startling images. A waist-level viewfinder will make such shots easier and more comfortable to take. ▼ ▶

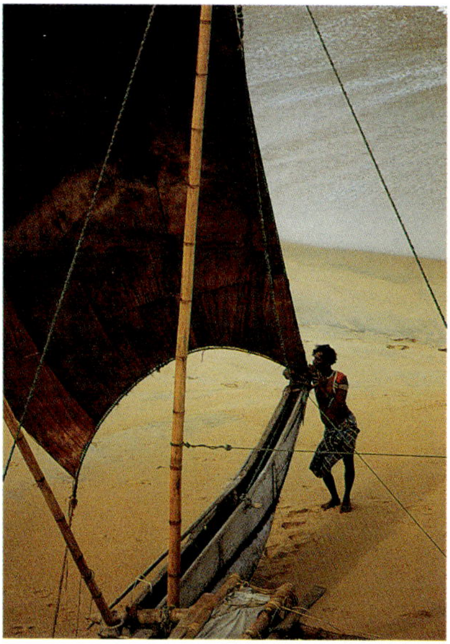

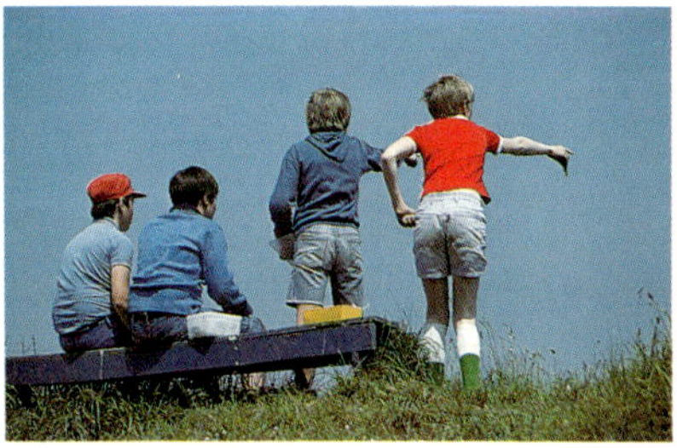

5.20 ● Photographs will have a stronger and more positive quality when the image's centre of interest stands out clearly from its surroundings, so choose your viewpoint with this consideration uppermost in mind. Place a light-toned object against a darker area of background, and vice versa, and juxtapose a subject with a dominant colour against a neutral or complimentary colour. You can also achieve a suitable contrast by opposing elements like lines, shapes and textures; the vertical line of a tree, for instance, will stand out clearly from the flowing horizontal lines of a landscape. ▼

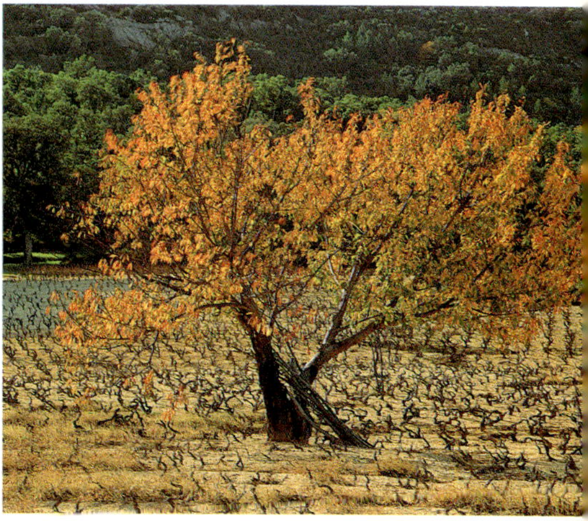

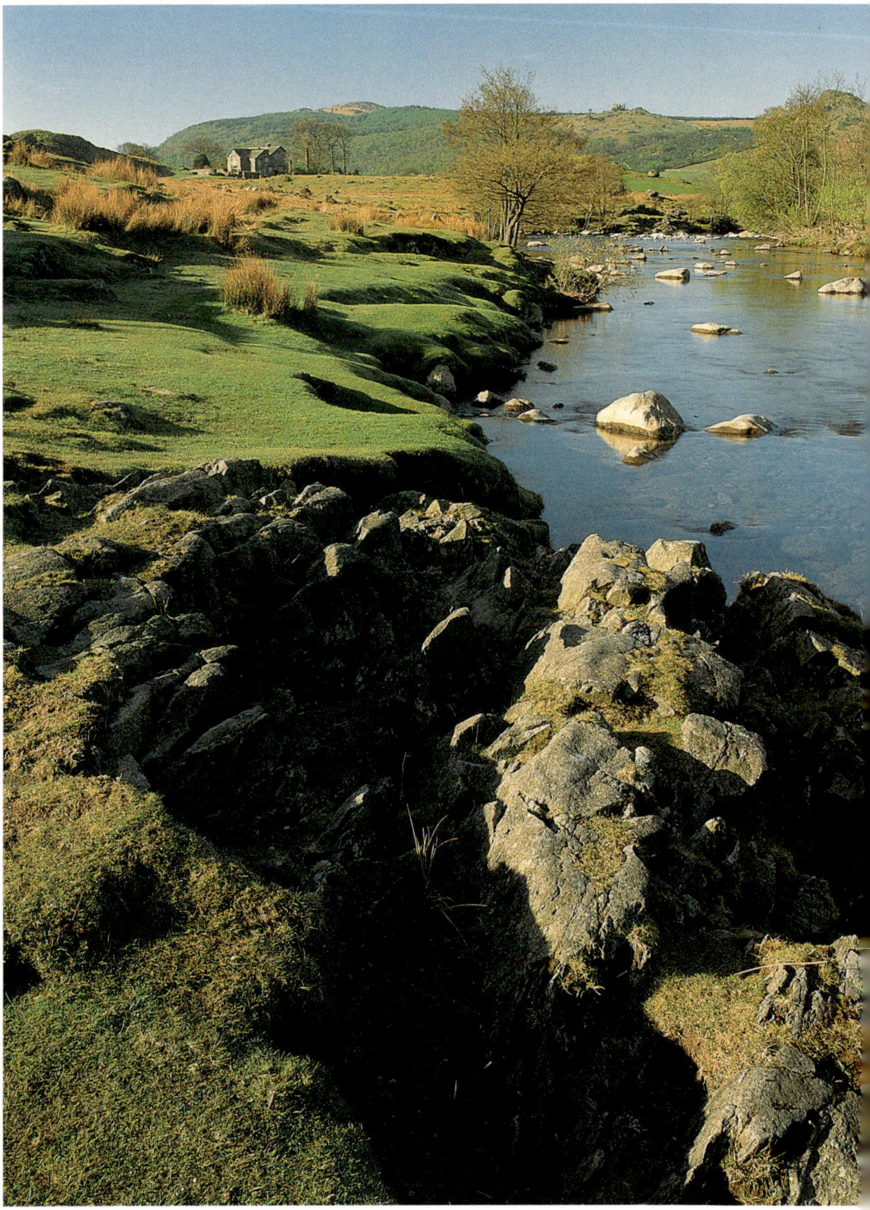

A wide-angle lens was used to include close foreground details and to exaggerate the effect of perspective.

5.21 ●● By minimising the perspective of a scene, you can create equally powerful, and often evocative, images. Use a long-focus lens to allow a more distant viewpoint and to exclude foreground details. The effect is heightened when two distant planes are juxtaposed so that the furthest objects appear disproportionately large, creating the impression of 'stacking'.

Pictures of cricket matches are a classic example, when the bowler appears to be hardly any distance from the batsman. These shots are invariably taken on very long-focus lenses, 800mm or more, but a similar effect can be obtained if objectives are more modest. The effect of a shot taken on a 300mm lens, for example, can be heightened by cropping and enlarging the central portion of the image. ▶

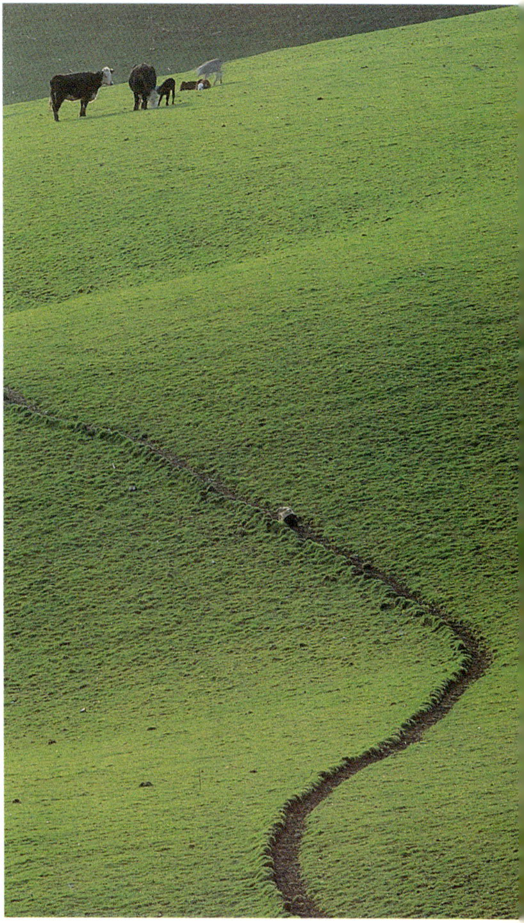

5.22 ●● A method certain to create bold eye-catching images is to exaggerate the perspective, a technique which can be applied to almost every subject from landscapes to portraits and still-life. Use a wide-angle lens and choose a viewpoint which allows the inclusion of both close foreground details and more distant objects. The effect will be especially strong when there are well-defined planes and receding lines in the subject. Although the most dramatic effects of this type will be produced with ultra-wide lenses, for instance an 18mm lens on a 35mm camera, a marked perspective effect can be obtained with a 28mm or 35mm lens when photographing the right subject from the most telling viewpoint. For this type of picture, use a small aperture so that both foreground and background details are in sharp focus. ◀

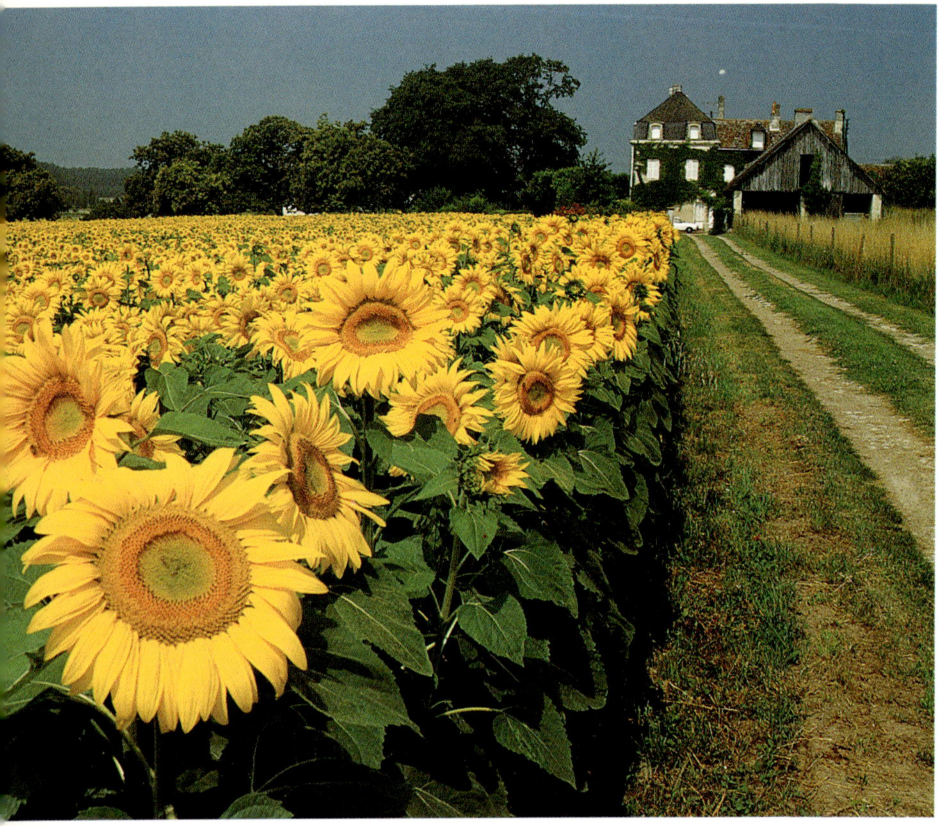

5.23 ● Linear perspective, caused when parallel lines appear to converge as they travel further from the camera, is one of the most powerful features in a composition. This effect can be created by objects of a similar size, such as a row of houses, or by natural lines in a landscape, like the furrows in a ploughed field or bands of hedgerows. In landscape pictures, I often use a track, road or pathway going into the distance, which can have a striking effect, especially when its colour or tone contrasts strongly with the rest of the image. ▲

TECHNICAL TIP

- The linear perspective effect will be much stronger when you use a wide-angle lens as this allows you to include close foreground details which make any natural lines appear to converge at a much steeper angle.

5.24 One of the most striking ways of using colour as an element of composition is to set primary and complimentary colours against each other. The primary colours of red, green and blue create the greatest degree of contrast and impact when juxtaposed with their opposites: red against a mixture of green and blue, known as cyan; green against magenta, the mixture of blue and red; blue against yellow, the combination of green and red. In practice, of course, natural colours are rarely as pure as those above, but the principle remains the same and the further apart two colours are, the greater will be the effect. Remember that most colours will tend to have a greater impact when viewed against black, or a very dark tone. ▶

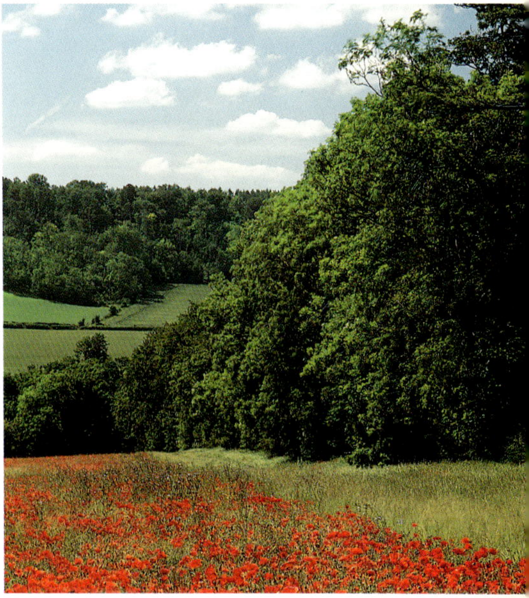

5.25 By closing one eye and squinting with the other, you will see a potential picture in a simplified way, reducing the colours and tones to basic shapes and lines, thus making distracting elements of objects more noticeable.

TECHNICAL TIP

- You will obtain the maximum degree of colour saturation when objects are lit with a soft diffused light and there is a slight degree of underexposure. In many cases, subjects with a reflective surface will show increased colour saturation when a polarising filter is used.

5.26 When you shoot in colour, always consider the individual hues within the image as elements of the composition, in the same way as you consider objects, shapes and lines. The presence of an unwanted patch of colour in the background of a portrait, for example, can be just as distracting as an ugly pylon in a landscape. ▶

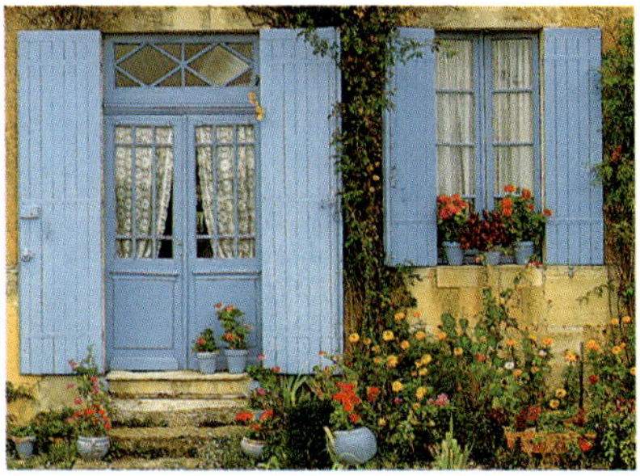

Dramatic hues are vital elements of composition.

5.27 ●●

Shadows are an inherent element of most pictures, helping to create a feeling of depth and form in the image. They can also be used as a much more dominant feature of the composition, however. On a sunny day, look for interesting shapes and formations in the shadows cast by objects within a scene to see how you might use them to create more impact in the photograph. They can form striking patterns, like those cast on a forest floor by the branches of trees, while a single shadow thrown on to a wall from an interestingly shaped object can create an almost surreal impression. You can also use shadows effectively to provide foreground interest in a picture or to form a frame at the top or sides of the image. ▼ ▶

TECHNICAL TIP

- If shadows occupy quite a large area of the subject that you are photographing, it will be necessary to make an allowance when calculating the exposure. A shadow filling the foreground of a shot will result in more distant details being overexposed. As a general rule, if areas of dense shadow occupy more than one-third of the image area, one stop less exposure should be given. A more certain method, however, is to take a selective reading from a fully-lit representative area of the scene.

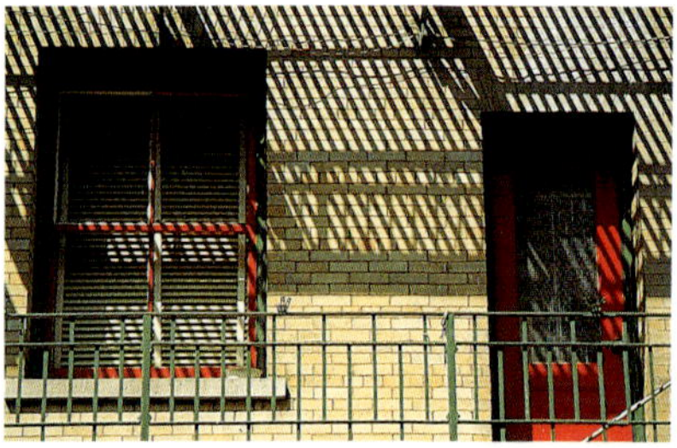

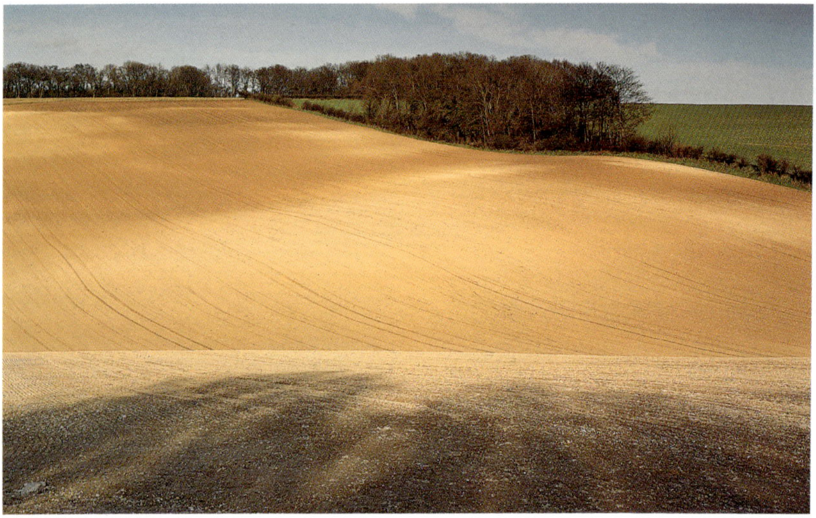

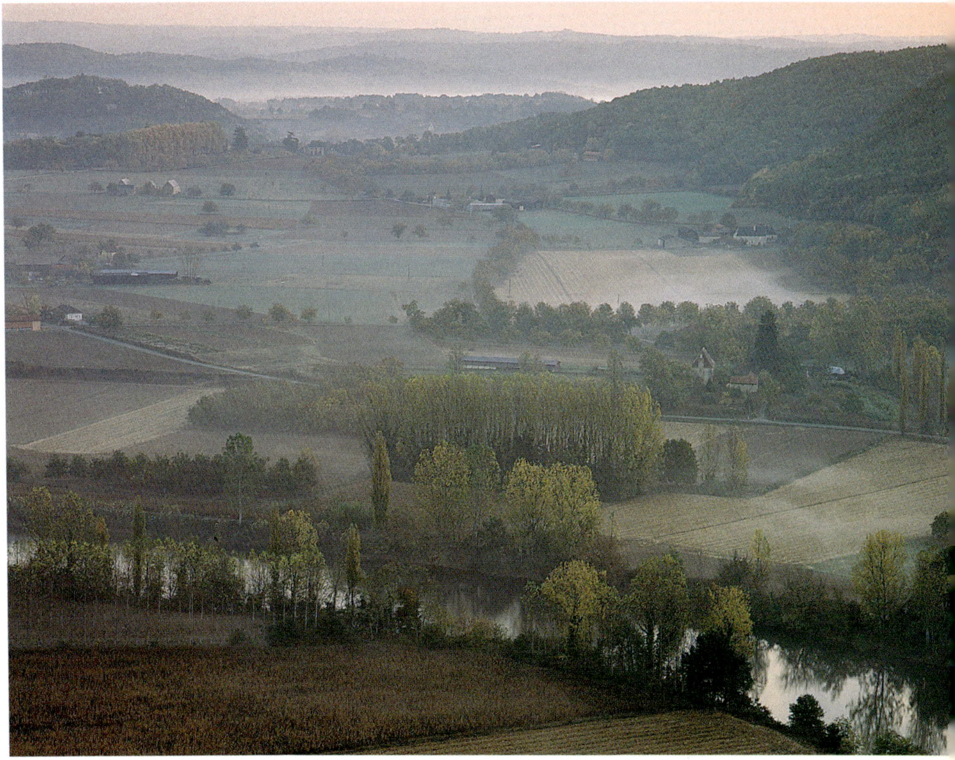

5.28 ●● One of the most effective ways to use colour in a photograph is to limit the range severely, to the point where it is almost monochromatic. To achieve this, shoot at dawn or dusk when the light is almost exclusively reflected from the sky; such photographs frequently display an interesting and unusual colour quality which can add an element of atmosphere and mood to the image. Since pictures taken at dawn or dusk invariably need long exposures of several seconds or more, you must use a tripod. ▲

TECHNICAL TIP

- Most films display a degree of reciprocity failure when exposures of more than 1 sec are given. Effectively this means that the stated film speed decreases as the exposure lengthens, and giving twice the exposure will not have as much effect as opening up the aperture by one stop. In addition, the individual colour layers of the film are not always affected proportionately, so a colour cast is likely. The solution is to make some experiments with your favoured film and to use the results as a basis for exposure calculations and filtration for future pictures of this type.

5 Foregrounds and Backgrounds

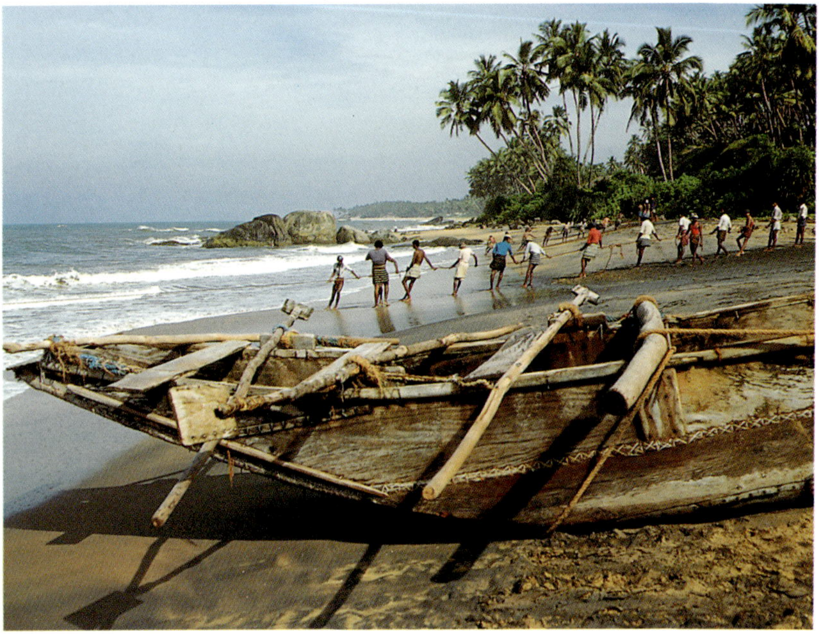

5.29 ● Always try to view a potential picture in terms of foreground, middle ground and background. This will help to make you more aware of an image's perspective, and will enable you to decide on the most effective viewpoint and best choice of lens. ▲

5.30 ●● To help you choose the best viewpoint, consider the process in three separate stages:

① Think of your camera as being fixed to a track between you and the subject.

② Walk along this track to determine the point at which the perspective created by the foreground, middle ground and background is the most impressive and striking.

③ Select the area you wish to include within the frame by trying different lenses.

5.31 ●● When you have chosen your viewpoint and lens, consider how the objects at different distances within the image relate to each other laterally. If you move to the left, closer objects move to the right of more distant objects, and vice versa. Raise the viewpoint, and objects in the foreground move lower in relation to more distant details, and vice versa.

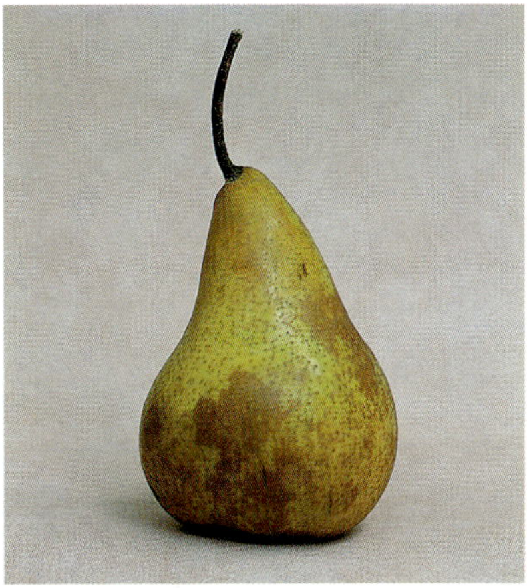

5.32 ●● The background is an important element of the composition in home and studio photography with subjects like portraits, nudes and still-life. While a plain paper background will be satisfactory for some pictures, a patterned or textured background can add additional interest and atmosphere to a picture, and play a much stronger role in the composition. You can buy ready-made painted backgrounds from professional photographic suppliers, although it is a fairly simple matter to make and customise your own. Paper is a suitable base, and emulsion or acrylic paint can be applied with a brush in the normal way, or with a spray gun for a more subtle effect. Calico, hessian or canvas have the advantage that they can be repainted easily a number of times and rolled up when not in use: these fabrics are sold in rolls of varying widths up to 3 metres, or sometimes more. ◀

PRACTICAL HINT

- Don't overlook the possibilities afforded by wallpaper when choosing a background – many patterns are suitable for photography, especially those which simulate the effect of rag painting or textures like grass paper. A single width of wallpaper will be sufficient for small still-life works and, with care, you can paste a larger seamless area flat on to a wall for portrait shots.

5.33 ● An impression of depth and distance is a quality sometimes lacking in photographs, but it is one that you can create by including foreground details. Adopt the habit of looking behind you before you take a photograph to see if there is an object or details which can be used to enhance the picture, then move back to include them. ▼

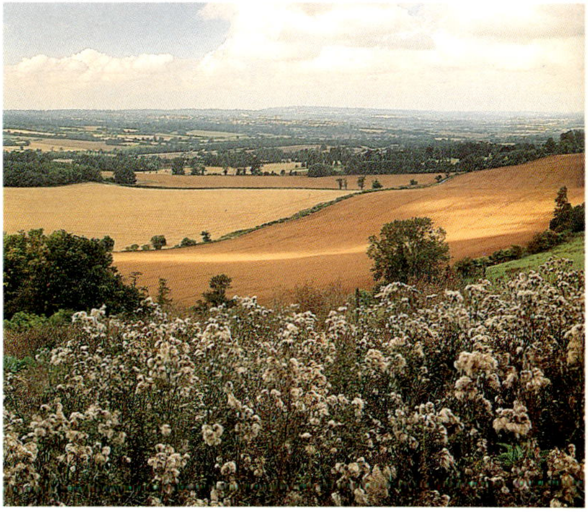

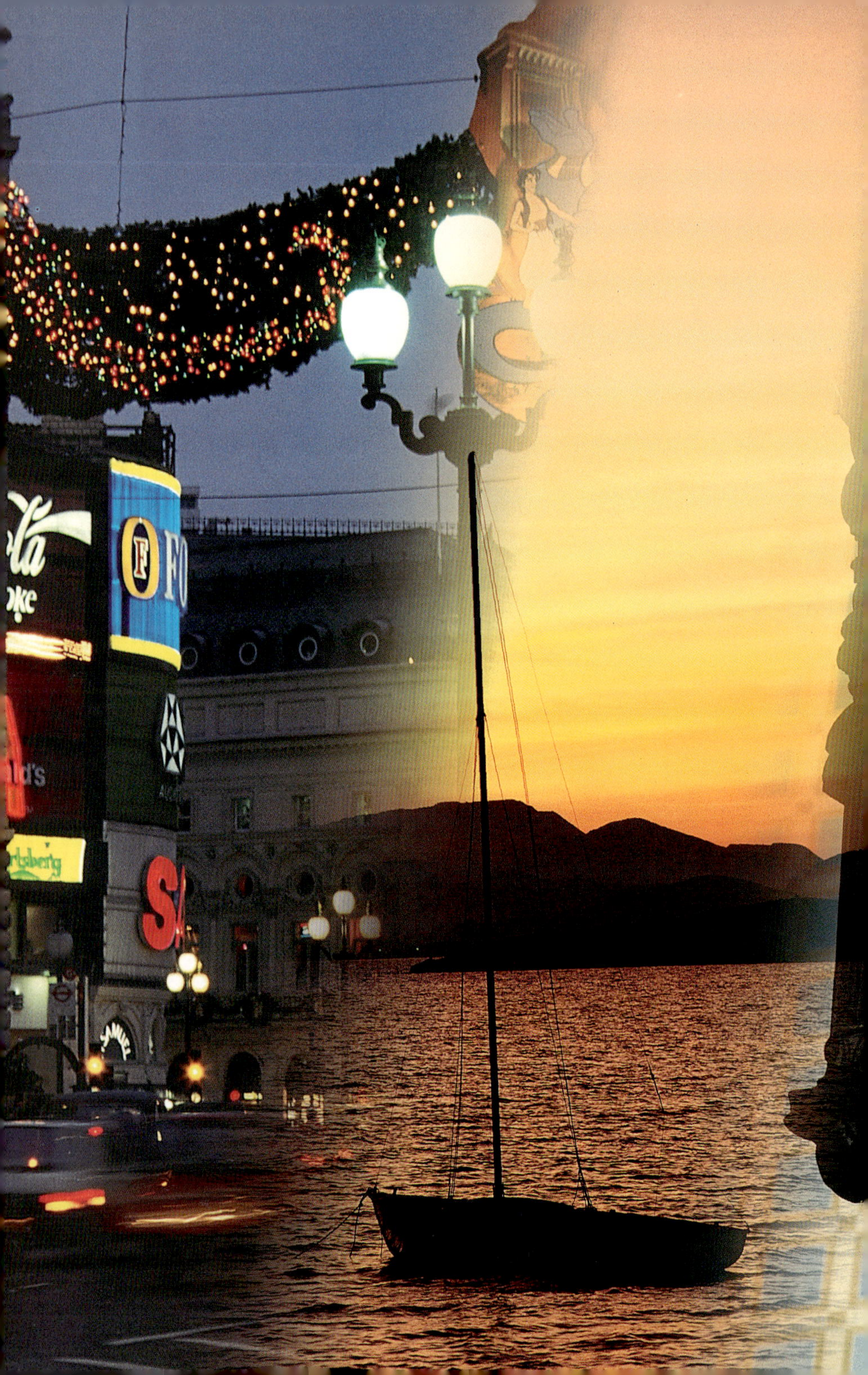

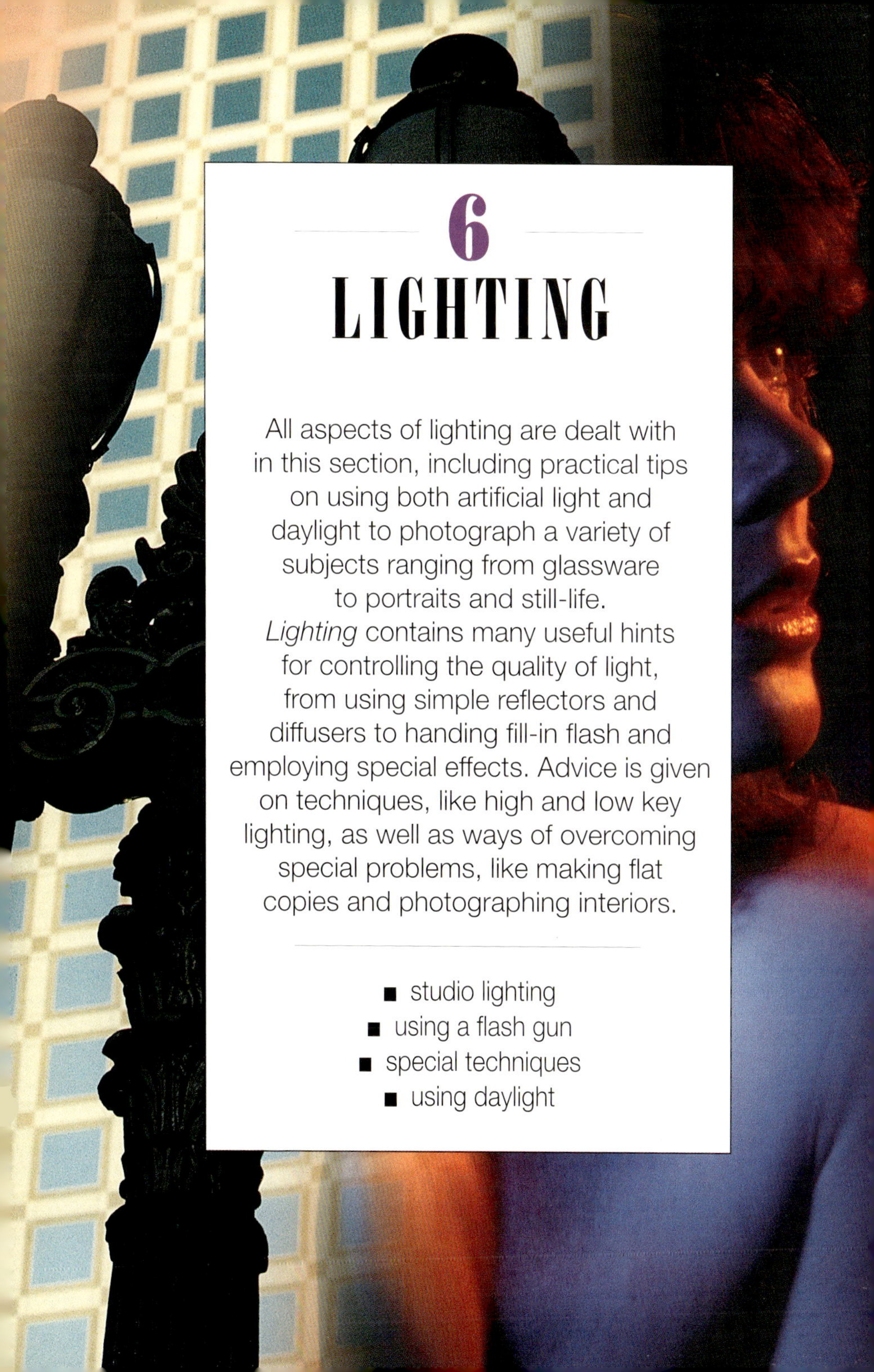

6
LIGHTING

All aspects of lighting are dealt with in this section, including practical tips on using both artificial light and daylight to photograph a variety of subjects ranging from glassware to portraits and still-life. *Lighting* contains many useful hints for controlling the quality of light, from using simple reflectors and diffusers to handing fill-in flash and employing special effects. Advice is given on techniques, like high and low key lighting, as well as ways of overcoming special problems, like making flat copies and photographing interiors.

- studio lighting
- using a flash gun
- special techniques
- using daylight

6.01 ●●● One of the best ways of lighting glassware to create a high-key, translucent effect is to place the objects on a surface about a metre in front of a white background, and illuminate this evenly from a light on each side. You can introduce dark tones, which give shape and form to any decorative mouldings or round the edges of the glass, by placing pieces of black card close to the glass in appropriate positions.

Make sure that the light sources illuminating the background do not spill on to the objects being photographed: you can limit the spread of light by taping pieces of black card to the reflectors. A more dramatic effect with greater tonal variation can be produced by using a snoot or spotlight to create a pool of light on the background. ▼▶

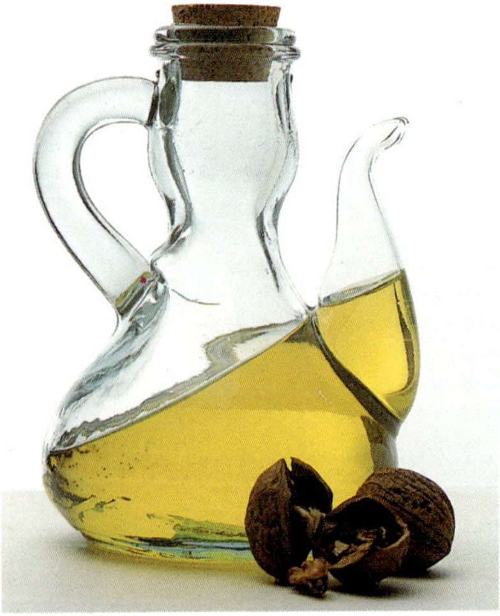

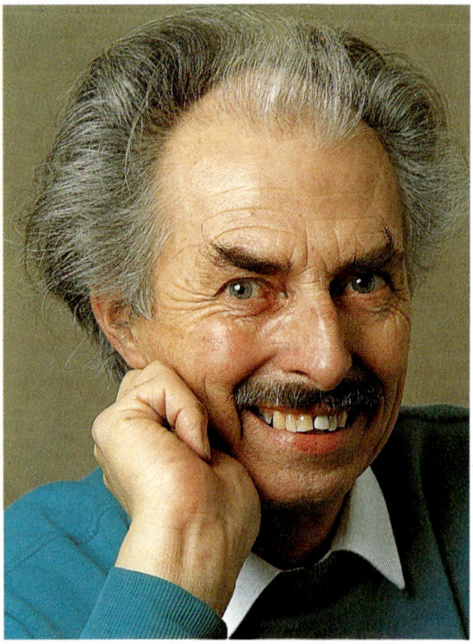

To create strong modelling use a single diffuser at almost right angles to the subject.

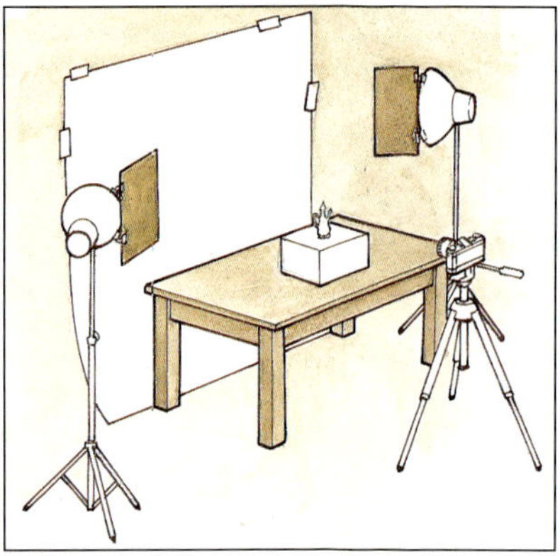

Lighting glassware with a high-key translucent effect.

6.02 ● Study the shadow cast by the model's nose to judge the effect of portrait lighting. If the shadow is too small there will be little modelling or form in the face. If it is too large and long

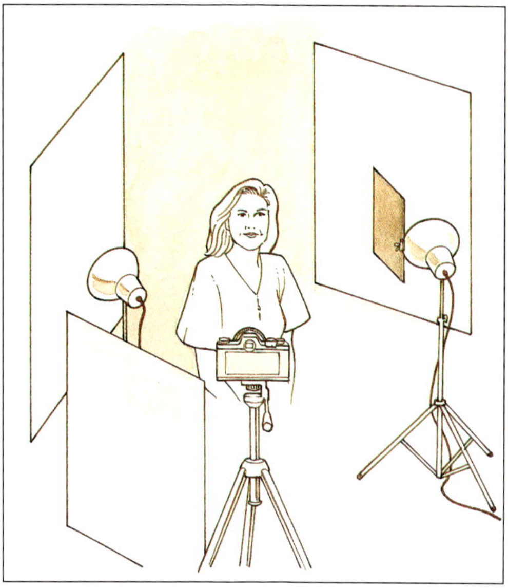

there is a danger that it will be too intense in the eye sockets and under the mouth and chin.

PRACTICAL HINT

When lighting a portrait, always start by positioning one key light to produce the basic shadows and highlights. You can then assess the degree of diffusion needed, and where you should place other lights or reflectors in order to add further highlights or to control the density of shadows.

6.03 ●●● Although the majority of studio portraits and figure shots use one dominant key light with supplementary lights for shadow control and extra highlights, indirect lighting from more than one source can be very effective for some subjects, especially when an overall low-key effect is required and a dark background tone is used. The method I favour is to place two large, white reflectors either side of, and a couple of metres behind, the subject. By placing two lights far enough from the reflectors to illuminate them fairly evenly, and by varying the angle and position of the subject, a range of subtle tonal effects can be created. If you are working in a large room or studio, you may need to place another white reflector close to the camera to bounce some light back into the shadows, or you can use a low-power diffused light source instead. ▲

TECHNICAL TIP

- A light reading taken in the conventional way from a dark, low-key subject will suggest more exposure than is needed, giving an overexposed result and the loss of the low-key quality. As a guide, you will need between one and two stops less depending upon the depth and extent of the shadows. Alternatively, take a close-up reading from the lightest area, avoiding bright highlights. If you are shooting on colour transparency film, bracket exposures or make a clip test.

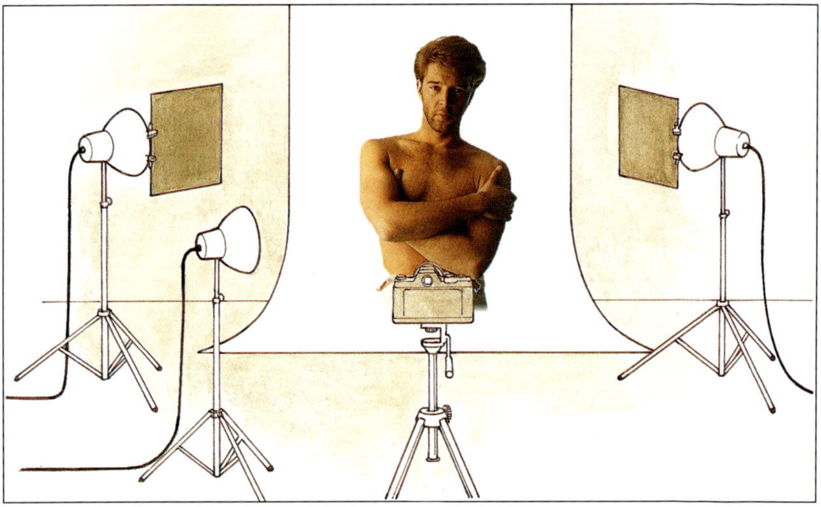
Shooting a portrait against a pure white background.

6.04 ●●● White card or polystyrene reflectors can be very useful for making shadow areas lighter, but they will not create additional highlights. For this purpose a mirror can often provide an alternative to an additional light source, especially for small still-life arrangements. Sheets of mirror foil, obtainable from artists' materials suppliers, are a good substitute for normal glass mirrors. Cut the sheets to size, place them close to the shadow side of an arrangement and angle them to reflect the key light into the desired area.

6.05 ●●● To obtain a pure white background for a portrait, place your model about 2 metres in front of a white-painted wall or white background paper. Place two lights just behind the model, a metre or so to each side of the background and aimed towards it. Fit a reflector or diffuser which creates a wide, even spread of light. Use pieces of black card taped to the outside and top edges of the reflectors to reduce light spill. Adjust the relative brightness of the background and subject lights so that the former is at least one stop brighter than the latter. ▲

TECHNICAL TIP

- Take your exposure readings with the background lights switched off, as these will give a misleadingly high measurement resulting in underexposure. Mask out any unwanted areas of white background to prevent the possibility of lens flare.

6.06 ●● Most portrait lighting is aimed into the face, so the model's nose points towards the direction of the light, but lighting across the face can create interesting effects. Three-quarter head angles and profile shots, where the model's face is turned away from the light source so that only one side of the face is illuminated, can look especially striking when a diffused light source from a soft-box is used. ▶

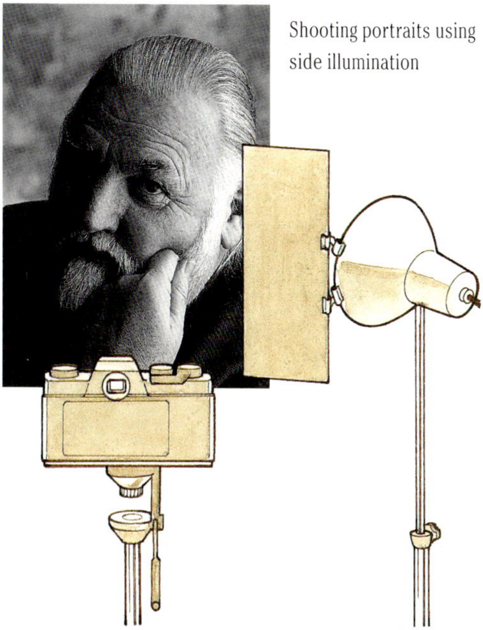

Shooting portraits using side illumination

PRACTICAL HINT

- To deflect light from a set-up towards a model you can fix a small pocket mirror near the camera and angle the mirror to light the model's eyes.

6.07 ●●● When shooting studio portraits using diffused side lighting, the model's eyes can sometimes appear rather lifeless. Create catch lights by using a small, low-power light source close to the camera; a small flash gun is ideal. If it is too powerful and detracts from the main lighting, you can diffuse its output with a layer or two of tracing or tissue paper.

6.08 ●● Portraits of people who wear glasses can present lighting problems. The lenses can be removed from many modern spectacle frames, however, allowing far greater freedom in the way the lights are positioned. Alternatively, use a polarising filter to eliminate any unwanted reflections in the lenses.

TECHNICAL TIP

- Reflections in spectacle lenses are easy to avoid or control if you use a small undiffused light source, like a lamp in a standard reflector, or a low-power light to fill in the shadows instead of a large white reflector.

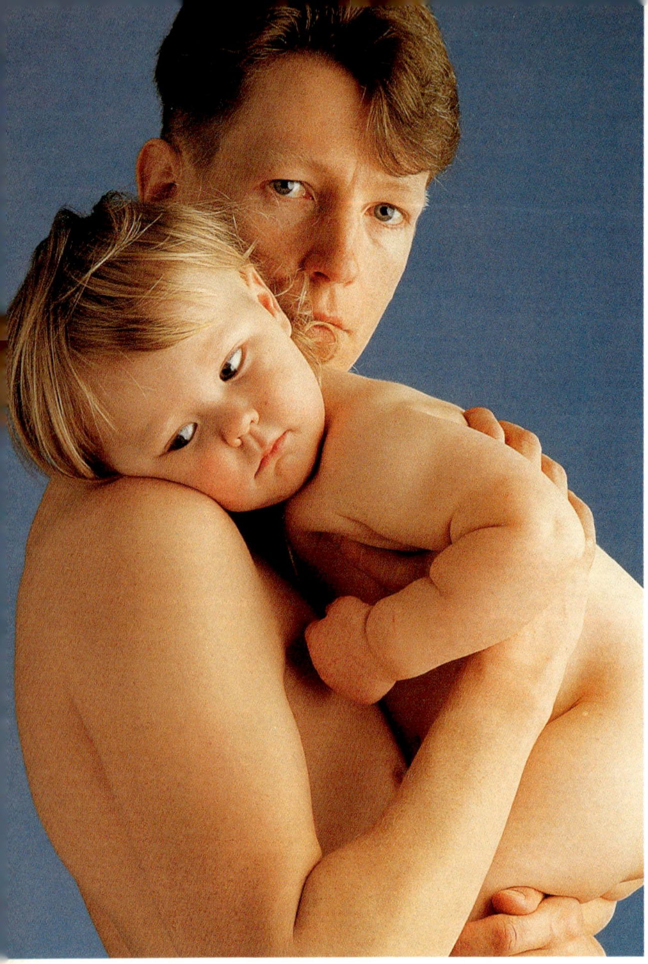

6.10 ●●● You can determine the exposure when using studio flash by using a flash meter. However, you can also use either TTL metering, or a conventional exposure meter, by calibrating the power of your modelling lamp against the power of the flash. To do this, establish the correct aperture for the flash at a given distance or power setting by making a test. Using modelling lights and the camera's meter, take a reading from the subject in the normal way to find the necessary shutter speed to give the correct exposure at the same aperture. Providing you maintain the power of the flash and modelling lights in the same ratio, you can set this shutter speed on your exposure meter or camera, and the correct aperture for the flash will always be indicated, irrespective of the lighting arrangement.

6.09 ●● The effectiveness of a diffused light source such as a soft-box, is dependent upon its size in relation to the object it is illuminating. A soft-box 1 metre square, for example, will create a very soft illumination with imperceptible shadows when used close to the subject, but at 4 metres away the illumination will be quite hard with clearly defined shadows. As a general rule, the maximum degree of softness will be obtained when the diffuser is larger than the object it illuminates. ▲

PRACTICAL HINT

- Remember to reset the shutter speed to the flash synch setting before shooting pictures using studio flash, otherwise the effect of the modelling lights will also be recorded.

6.11 ●●● Intense shadows can be difficult to achieve in a small light-toned studio. Use a 'black reflector' close to the model, on the opposite side to the light, to prevent spilt light being reflected into the shadows and weakening them. You can make a black reflector by painting one side of a white polystyrene reflector with matt black emulsion paint. Alternatively, you can attach a large piece of black felt to a white reflector, or any other support, with self-adhesive Velcro strips.

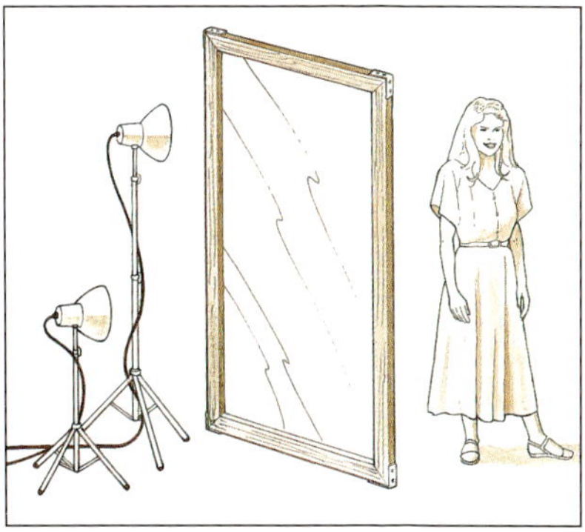

Using a home-made light diffuser in the studio.

PRACTICAL HINT

- To make an inexpensive, highly effective diffuser, cover a 1 x 2 metre softwood frame with one or more layers of a white translucent fabric such as tracing paper, frosted acetate or white nylon. Place this frame close to the subject and illuminate it from two light sources positioned about 2 metres behind. A very soft illumination will be created, even on a full-length figure.

6.12 ●● While graduated filters are most commonly used for outdoor photography such as landscapes, they can also be useful in the studio. A neutral graduated filter will darken the top of a plain background in a portrait or still-life shot to create a graduated tone. Coloured graduates will introduce a tint into a white background or change the hue of a coloured background. In a similar way, graduated filters can also darken or add colour to the foreground of shots. The lighting for a still-life shot on a white background, for instance, can often result in the foreground being too light. A graduated filter will correct this more easily and effectively than by masking the light source with barn doors. ▼

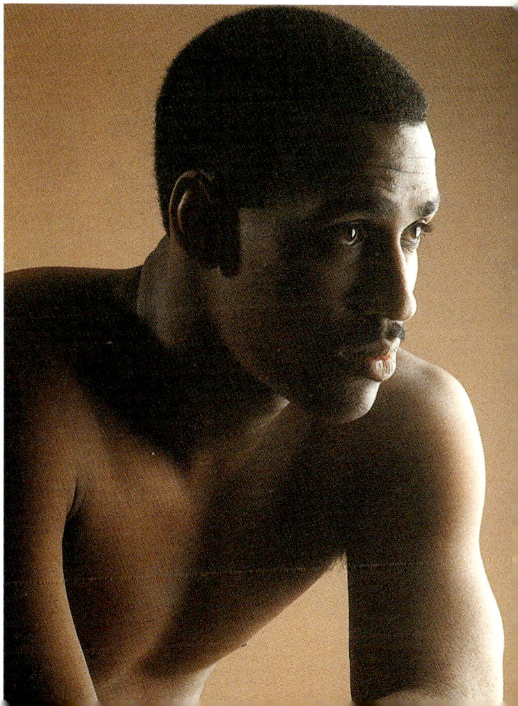

6.13 ●● You will get better results when taking interior photographs with flash if you do not select the flash setting on your camera's shutter speed dial, usually about 1/125 sec. By using a much slower speed, 1/30 sec for example, you will be able to record some of the background ambient light. Determine the best shutter speed by using the exposure meter in the usual way. If your camera is supported firmly, you can give exposures as slow as 1/2 sec, or even longer. ▼

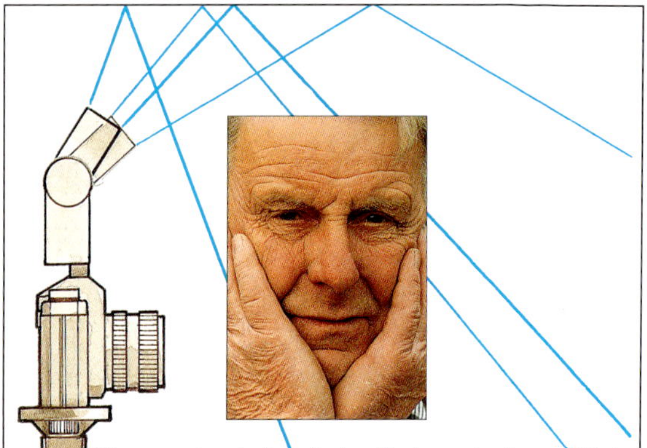
The correct angle for a flash unit when using bounced light

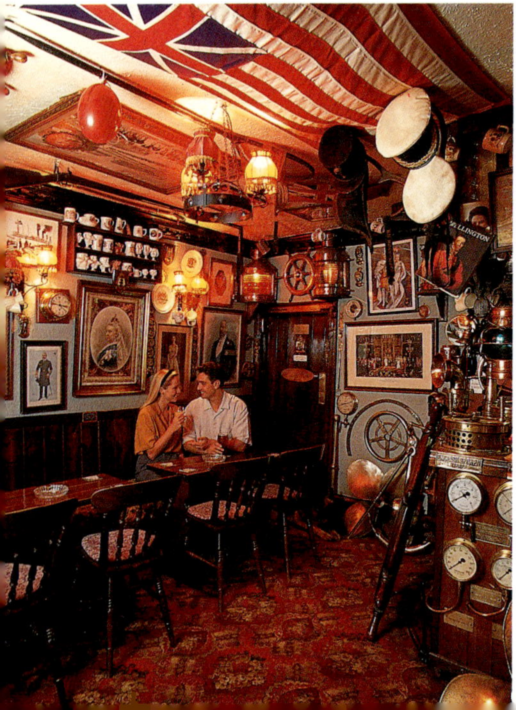

6.14 ●● Use bounced flash when shooting portraits, aiming the gun at the ceiling immediately above the camera rather than in front: if it is too close to the subject it will cause excessive top light and create unsightly shadows in the eyes. Fit a long-focus lens and take a more distant viewpoint when using this technique. ▲

PRACTICAL HINT

- To offset the effect of top lighting and create a more flattering effect with fairly close-up portraits, place a white reflector near to the subject and angle it up from under his or her chin.

6.15 ●● One of the most common faults with photographs lit by on-camera flash guns is that the subject's background and surroundings appear as a black void. This is because the intensity of a light source diminishes in inverse

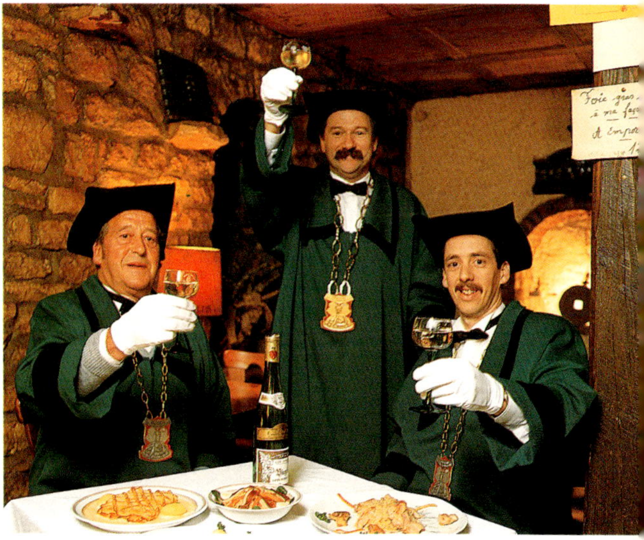

ratio to the square of the distance from its source. More simply, if a subject is 2 metres from the camera and the background is 4 metres away, the latter will receive only a quarter of the light falling on the subject. With the exposure set correctly for the subject, the background will be two stops underexposed. This effect will be exacerbated when a wide-angle lens is used. A long-focus lens using a more distant viewpoint will help to limit the fall-off of illumination between the subject and background. The quality of your flash photographs will be greatly improved if you remember that the distance between the camera and the subject should be at least twice the distance between the subject and the background. ▲

6.16 ●● Most flash guns are controlled by computer systems which are regulated by a light-sensitive cell to give the correct exposure. Remember that the principle is exactly the same as the camera's TTL metering system, however, and you must modify it in the same way when photographing abnormal subjects. In other words, give less exposure for dark-toned subjects and more for those with an inherently light tone. In addition, the flash itself can create an abnormal tonal range: one of the most common situations occurs when shooting head-and-shoulder pictures of people indoors when they are much closer to the camera than the background. In this case, because the background is receiving much less light than the foreground, the camera will tell the flash to give more exposure than is necessary for the foreground and the picture will be overexposed.

As a general rule, in a large or dark room, if the subject is closer than one-third of the distance between the camera and the background, give one stop less exposure than indicated. If it is closer than half the distance, give two stops less exposure.

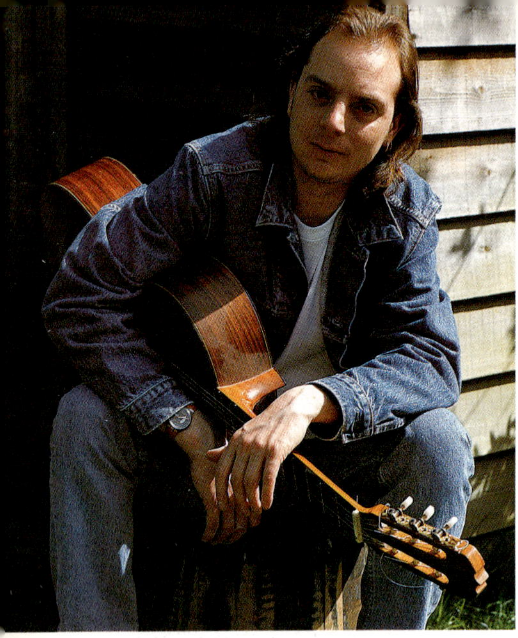

Above: The highlights are correctly exposed in this daylight shot, but the shadows are underexposed. Below: Add in a flash calculated to one stop less than required and the shadows are correctly exposed.

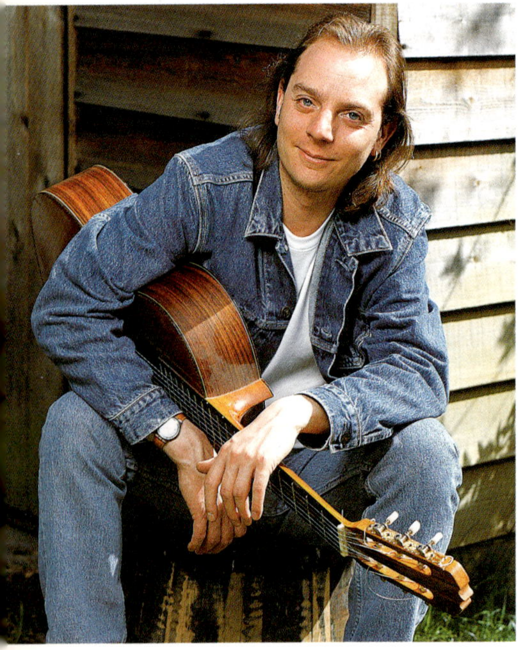

6.17 ●● If you want to combine daylight with fill-in flash, for example, the correct exposure setting will be easier to determine if you consider it as two simultaneous exposures. Calculate the aperture needed to give the correct exposure for the flash. Set this on the camera and then use an exposure meter to establish the shutter speed indicated for the correct daylight exposure at that aperture. ◀◀

TECHNICAL TIP

- Use a faster shutter speed to make the areas of the subject lit predominantly by daylight darker; use a slower shutter speed to make them lighter. The areas of the subject lit by flash can be made darker by selecting a smaller aperture, and lighter with a larger aperture. In each case, however, you must alter the shutter speed accordingly to maintain the same level of exposure for the areas lit by daylight.

6.18 ●● The effect of fill-in flash will be more natural if you use a soft-box to provide some form of diffusion, in preference to direct flash. It also helps if the flash is slightly off camera, creating a degree of modelling in the subject's face.

TECHNICAL TIP

- You can create a diffused and more evenly distributed illumination when using flash by aiming the flash at a white ceiling or wall, thereby reflecting it on to the subject.

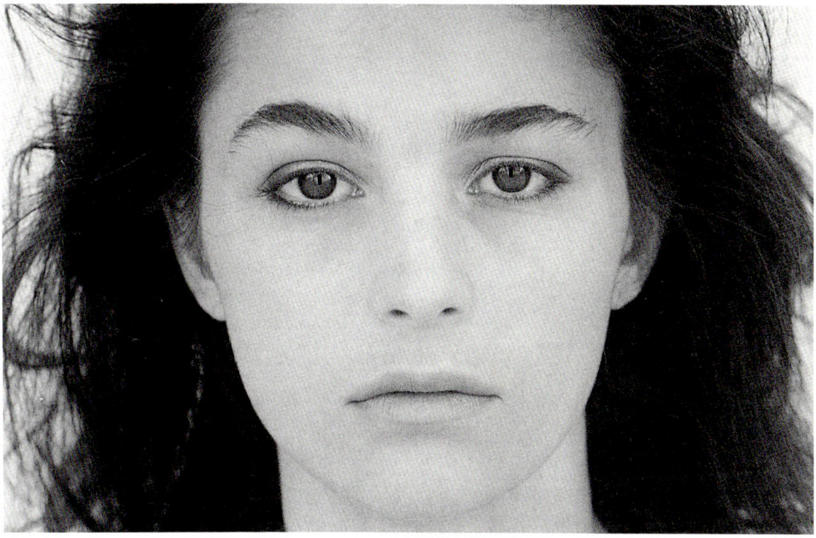

6.19 ●●● A simple way to create a soft, shadowless light for a portrait is to place two large white reflectors in a 'V' shape either side of the model, with the camera aimed through a gap in the narrow end. Two lights, one on each side of the model, are then aimed at the reflectors; place the lights far enough away from the reflectors to light them as evenly as possible. Use pieces of black card taped to the reflectors to make sure that the illumination from the lights does not spill over on to the model. ▲

PRACTICAL HINT

- ☐ Sheets of 1-inch thick polystyrene, obtainable from builders' merchants, are ideal as reflectors because they are rigid, light and inexpensive. They are supplied as 8 x 4 feet sheets, but you can easily cut these to size using a Stanley knife.

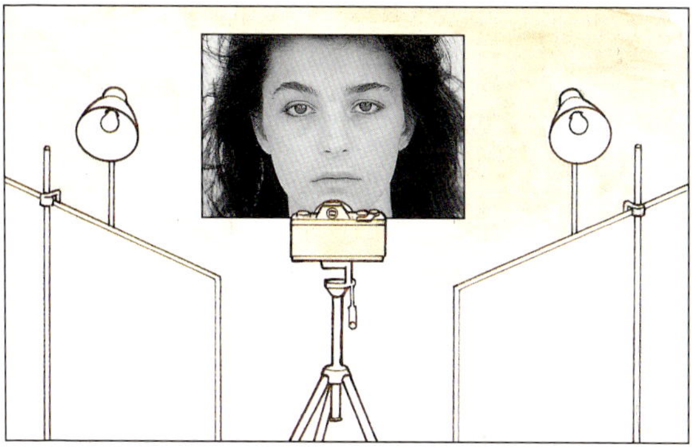

Using polystyrene sheets as reflectors to create soft lighting.

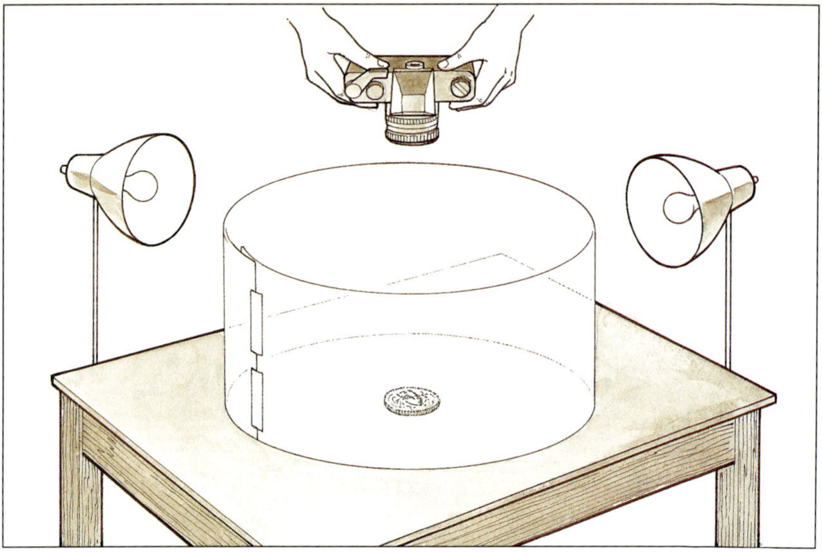

Using a tube of translucent plastic to obtain soft lighting for small flat objects.

PRACTICAL HINT

- Light small, flat objects such as coins, jewellery or watches, when photographing from above, by curling a piece of translucent plastic about 30cm wide into a tube 30cm or so in diameter. Place the object to be photographed within it and aim two or more light sources at its exterior. This will give soft high-key lighting without reflections.

6.20 ●●● When shooting head and shoulder portraits, a lap reflector is a useful way to reduce the shadows created under the eyes and chin, and gives a flattering or high-key effect. Balance a piece of white card or polystyrene on the model's knees, or support it on a low stand, under his or her face as close to it as the framing allows. You can gain a stronger effect by using a silvered reflector, and fashion or beauty photographers often use a low-powered soft-box placed on the floor and aimed upwards.

6.21 ●●● The best way to light a highly reflective object with an irregular surface is to construct a 'tent' of white translucent material around it, leaving a small gap for the camera to see through. Fine nylon is ideal. Light this evenly from two or more sources to create an even tone on the object's surface. You can achieve definition and shape within the object by introducing small pieces of black or tinted card, within or outside the tent, to create localised variations in tone.

6.22 ●●● A single continuous source of illumination, such as a photoflood, gives a soft, shadowless light which is best for static subjects like still-life arrangements. Move the light from side to side and up and down in a painting motion while you give a long exposure of 10 sec or more. You must do this in a darkened room so that the only source of illumination is the light being used.

6.23 ●● To photograph a document or piece of artwork, place a light on either side of it, between 30cm and 1 metre away, ensuring that the lights are equidistant and at the same angle. Check that the subject is evenly lit by holding a pencil in the centre of the subject at right angles to it: the two shadows should be of equal density and length. ▲

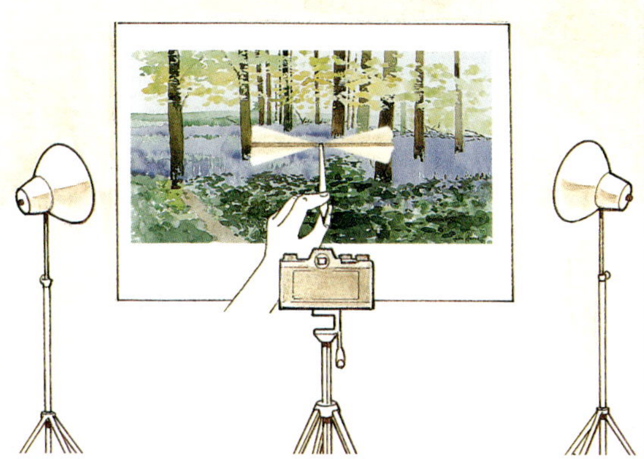

Balancing lighting for photographing artworks and documents

TECHNICAL TIP

□ Oil paintings can present a special lighting problem because of the paint's natural gloss, but a polarising filter will eliminate the reflections. Use polarising filters over both the light sources and the camera. Although this type of filter can also help to eliminate most reflections when photographing artwork under glass, it may not prevent the reflection of the camera and tripod, so position a large black screen in front of the camera with a hole cut for the lens to see through.

6.24 ●●● One of the difficulties with macro photography is that the distance between the camera and subject is often so small that side lighting is the only feasible option. This does not suit all subjects, however, and some small reflective objects are more effectively lit from the front. A simple way to overcome this problem is to place a thin piece of optical quality glass at an angle of 45 degrees in front of the lens. Aim a narrow beam of light (a projector or light fitted with a snoot is ideal) on to the glass at right angles to the camera, directing it along the optical path of the lens to create a shadowless frontal light. ▼

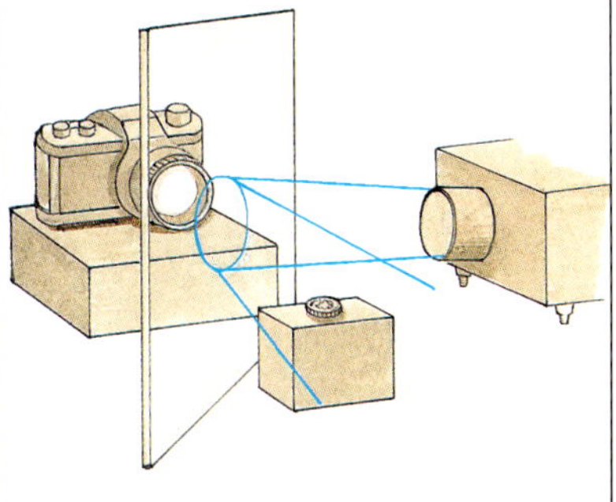

Using glass as a reflector in close-up shots

TECHNICAL TIP

- Filters are useful in enabling you to correct an imbalance between two light sources of different colour temperatures. An 80A or 80B, for instance, can be used over a tungsten light to remove the orange cast created on daylight type film when you are shooting in a room that is also lit by daylight.

6.25 ●●● To photograph objects with a pure white background, construct a light box. Support a large piece of translucent white plastic about 1 metre above the floor and position two lights underneath, one each side, so that the area of plastic is evenly lit. Place the subject of the photograph, lit independently, on the surface of the plastic, ensuring that the level of illumination on the subject is at least three stops lower than that on the plastic surface.

Alternatively use a sheet of plain glass covered with tracing paper. Place a piece of white paper approximately 1 metre below the glass and light that evenly from an independent source.

TECHNICAL TIP

- You can minimise the risk of flare, when using the technique described above to create a pure white background, by positioning pieces of black card around the subject to be photographed. These will mask any unwanted areas of white background.

6.26 ●●● Sheets of coloured acetate can be used to create a number of useful effects in the studio by placing them over one or more of the light sources. In portraiture, the highlights created by a hair light or rim light often provide more impact and interest when tinted to an appropriate hue. In food photography, a yellow or orange filter over a backlight or spotlight creates warm, inviting highlights on the surface of sauces and glazed or roasted meats. A filtered background light adds colour to a white or neutral background, while the hue of a coloured background is intensified when a filter of the same colour is used.

6.27 ● Late afternoon and evening light can be ideal for nude and glamour photography. The warmer colour temperature can emphasise the quality of tanned skin and the softer, lower angle of evening light can give more pleasing results than the bright midday sun.

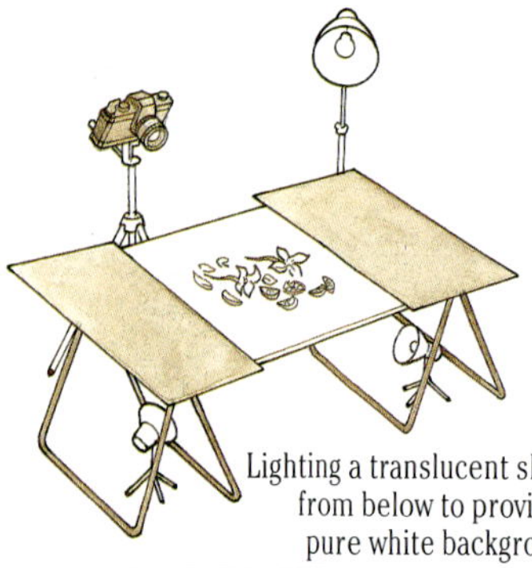

Lighting a translucent sheet from below to provide a pure white background

TECHNICAL TIP

- In subjects where large areas of shadow are included in the image, a normal reading will indicate more exposure than is actually needed, so take a close-up reading from a fully-lit mid tone within the subject.

6.28 ●●● The duration of flash from most tubes is often much shorter than the fastest shutter speed: the flash duration is briefer at lower power settings. This characteristic can be used to create effective frozen action shots. The simplest method is to photograph a continuous action, a pack of cards being shuffled, for example, or a golf swing, visually judging when to shoot. You can also freeze moments of action – glass breaking on impact or a stone falling into a bowl of water – by setting up the shot in a darkened room, leaving the shutter open on a time exposure and arranging for the flash to be fired at the required moment. Devices are available which will fire the shutter when an infra-red beam is broken, when impact is made or when a sound is emitted. ▶

TECHNICAL TIP

- If you are shooting in colour and wish to combine flash with light from a projector, you will need to use daylight type film with an 80A colour balancing filter over the projector lens or artificial light film with a 85B filter over the flash tube.

6.29 ●●● A projector is useful for portraits and still-life subjects to create a spotlight effect. A projector can be used as a key light in a portrait to produce the sharp, hard-edged shadows typical of 1940s Hollywood-style shots, especially when you are using black-and-white film. Set slightly higher than the subject's eye-level and angled so that it creates a strong modelling within the facial contours (but not so high that it produces shadows in the eye sockets) the spotlight effect can be both dramatic and flattering. With female portraits especially, a degree of soft focus can mellow the slightly harsh skin quality this type of lighting tends to produce.

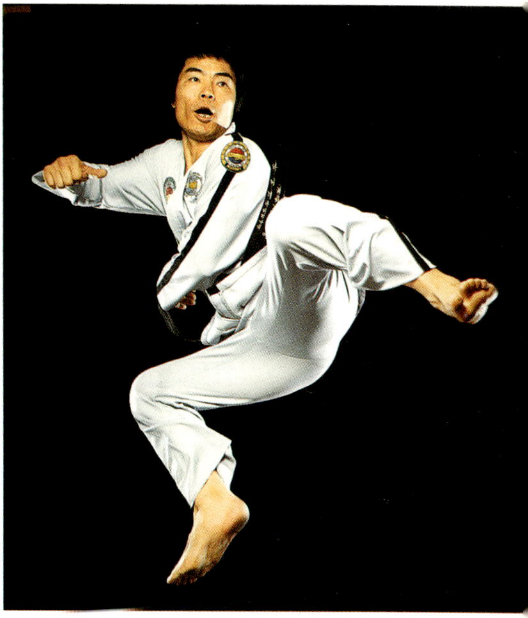

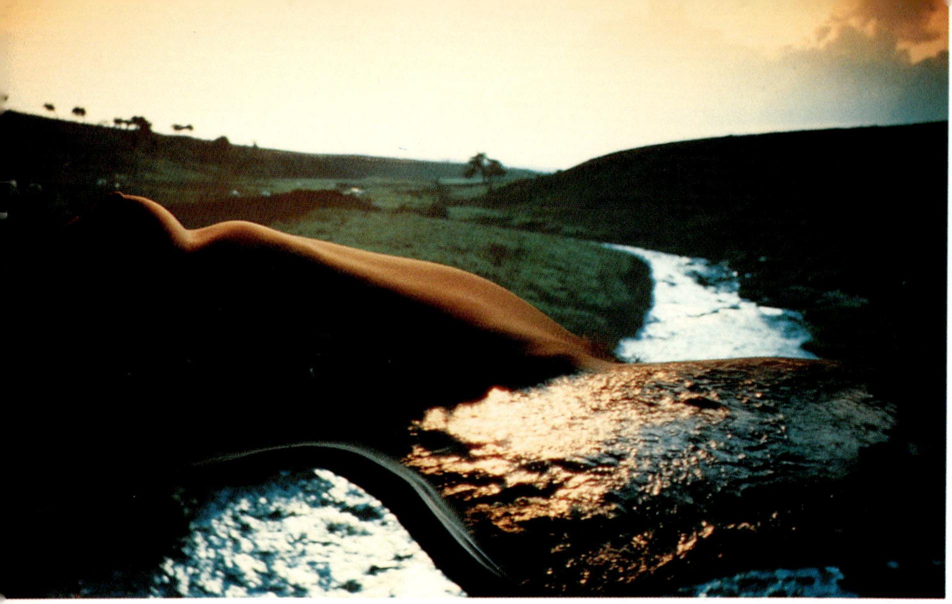

6.30 ●●● A projected image used as a light source can create unusual, abstract effects. A transparency of a landscape for example, could illuminate a portrait or a nude. If the projector is placed close to the camera, the image will cover most of the subject creating little or no modelling. However, if the projector is placed well to one side of the subject there will be large areas of shadow and a greater impression of form. A small, carefully controlled amount of normal lighting can be used to create additional modelling and to make the image less abstract. ▲

TECHNICAL TIP

- Try placing a strong primary coloured filter over the camera lens and a complimentary coloured filter of the same strength over the flash. Foreground objects lit by the flash will appear quite neutral, but the more distant details will have a pronounced red cast.

TECHNICAL TIP

- A small portable flash gun can be used to light large interiors like a church. Stop the lens down so that a very long exposure, of a minute or more can be given for the ambient light. Hold the shutter open on the time setting, and hand hold the flash gun in various positions, aiming it into the darkest corners and firing it manually. A certain amount of trial and error is involved with this technique, so check the lighting balance and exposure with a Polaroid, or bracket widely.

6.31 ●● One of the most effective ways of photographing large interiors is to combine flash lighting with ambient light. Use a combination of these two light sources, to vary the mood and appearance of the interior. By using flash combined with a long exposure you can use the effects of both, the flash to illuminate the darker areas but allowing existing light to create the lighter tones. ▶

6.32 ●● Balance the colour quality when combining flash with ambient light of a different colour temperature by using complimentary filters over both the flash and the camera lens. A foreground subject lit by flash in a room lit by fluorescent light is a good example, since a strong magenta filter is usually needed to overcome the green cast of the room lighting. Place a magenta filter over the camera lens and a green filter of the same strength over the flash tube to give an image with an overall neutral balance. The green tinted light of the flash will cancel out the magenta cast in the areas lit by the flash, but not the more distant details lit by the fluorescent light.

6.33 ●●● Light masking is a technique which can be used under studio conditions to create unusual and dramatic effects on a range of subjects including still-life, portraits and nudes. It involves the use of one or more light sources to produce selective pools of illumination on the subject. Use undiffused lights (bare bulbs or flash tubes in polished reflectors), and spotlights which will give you maximum control. Position screens of black cartridge paper or card about 1 metre from the subject, with the lights about 2 metres behind the screens.
Cut apertures of the desired size and shape into the screen and you will be able to vary the respective positions of the lights to illuminate precise areas.

If you use a sharply focussed light source from a spotlight or projector, you can play clearly defined patterns of light on to the subject to give a particular effect such as that produced by a Venetian blind. Limit the spill of stray light as much as possible by using barn doors, honeycombs or snoots fitted to the reflectors. To obtain detail in the shadow areas, use a low-power, diffused light from a position near the camera.

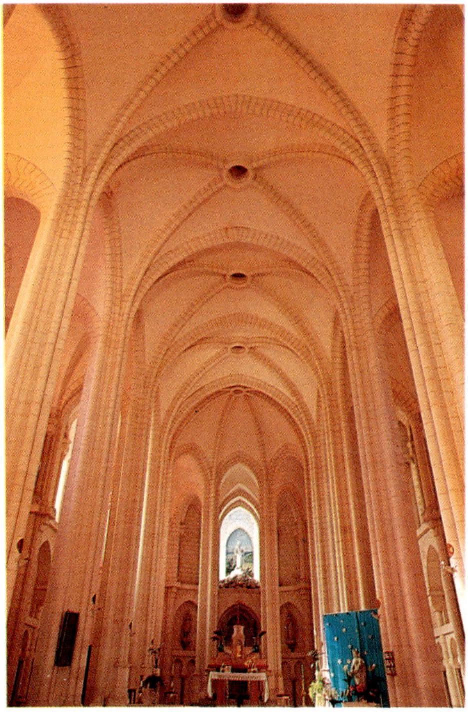

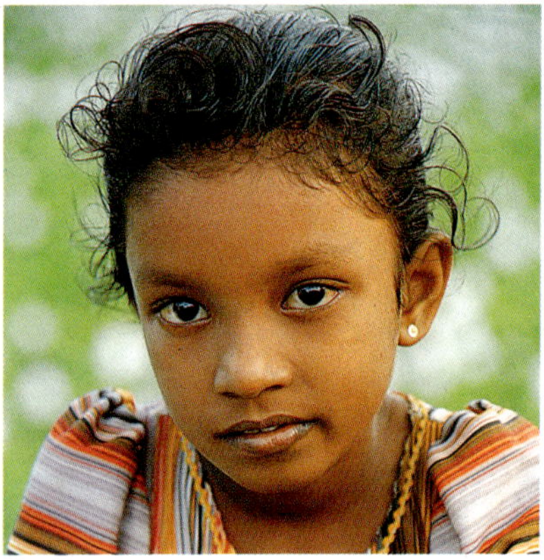

6.35 ● For a very flattering light when shooting portraits outdoors, place your model just inside a doorway or under a tree. This eliminates the effect of excessive top light from the sky which can create unpleasing shadows in the model's eyes and on facial contours. ◀

6.34 ●● Glassware can be lit effectively using daylight. For a high-key, translucent effect, place a piece of tracing paper, or translucent white fabric, such as nylon, over a window and set the glassware composition in front of it. You can create darker tones and greater definition by placing small pieces of black card close to the objects to control the light. ▶

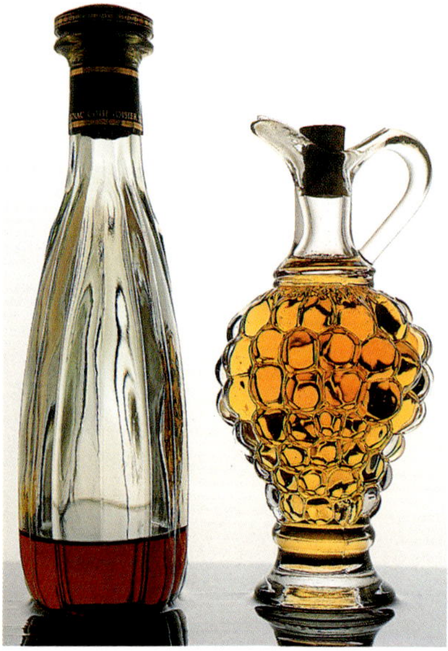

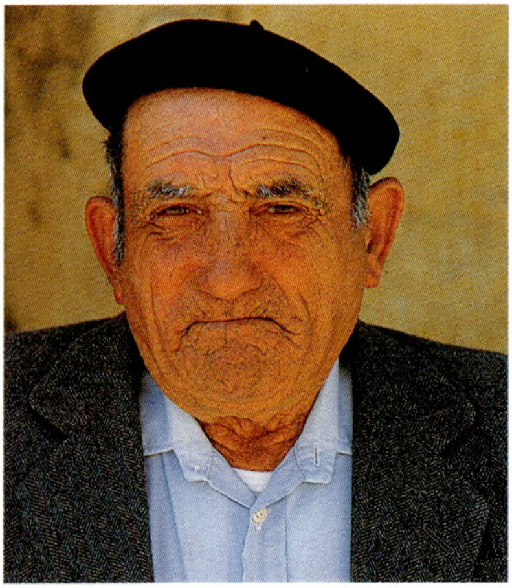

6.36 ●● Avoid direct sunlight when shooting portraits outdoors, as it can create dense shadows and a high degree of contrast which will result in your model's skin having an uncomplimentary quality. Place the subject in an area of open shade, beside a wall is a good choice. If you are shooting in the garden use a large sheet of hardboard or a reflector to create an area of shade, wherever it is needed. ◀

PRACTICAL HINT

- Some fashion photographers use white location umbrellas to eliminate excessive top light, but you can easily construct a 'roof' from a sheet of white polystyrene supported by lighting stands.

6.37 ●●● Still-life photography is generally best dealt with in the studio, but daylight can be an ideal source of illumination. A suitable bench or table in a garden can be used to help produce effective and nicely lit still-life shots. Use mirrors, reflectors, diffusing screens and pieces of black card to control and direct the light. Remember that the quality of light found in open shade closely resembles that created by studio photographers using large overhead soft-boxes. ▶

6.38 ●● Daylight indoors can provide a very satisfactory alternative for those who do not have access to studio lighting, giving a rather more formal and controlled quality than can be obtained with outdoor portraits. A large north-facing window is ideal as it will not be subjected to direct sunlight, thereby providing a softer light. You can, however, diffuse a sunny window with tracing paper or with a white translucent material like nylon. Vary the angle and direction of the lighting by altering the relative positions of the camera and model, and control the contrast by the use of white reflectors or mirrors.

6.39 ● When taking exposure readings for a an abnormally light subject, give more exposure than will be indicated by a conventional averaging reading. If you increase this by three stops over that read from the white background is likely to be correct, however it is best to bracket exposures one stop each side of this in half-stop increments.

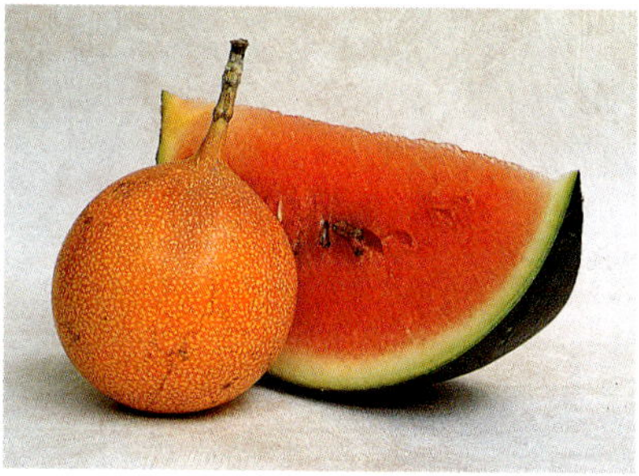

A typical studio shot taken outdoors.

PRACTICAL HINT

- A movable background will allow you to provide a suitable tone or colour to compliment your portrait or still-life subject, regardless of the set-up and camera positions, and will create a less cluttered and more studio type look to outdoor compositions. A hardboard panel is suitable for head and shoulder or close-up shots; it can be papered, painted or covered with fabric and simply propped against a chair. For full-length or more distant shots, use a cartridge paper roll which can be obtained in a wide range of colours from professional photographic stores . Support the roll on its cardboard core from a pair of lighting stands and allow it to drape in a curve on to the ground, giving a seamless join behind the subject.

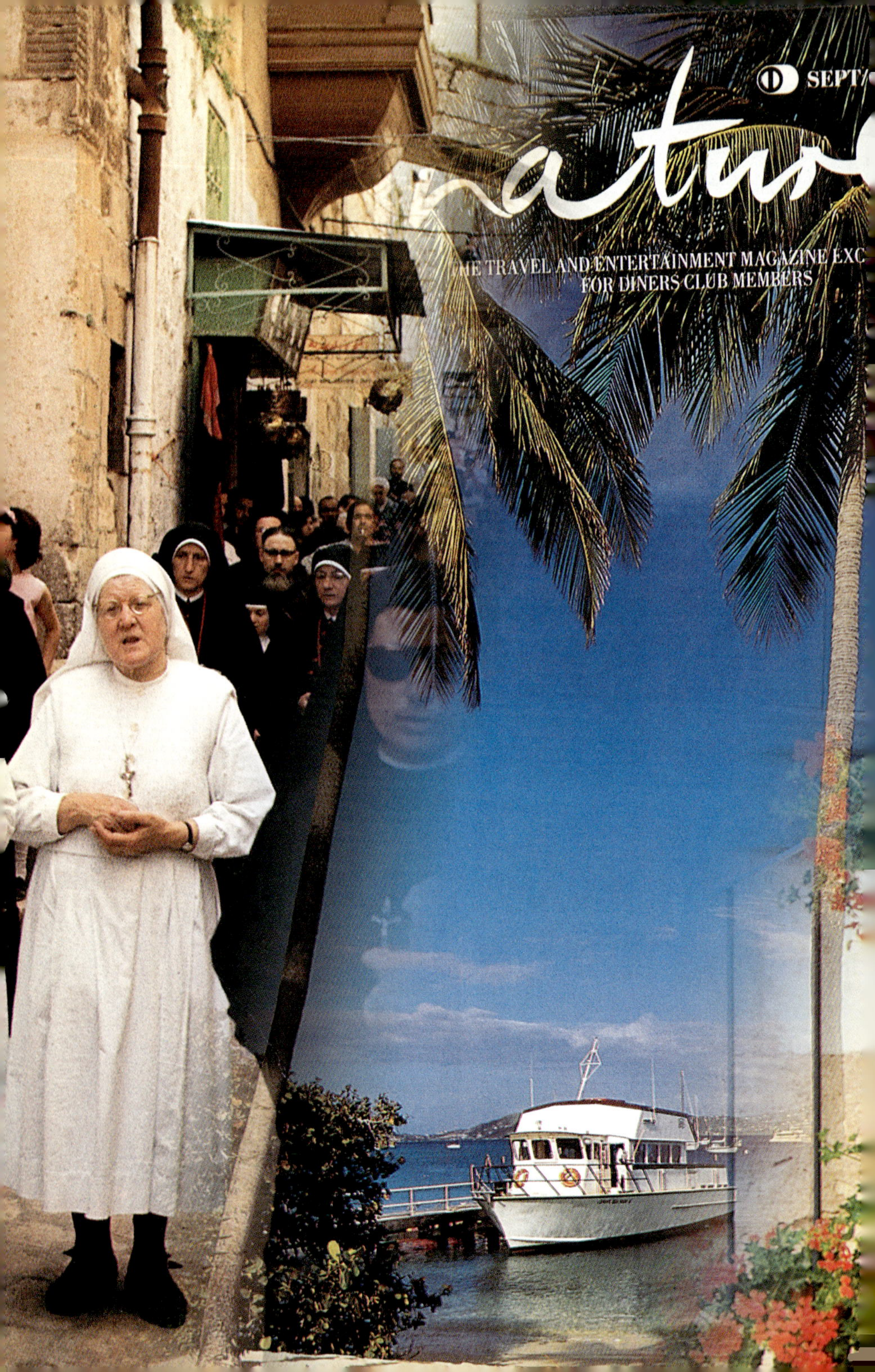
SEPT
THE TRAVEL AND ENTERTAINMENT MAGAZINE EXC
FOR DINERS CLUB MEMBERS

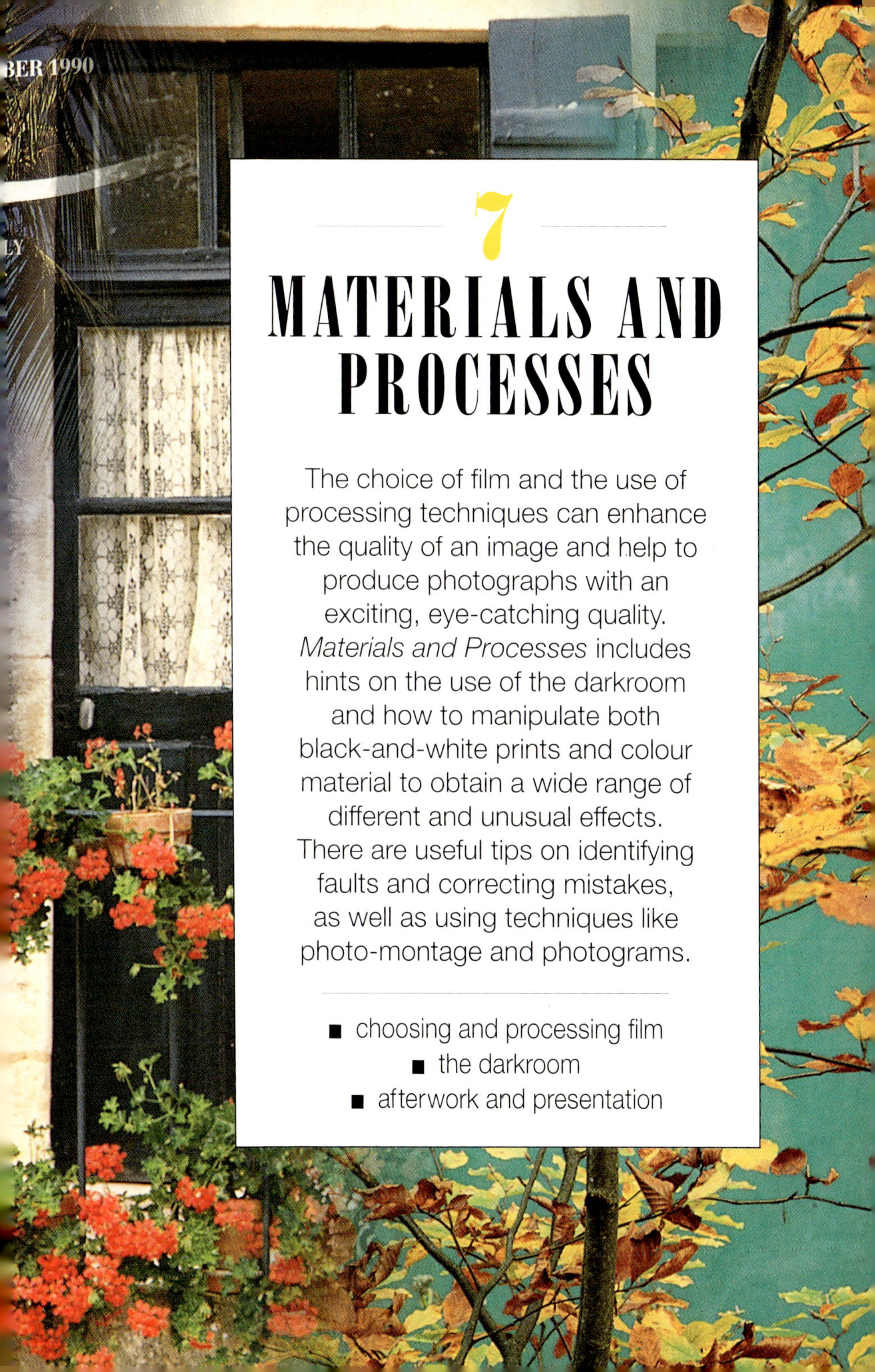

7

MATERIALS AND PROCESSES

The choice of film and the use of processing techniques can enhance the quality of an image and help to produce photographs with an exciting, eye-catching quality. *Materials and Processes* includes hints on the use of the darkroom and how to manipulate both black-and-white prints and colour material to obtain a wide range of different and unusual effects. There are useful tips on identifying faults and correcting mistakes, as well as using techniques like photo-montage and photograms.

- choosing and processing film
- the darkroom
- afterwork and presentation

7 Choosing and Processing Film

7.01 ● If you would like to experiment with black-and-white film but do not have access to darkroom facilities, try a roll of Ilford XP2. It can be processed like colour negative film at your usual lab to produce monochromatic enprints, usually with a slightly sepia tint. The resulting negatives are printed in the normal way using bromide printing papers. ▼

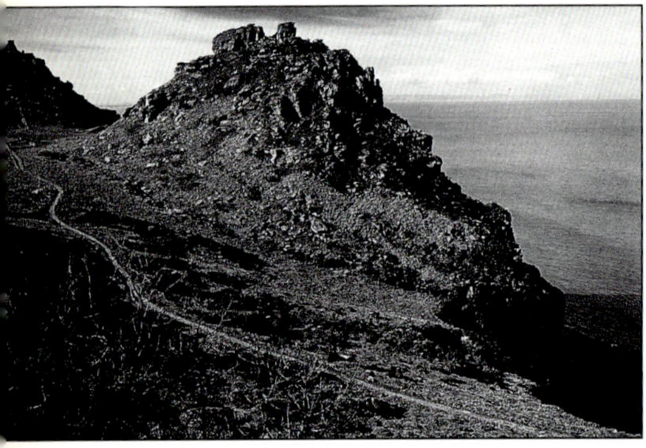

7.02 ● When you are going away for a period of time and anticipate using a large quantity of film, it is best to take it with you rather than relying on local sources. This applies particularly to transparency film where storage conditions, age and variations in individual batches can have a significant effect. Buy the freshest film available of the same batch from a reliable supplier, and test it under your normal working conditions before you leave. Buying film in Pro-Packs will save on both luggage space and rubbish output. You can also remove cassettes and foil-wrapped roll films from their boxes and discard the packaging to save space or weight in your luggage.

PRACTICAL HINT

- Although tests have been carried out which indicate that modern X-ray security equipment at airports does not cause fogging, try to pack your film separately, wait until there is a lull in the security line and ask, very politely, for a hand search. This applies particularly when carrying very fast film, when older X-ray machines are in use, or when the same film stock may pass through a sequence of checks.

7.03 ●● Black-and-white slides can be produced by using Agfa's Dia-Direct 35mm film which is processed to give a reversal image. Polaroid's Polapan instant 35mm black-and-white slide film is an alternative, but this must be developed using Polaroid's special processing device. Polaroid also produces colour transparency and high contrast black-and-white 35mm instant slide film.

7.04 ● Keep a quantity of film for future use in a freezer to arrest the deterioration of the chemicals and dyes, but always remove it an hour before use. Use the film before its expiry date as low temperatures do not prevent other factors, such as radiation, from building up fog levels.

7.05 ● A wide range of types and qualities of film for both colour transparency and prints is available, and it is worth considering the choices on offer according to the type of subject to be photographed. In general, relatively high contrast fully-saturated films, including Kodak Ektar and Fuji Velvia, are best suited to subjects like landscapes and architecture, whereas a lower contrast film, with slightly more muted colours, such as Agfacolor Portrait or Kodak EPN, is better suited to photographing people. Even within the same film types there are differences in colour rendition. Kodak's Panther X, for example, gives a warmer quality for outdoor photography than the more neutral balance of normal Panther and Fuji Provia and offers a less saturated emulsion than Velvia with more natural skin tones. ▲ ▶

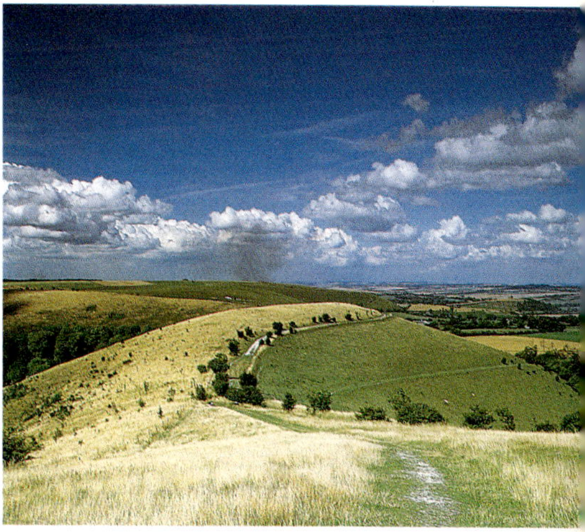

Above: Fuji Velvia was used to maximise the image contrast and colour saturation in this landscape.

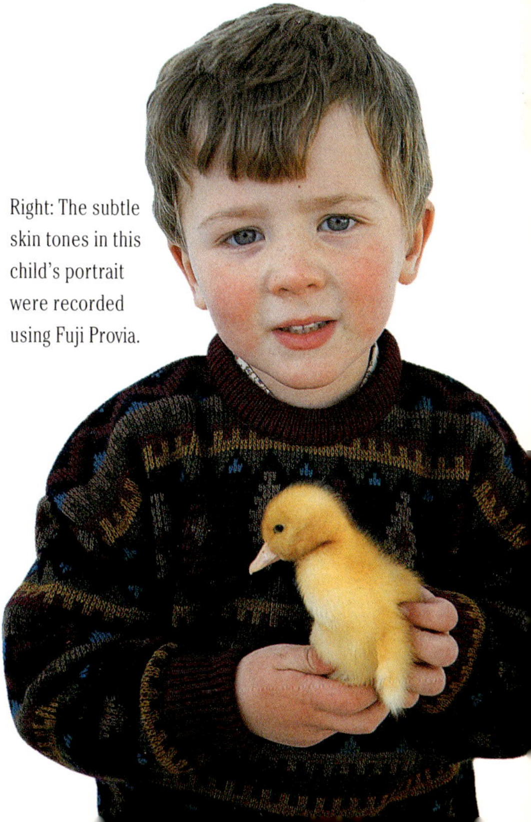

Right: The subtle skin tones in this child's portrait were recorded using Fuji Provia.

7.06 ●● Today's films are so good that colour fidelity is taken for granted, but there are occasions when you might want to create a more unusual and less predictable effect. If you shoot on colour transparency film but process it as a colour negative, it will produce an image in which the colours are slightly distorted due to the lack of colour masking layers in the transparency film. There will also be a significant increase in contrast which will add a further degree of strangeness to the image. You can reduce the contrast by using a fog or pastel filter; the effect will vary according to the choice of film and subject matter. The stated film speed may need adjustment, so it is worth experimenting to discover which film produces the most pleasing result.

7.07 ●● A variation of this technique can be used for abstract effects by treating the resulting negative as a transparency. Shoot boldly coloured subjects in which the tonal range is quite limited, and you can obtain images which give curious effects like green oranges and blue bananas.

TECHNICAL TIP

- A negative produced from colour transparency film will need heavy filtration when printed due to the lack of colour masking layers in the film. To overcome this, use an artificial type film in daylight, with an 82A colour conversion filter, or make prints with a piece of unexposed but processed C41 film in contact with the negative. I have found that Scotch Chrome 640T produces good results with an added granular quality.

Processing transparency film in C41 colour negative chemistry created the strange effect in this shot.

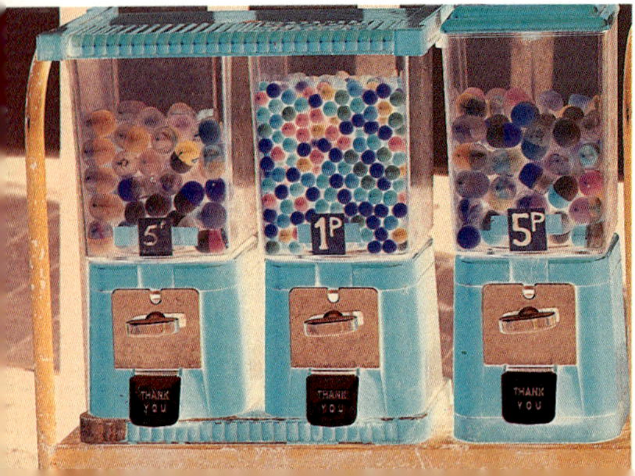

7.08 ● If you are disappointed with a set of colour prints from a processing lab, always look at the negatives: it may not be your fault. Where a print is dark and muddy, the negative should be thin and weak; where the print is pale with bleached colours, the negative should be dense and difficult to see through. If the negatives have good detail, however, it is likely that the prints have been badly processed and you should ask the lab to do them again.

7.09 ● When only the occasional frame on a roll of film is too light or too dark, the fault is most likely to be the result of abnormal subject or lighting conditions which you failed to recognise and compensate for. If you have a complete roll of negatives or transparencies which are either under or overexposed, the fault is more likely to be with the camera and its settings.

7.10 ● There is little point in using colour correction filters when shooting on colour negative film, since machine-made prints in processing labs adjust the colour balance automatically. If your prints are noticeably different in colour from the subject, ask to have them made again. For the finest results and to obtain precisely the effect you want for a special picture, ask for a hand-made print. Bear in mind that this will cost more than machine prints.

7.11 Overexposure of a complete roll of film can be caused by a number of factors:

- The film-speed dial is set to a slower ISO number than its recommended index;
- The auto-iris mechanism fails and the lens is not stopping down to its preset aperture;
- The shutter is operating at a slower speed than the setting indicates;
- The exposure compensating dial is inadvertently set to a plus factor;
- A spot metering mode is aimed at a small dark area in a normal-toned subject.

If none of the above are applicable, the film has probably been processed incorrectly.

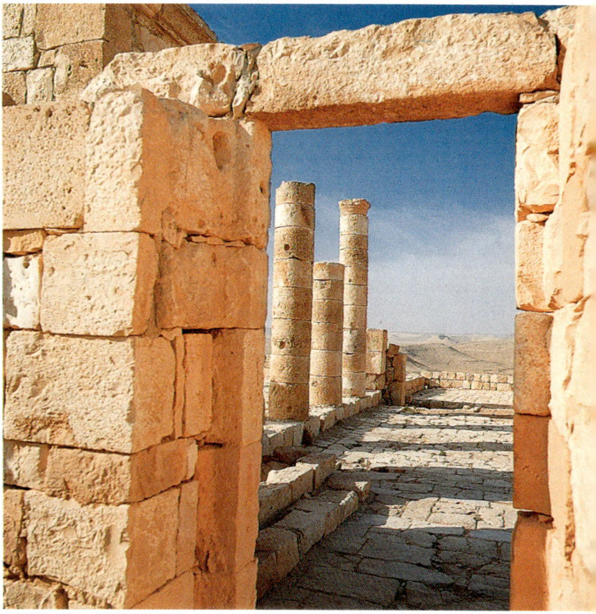

In strong light such as this always change your film in the shade to avoid it getting damaged.

7.12 Underexposure of a complete roll can be caused by any of the following:

- The film-speed dial is set to a higher number ISO than is indicated on the pack;
- The film is very old;
- The selected shutter speed is operating at a faster speed than indicated;
- The exposure compensating dial is inadvertently set to a minus factor:
- A spot-metering reading is made from a small, light area of a subject of normal tone.

If none of the above apply, the film has probably been processed incorrectly.

7.13 When using a separate exposure meter, underexposure can also be caused if you have not made sufficient allowance for any attachments such as filters and extension tubes.

7.14 ●● The most effective way to dry prints made on fibre-based paper so that they remain flat is to squeegee the surface dry and then stretch them on to a sheet of glass, securing them with masking tape along each border.

7.15 ●● Handle fibre-based paper carefully as the slightest stress will cause marks or kinking. Always use trays a size or two larger than the paper, slide the paper into the solutions smoothly, handle and drain only by the corners and avoid the use of print tongs – or be very careful with them.

PRACTICAL HINT

- When fibre-based prints are pegged at each corner back-to-back on the line, the worst of the cockling is eliminated. If you then place them under a weight before they are bone dry, they will be quite flat after a few hours.

7.16 ● Make a useful light switch for the darkroom by stretching a piece of wire 30cm or so above head height across the part of the room you use most, and attaching to it the end of a string pull-switch. You can operate the room light from anywhere within reach of the wire.

7.17 ● If you process film regularly in daylight tanks, it is worth buying a tank and lid for each stage of the process and marking them, for example 'developer', 'stop bath' and 'fix'.This will eliminate the need to wash and dry the tanks thoroughly in between each processing session and will drastically reduce any risk of contamination. You can leave the stop bath and fix in their respective tanks during their useful life. If you adopt the habit of filling the developing tank before loading the spirals, you can immerse them in the developer more rapidly, and remove air bubbles more effectively by up-and-down agitation before you put on the lid and switch on the room light.

7.18 ● When you process film in a daylight tank, it is a good idea to tap the tank sharply from time to time on the edge of the sink to dislodge any air bubbles which may have formed on the film surface.

7.19 ● Keep a large, thick plastic bag within reach while you work in the dark; the inner lining of a 40 x 50cm (16 x 20in) paper pack is ideal. This will provide you with somewhere safe to store a film or sheet of paper if you need to switch on the room light suddenly – to find the tank lid, for instance.

7.20 ●● A useful gadget for film and print drying is a tripod-based clothes dryer, the type with umbrella arms supporting parallel circular strings. Place it in a dust-free, well-ventilated spot. A shot of wetting agent in the final rinse will help the fibre to dry quickly and, in hard-water areas, a drop of acetic acid will prevent the formation of scum.

7.21 ●●● Use archival processing methods for maximum keeping qualities when you make black-and-white prints on fibre-based papers. You should always:

1. Use a stop bath after development.
2. Use two fixing baths, discard the first when it is exhausted and replace it with the second which is made up fresh.
3. Immerse the prints after an initial wash, in a hypo-eliminator bath for the recommended period before giving them a final wash.

The best possible archival permanence can be obtained by selenium or gold toning.

7.22 ●●● A useful technique for gaining a little extra print contrast without changing to a harder grade of paper is to expose and develop a print to the required shadow density, and then make the highlights brighter by immersing the print briefly in a dilute bath of potassium ferricyanide after a short period in the fix. You can then fix and wash it normally. With a little care, and the use of a cotton-wool swab or brush, you can apply this technique locally to a print which just needs to be lifted in some areas. ▼

TECHNICAL TIP

- To produce an interesting creative effect, you can lighten selected areas of an image in an exaggerated way by bleaching using the technique described above.

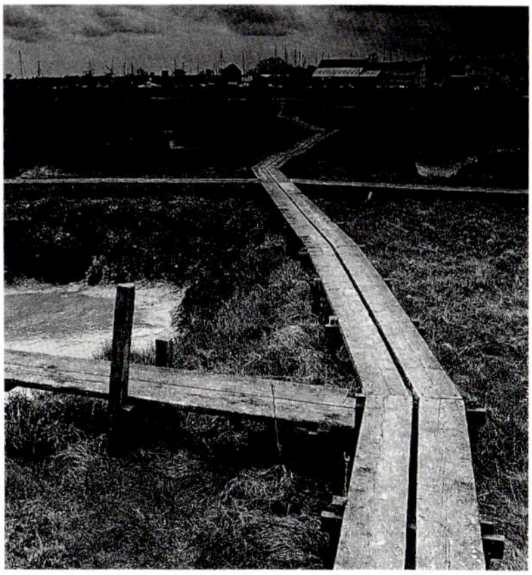

A normally exposed and processed print on grade 3 bromide paper.

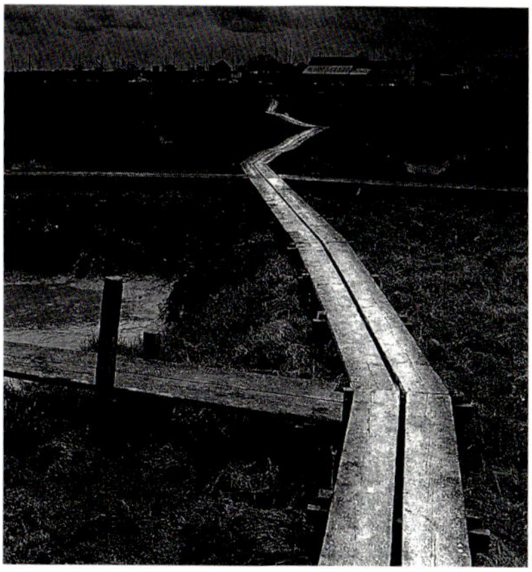

Create a dramatic effect with a darker print on the same paper, with localised brushed bleaching.

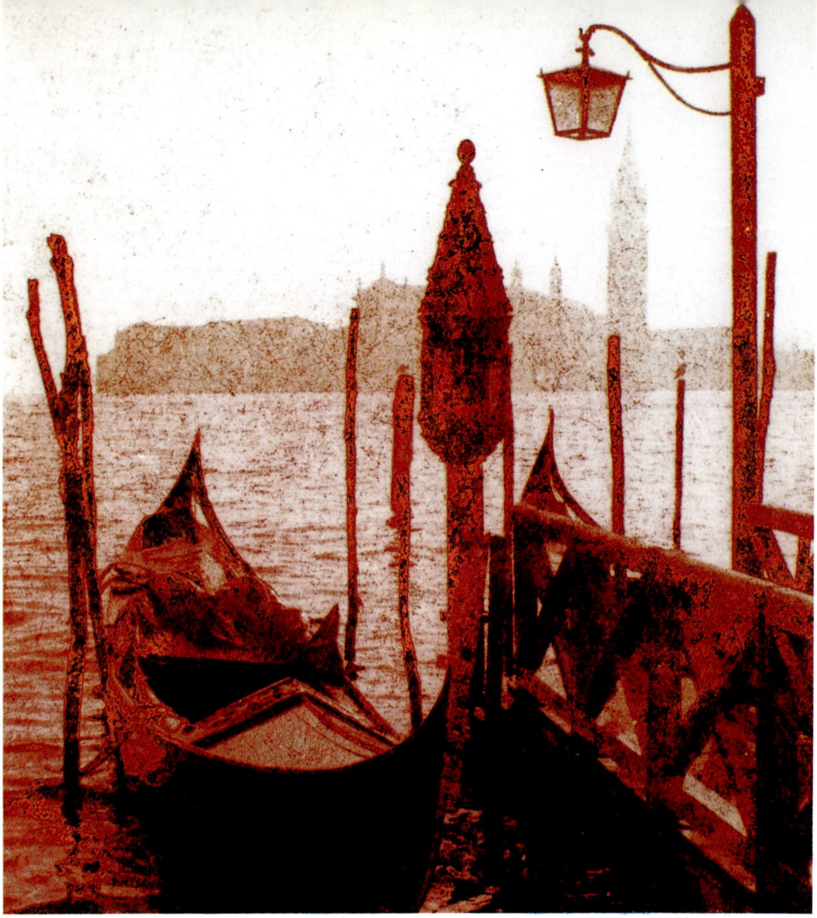

7.23 ●●● Skin blemishes on portraits can be eliminated, and interesting effects created with many other subjects, by the use of a texture screen. This is a transparent material which is held in contact with a negative or transparency in the enlarger's carrier while it is printed. It is possible to buy ready-made texture screens from photographic suppliers, which imitate the effects of film grain, canvas and burnished metal, among others, but you can also make your own by photographing suitable, finely-detailed surfaces and then exposing to create very light negatives or transparencies. The material used to make the semi-transparent sleeves for storing negatives can create an interesting granular effect. ▲

7.24 ●●● To improve skin quality on portraits, use a controlled amount of diffusion when making prints. The simplest technique is to introduce a piece of fine gauze or nylon between the enlarging lens and paper for all or part of the exposure. You can use conventional soft-focus camera attachments and other materials:

try experimenting with sellotape and crinkled cellophane, and with petroleum jelly smeared on to a clear filter or glass slide cover. You can vary the effect by altering the proportion of the exposure for which the diffuser is used and by moving it gently.

7.25 ●●● It is possible to reduce the contrast of a black-and-white print and obtain more detail in the highlights without changing paper grades by the technique of 'flashing'. This involves exposing the paper briefly before or after the basic exposure – it should be slightly less than is necessary to create a distinguishable tone. This is most easily achieved by giving a timed exposure under the enlarger without a negative in the carrier and with the lens stopped down. You will need to make tests to determine the amount of exposure needed.

7.26 ●●● The normal way to make a test strip is to give a series of exposures in regular units, progressively covering a strip of the paper each time. In this way five exposures of, say, 5 seconds will produce a test strip of 5, 10, 15, 20 and 25 seconds. It can however, be more informative to make a zonal test strip. This involves giving a basic exposure of 5 seconds and then progressively covering the paper while exposures of 2, 3, 4, 6 and 10 seconds are given. This will produce a test strip in which the stages represent exposures of 5, 7, 10, 14, 20 and 30 seconds. ▶

TECHNICAL TIP

- If the recommended test strip exposure range is too short, simply multiply each stage by a factor, x4 for instance, to produce a test strip with stages of 20, 28, 40, 64, 80 and 120 seconds.

7.27 ●● You can check the efficiency of your safe light by exposing a piece of bromide paper briefly to the room light – just enough to create a light grey tone – and then placing it on the workbench or sink for about 10 minutes with a coin laid on the surface. If the shape of the coin is visible after development you should adjust the position or brightness of the safe light and test again.

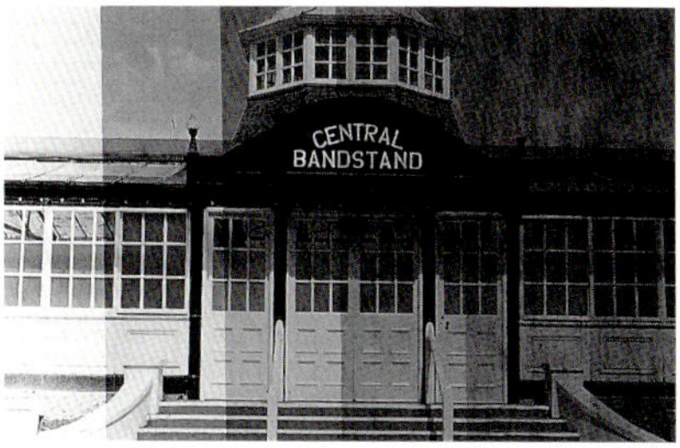

A test strip made in the normal way.

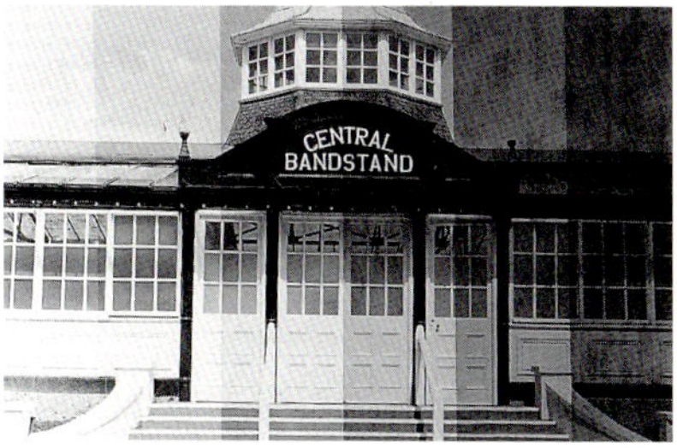

A test strip made using the zonal method.

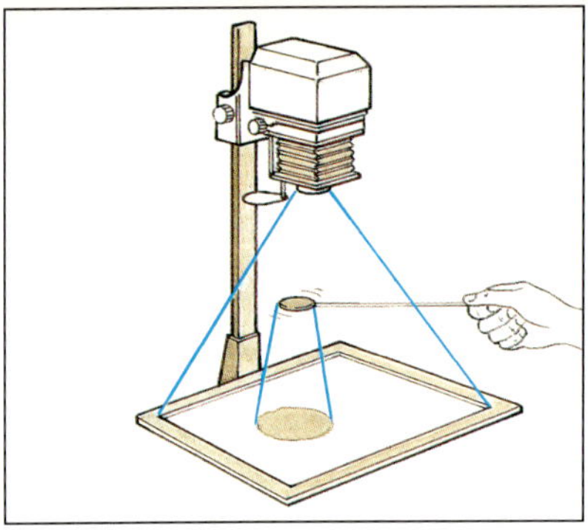

7.28 ●●● You can make an effective aid to shading and dodging when printing by bending strands of flower arranging wire into a loop at one end. Use this to support a small piece of modelling clay, moulded into the shape required. ▲

7.30 ●● Marks are sometimes visible on the back of negatives, which have been left as a result of drying. These can be removed easily if you touch the side of your nose with your finger tip, then lightly polish the offending area: the natural oils in the skin make an effective cleanser. Remove any marks left on the emulsion side of the film with a special film cleaner, These cleaners are available from professional photographic suppliers.

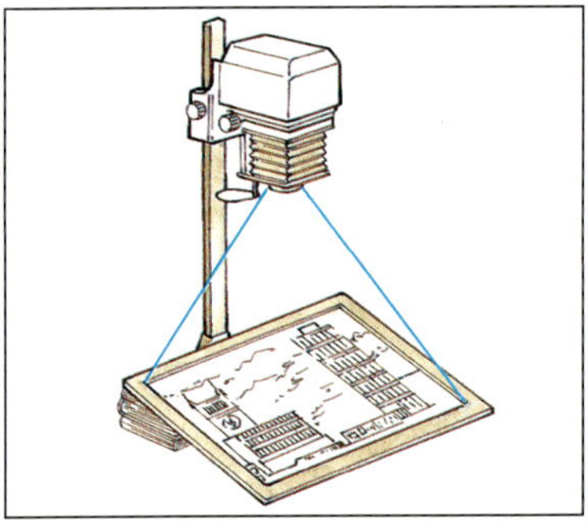

Tilting the baseboard to correct parallax error.

7.29 ●●● A photograph of a building which has converging verticals – caused by the camera being tilted upwards when the picture was taken – can be corrected during the printing process. Simply tilt the paper easel so that the base of the image is closer to the enlarger lens. You will need to use a small aperture to increase depth of focus and to ensure that the print is sharp from top to bottom. Some enlargers have a tilting negative holder which can be tipped in the opposite direction to the paper easel and so help to maintain sharp focus. ▼

PRACTICAL HINT

- This technique can also be used to create deliberate distortion for unusual effects with many subjects such as portraits and nudes.

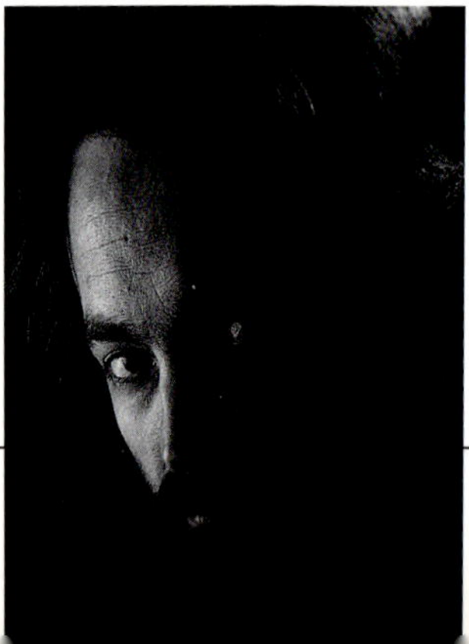

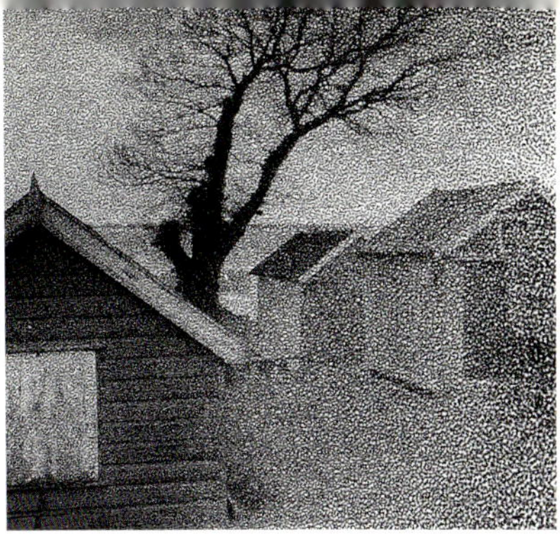

Texture your prints by exposing the paper through a clear portfolio sleeve.

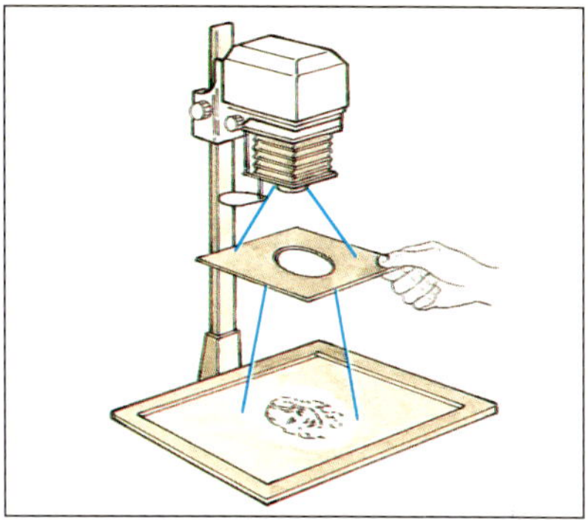

A simple method of creating an oval vignette print from a standard portrait shot.

7.31 ●●● You can make some interesting effects when printing by placing a piece of textured glass in contact with the paper, or coat a piece of plain glass with a thick layer of clear petroleum jelly and swirl it around with your finger tip, a serrated knife edge, or something similar, for a more subtle and controllable effect. When printing in colour, you can add transparent water colour to the glass for a limitless variety of interesting effects. In fact, you can use almost any semi-transparent material – muslin, lace or bubble plastic, for example. ▲

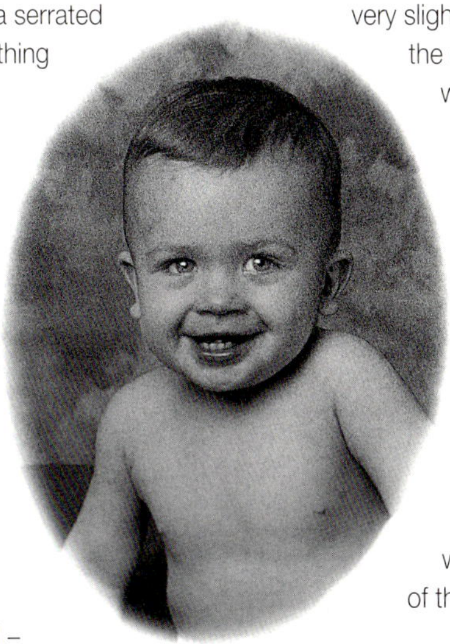

7.32 ●●● Create an appealing, old-fashioned effect when printing portraits by using the vignetting technique. Cut a round or oval hole in a piece of card and hold it between the enlarger lens and the printing paper during exposure, so that the important area of the image is allowed through into the centre of the paper while the rest remains white. If you move the card very slightly and gently during the exposure, the image will have a soft graduated edge. If you hold the cut oval or round shape on a piece of wire over the most important part of the image after the exposure has been made, you can give additional exposure which will leave the rest of the image black. ◀▲

PRACTICAL HINT

- For the second exposure in the vignetting technique described above, open the enlarging lens to its widest aperture to allow a shorter exposure time.

7.33 ●●● Photograms are images created by making an exposure on a piece of photographic paper with objects placed on it, like a three-dimensional contact print. By mixing opaque, transparent and translucent objects a range of tones can be created, and the technique works equally well with coloured objects using colour reversal materials. Make the exposure using an enlarger as a light source without a negative in the carrier, or use an ordinary room light with the composition and photographic paper positioned immediately below it. ▼

7.34 ●●● To extend this technique further, make abstract slides on a piece of glass using a mixture of coloured and clear fluids, including water-colour inks, dyes, detergent, transparent glue and household bleach. Drip them on to the glass with an eye-dropper and allow them to mingle, then tease them around with a brush or blot them to create a wide range of effects.

7.35 ●●● Using an enlarger, the same principle can be employed to make magnified photograms, with small translucent objects placed in the enlarger carrier and treated as a negative. ▶

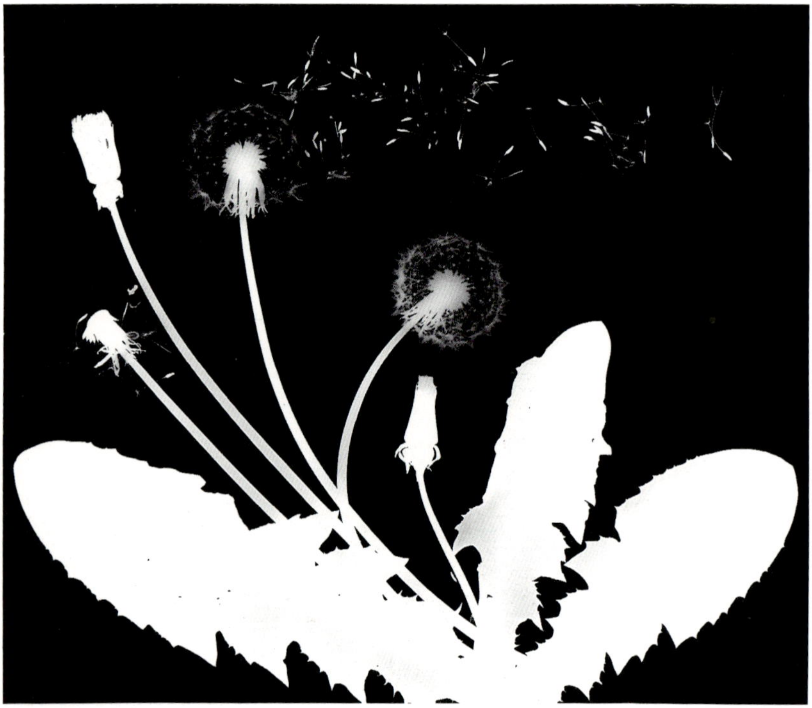

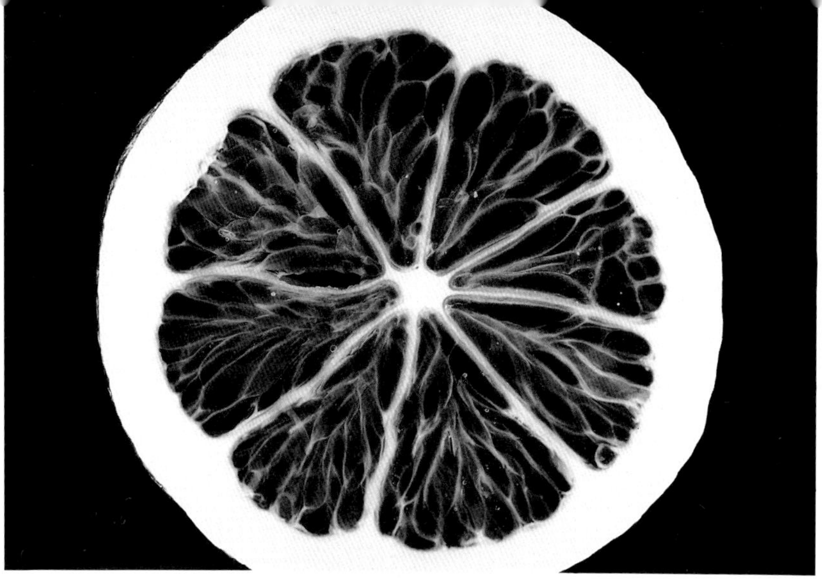

This effect was achieved by placing a lemon slice in the negative holder of the enlarger.

7.36 ●●● Always use lithographic film and paper in conjunction with the appropriate developer in order to eliminate half tones when printing from negatives. The resulting images will be recorded as pure black-and-white. You can create striking effects if you use this technique with the right kind of subject. If you would like to try to print pure black-and-white images but don't want to invest in the special materials needed, you can obtain similar effects using a photocopier or fax machine. ▶

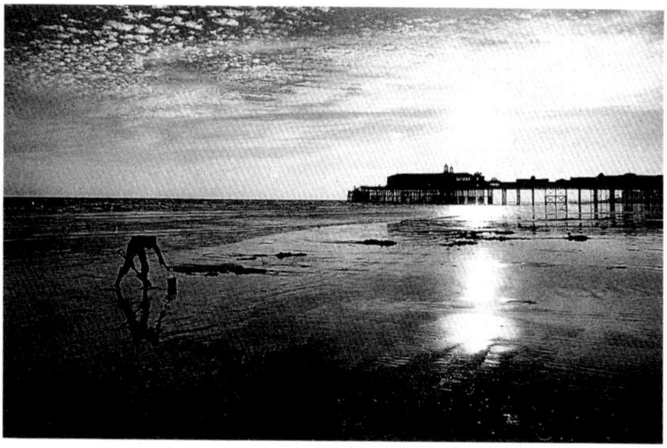

The image (below) was created by making a photocopy of the normal bromide print (above) using a fax machine.

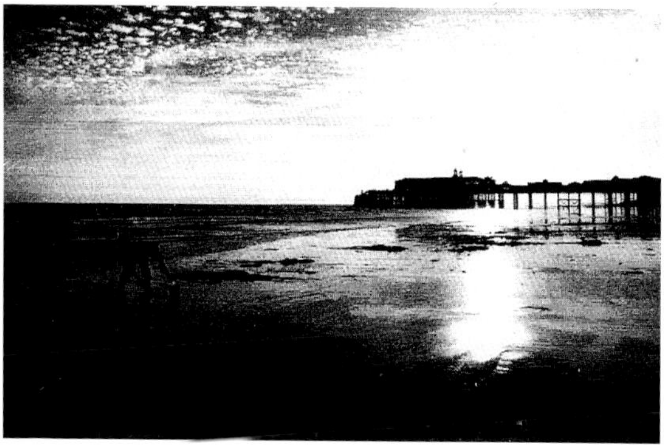

7.37 Add a sky from another negative or transparency to a photograph of a scene which is spoiled by a blank or uninteresting sky to make a striking image by using the montage technique. The process is as follows:

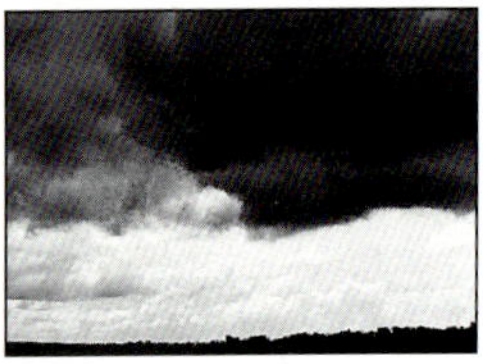

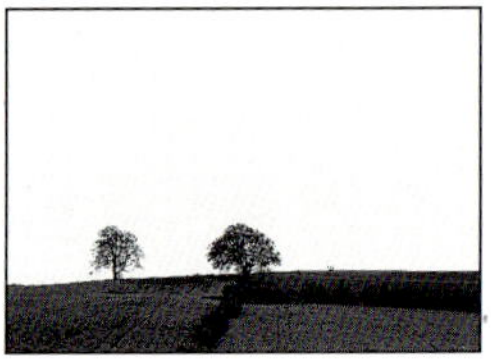

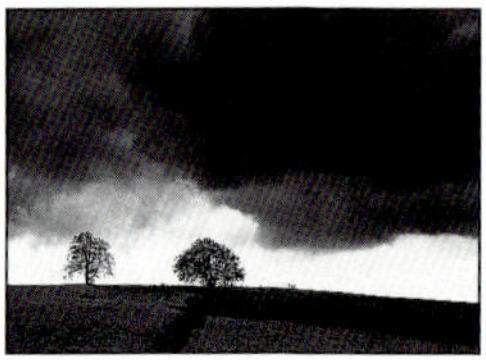

① Find, or take, a suitable sky picture in which the horizon is similar to the recipient picture.

② Size up the negative of the foreground subject in the enlarger, and with a piece of plain paper in the masking easel make a tracing of the image.

③ Make a test strip of this negative to determine the correct exposure.

④ Replace the foreground negative with the sky picture in the enlarger, size this up and position it using the tracing of the first negative, then make a test strip from this image.

⑤ Expose this negative on to a full-size piece of paper using your hand, or a piece of black card cut to shape, to hold back the image below the horizon, moving it slightly all the time to ensure the image has a softly graduated edge.

⑥ Mark one corner by clipping it or folding it over to ensure that it is replaced the correct way round in the masking easel for the second exposure, then store it in a light-tight box.

⑦ Resize the foreground negative and position it on the easel using the traced image.

⑧ Make the second exposure on the same piece of paper, this time holding back the area above the horizon in the same way as before.

The image can now be processed. You may find it necessary to make another print in order to refine the join between the vignetted edges.

7.38 Use liquid silver halide emulsion, which can be obtained from any specialist photographic supplier, to make prints on surfaces other than printing paper, such as wood, metal or pottery. Coat the surface and allow it to dry. Some absorbent surfaces must be primed first with a polyurethane varnish. The silver halide is supplied with a subbing solution for use with non-porous surfaces such as china. Bromide emulsion ready coated on to a linen base is also available, enabling you to make photographic cushion covers and dining-table place mats.

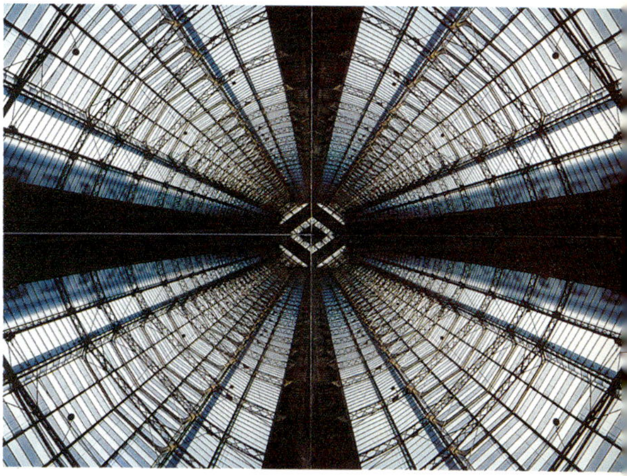

Join two normal and two reversed prints together to create an abstract image.

7.39 ● All photographers sometimes produce substandard or repetitive work, so rely upon careful editing to maximise the impact of their images – and to guard their reputations. Even your collection of family photographs will benefit enormously from rigorous selection and the rejection of second-rate images. Check transparencies with a magnifying loupe of at least x8 for 35mm slides – any which are not critically sharp and correctly exposed are unsuitable for photo library or presentation material. Selection work for a portfolio or album by choosing only the best from each sequence of the same subject and avoid the inclusion of similar or repetitive shots.

7.40 ●● Photographic prints can be cut and joined to create a number of unusual effects. One of the most amusing techniques takes advantage of the lack of symmetry in the human face. From a negative of a full-face portrait make four prints of exactly the same size, but with two of them place the negative upside down in the carrier so the prints are reversed left to right. With a sharp scalpel, cut each of the prints through exactly the same vertical line down the centre of the subject's face. Using Cow Gum or Photo Mount, and a piece of mounting board, paste the prints down with a butted join to create images where each full-face image consists of the same side.

7.41 ●● A set of two reversed pairs of prints can be joined to form a square. This works best if the image chosen has a strong diagonal line running from corner to corner. Alternatively, two or more reversed pairs of prints can be butted in line alternately to create a patterned frieze. ▲

7.42 ● The popular flip-over album may be a convenient and inexpensive method of storing prints, but it does little for

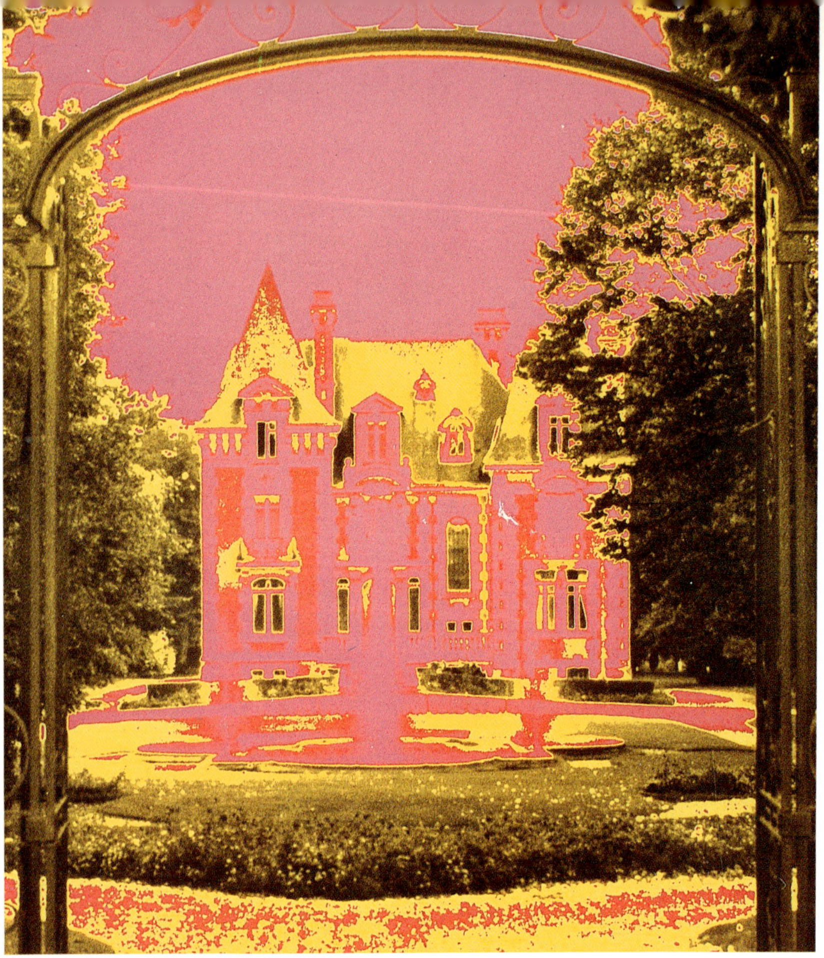

This surreal effect was created using the solarisation and toning chemicals of the Colovir process.

presentation. A larger album or portfolio is a far more satisfactory way to display photographs. You can combine individual pictures on a page to create a strong sense of design, in a way similar to the layout of books and magazines.

7.43 ● Lamination is a method many professional photographers use for their portfolio and presentation material. Magazine tear sheets, proofs or original prints are encased in a thin sandwich of clear, rigid plastic creating a stylish and unified collection of photographs which is durable and light. Laminated materials can be kept loose in a case; they are easy to change to suit your needs.

PRACTICAL HINT

- ☐ The Colorvir process provides a convenient mixture of toners, bleaches and dyes which can be used to create a wide range of effects.

PRACTICAL HINT

- To make a panoramic picture, shoot a sequence of two or more pictures of a suitable subject which allows a 180 degree, or greater, view using a standard lens. A wide-angle lens will cause too much distortion at the edges making them difficult to join. Use a tripod and ensure that the camera stays level throughout the sequence, and allow a generous overlap on each side of each shot. When cutting the picture, try to find a natural vertical line in the subject which will help to mask the join.

7.44 If you want to display framed colour prints on a home or office wall, select a place which is not subject to continuously bright daylight to avoid fading. Ilfochrome colour reversal paper is generally considered to be the most resistant to fading and it is quite safe to display archivally processed, fibre-based black-and-white prints even in a well-lit area.

7.45 A large proportion of photographs can be improved by cropping. Whether you make your own prints or use a processing lab, look for ways in which your pictures can be given extra impact; a more pleasing and balanced composition may be created by trimming the sides of a photograph. Don't feel that you have to conform to the conventional shape of a photograph which may well have a stronger effect cropped into a long thin upright or as a square picture. When photographs are laid out on

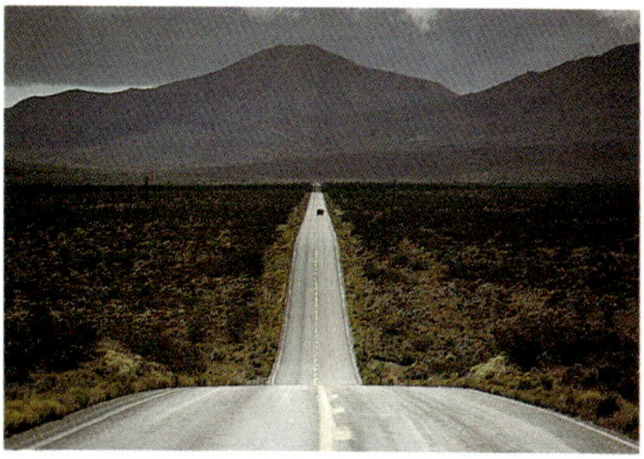

The complete image of a shot taken on 35mm film.

the pages of an album or portfolio, a variety of shapes and sizes is more interesting. ▲ ▼

PRACTICAL HINT

- You can make a useful gadget to help determine how a picture should be cropped. Cut two pieces of L-shaped white or black card the size of the prints you wish to crop. Lay these over the print to form an adjustable frame, then you can assess where cropping will be most effective.

The image above, cropped and enlarged.

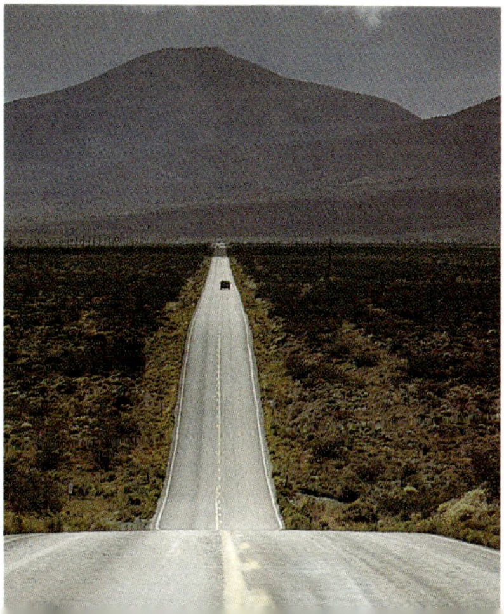

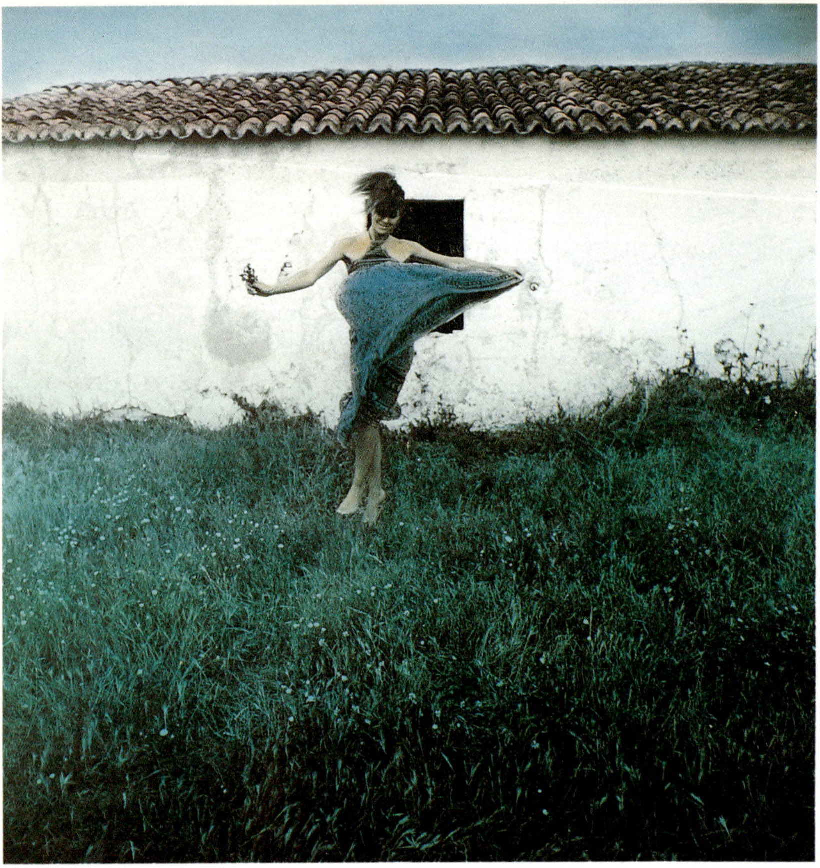

7.46 ●●● You can make subtle and unusual colour images by toning and tinting black-and-white prints; for most methods, this does not require the use of a darkroom. A wide variety of chemical toners is available from specialist photographic suppliers which enables colours, ranging from the familiar sepia to orange, green and blue, to be produced with ease and simplicity. Add further selective colours with a brush using transparent dyes or water colours. If you choose the right subject, and add the colour sparingly, you will need little painting skill to produce very pleasing results. You may find that working on resin-coated papers, in preference to fibre-based materials, is much easier. ▲

7.47 ●● Give a framed photograph a more polished presentation by the use of a bevel-cut overlay, or matt. With care and a sharp craft knife it is possible, but difficult, to cut them yourself. Most art shops, however, have ready-cut overlays in a range of standard sizes and colours. Alternatively, you can purchase a specially made matt cutter which makes the job quite simple.

7.48 ● By taking a picture especially for a photographic greetings card, you may be able to overcome the problem of finding an inexpensive but interesting means of incorporating the message. A still-life picture of a bunch of flowers, for instance, could include a label with a nicely handwritten message. Another possibility is to apply suitable 'graffiti' temporarily to a larger subject or scene, such as a message written in the sand of a seascape. Once you begin to think of the message as part of the image, you will find that there are numerous ways in which you can produce attractive results. ▶

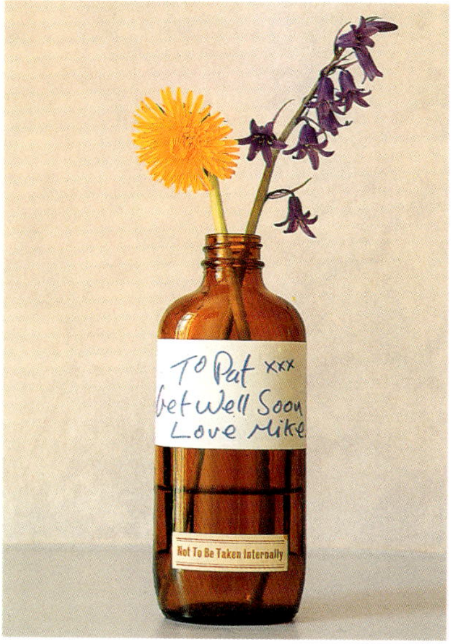

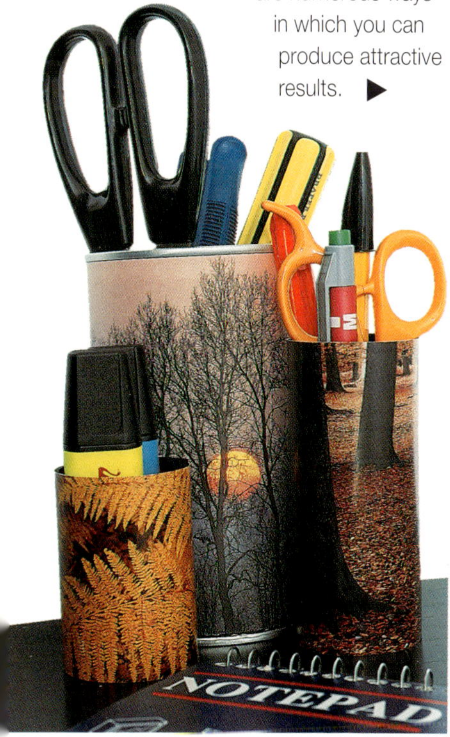

7.49 ● Although most photographs are destined for an album or portfolio, it is also well worthwhile considering their potential as an element of design in personal and gift items. In addition to the more obvious calendars, a photograph pasted around an empty tin makes an attractive desktop pencil holder.

Laminated photographs can be used extremely effectively as place mats to grace any dining table, or you can print on to fabric to make a photographic cushion cover.

Ideas like those described above work especially well if you remember to bear the end product in mind when you take the photograph, so that it becomes an integral part of the design. ◀

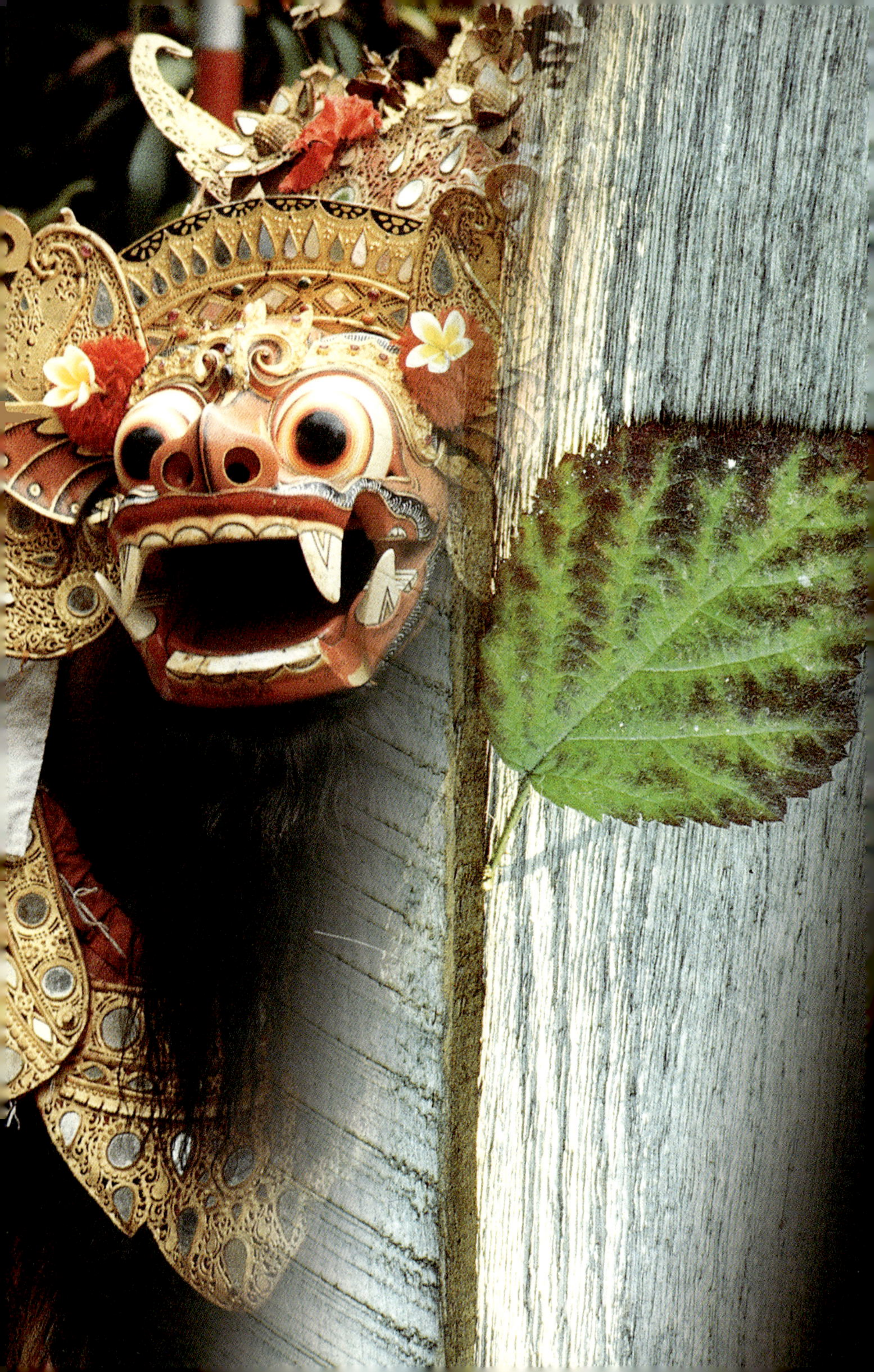

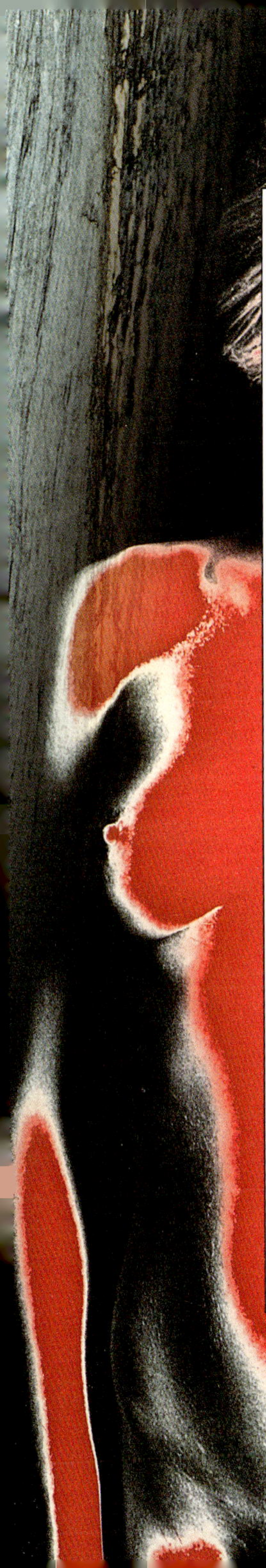

8

SPECIAL APPLICATIONS

Tips on taking photographs under difficult conditions, like mixed lighting, in snow, at special events and underwater are given in *Special Applications*. Techniques, like back projection, flare, texture screens and polarised light are described, as are the ways in which these techniques can be used to help create images with an unusual and ambiguous quality. There are also hints on filing, captioning, presenting your work to its best advantage, and how to submit your work for publication.

- special situations
- special effects
- still-life photography
- selling your work

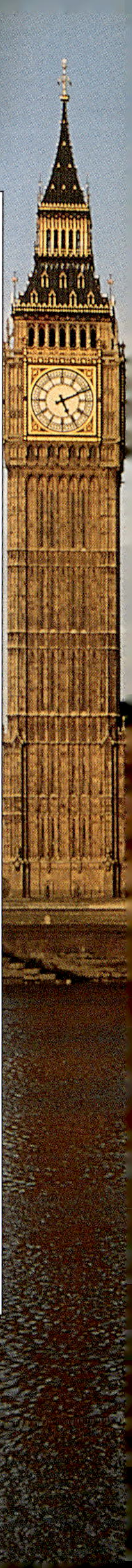

8 Special Situations

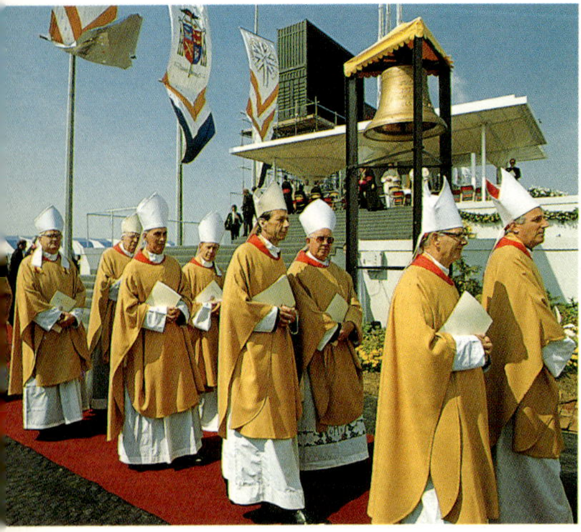

8.01 ● It is difficult to take photographs at public events such as street processions and spectator sports unless you have a good view of proceedings. All too often you are hemmed in by crowds and unable to see over peoples' heads. Take a leaf from the press photographers' book and use a small aluminium step ladder; a strong metal camera case would make an ideal alternative. As little as 30cm of extra height can make all the difference. ▲

PRACTICAL HINT

- If your camera has a waist-level viewfinder, hold it upside down above your head so that you can view the scene accurately. A wide-angle lens is useful as you can often obtain satisfactory pictures by aiming it at the scene at arm's length, using a combination of eye and guesswork.

8.02 ●● When photographing subjects lit by theatrical lighting, including rock concerts and discotheques, daylight type colour transparency film is the best choice. This is because the lighting effects are created by using a variety of coloured filters ranging from reds and yellows to blue, green or violet, over numerous light sources. The overall colour balance is impossible to predict as the filters, together with the angle and direction of the lights are often frequently and rapidly changed.

There is no such thing as an accurate colour balance in these circumstances, so opt for a film which is likely to give the best overall effect. In areas where the reddish filters predominate, daylight film will enhance the effect. Tungsten type film, however, will tend to accentuate the quality of the blue and green filtered areas in an adverse way, especially where skin tones are involved.

8.03 ●● The choice of filters when shooting pictures in the snow is not always straightforward. Shadow areas in snow scenes invariably have a pronounced blue cast, especially when a blue sky is present. You can use a warm filter, like an 81C, which will tend to create a sunnier, more 'normal' colour quality, but a blue cast can contribute to the mood of snow scenes, especially in dull light, giving them a colder and more realistic appearance. ▶

8.04 A number of cameras are available today which enable photographs to be taken under water at modest depths, in addition to those like the Nikonos which are designed for serious sub-aqua photography. Remember that water filters out the shorter wavelengths of light at the red end of the spectrum: even at only 1 metre or so beneath the surface, this may cause a noticeable blue cast, although it can be corrected by using a red filter. As a rule of thumb, in clear water you should use a CC10 red filter for each metre the camera is taken below the surface. At depths greater than 6 metres, it is not possible to correct the blue cast and you may have to use artificial lighting.

8.05 Capturing the colourful effervescence of firework displays can be an enormous challenge, even to a professional photographer. For striking results, record several individual bursts on one frame of film. Set the camera on a tripod and aim it at a likely area of sky, with the camera shutter held open on the time setting and the lens covered by its cap. When a suitable firework burst occurs in the targetted area, make an exposure by removing the cap for approximately 2 seconds. If you use a film of ISO 100, you should be able to make several exposures at around f11 without the risk of overexposure, but don't be tempted to include too many as the result will look confused.

The actual exposure you will need depends largely on how bright the individual bursts are. My advice is to bracket, both by varying the aperture and the number and duration of bursts that you include.

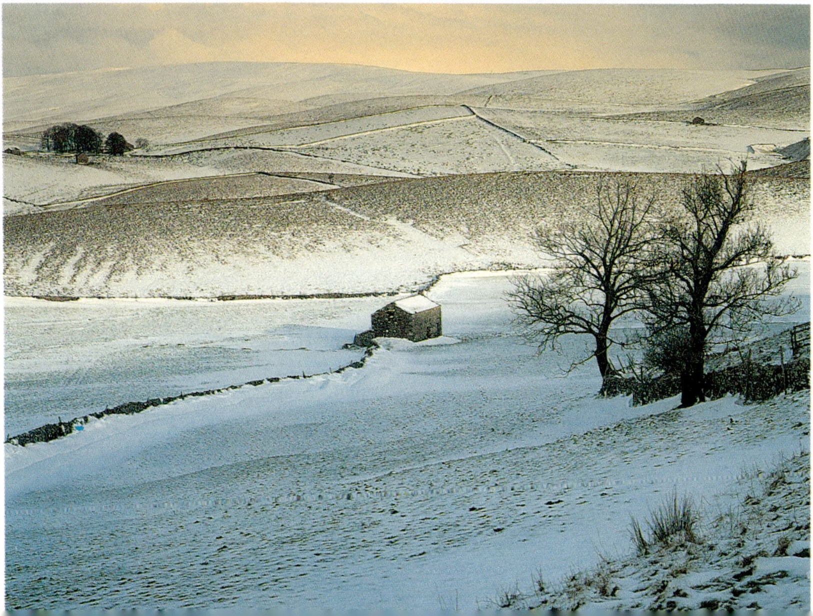

8.06 ●●● Create a striking impression of movement under studio conditions by using a combination of flash and a long exposure. Make a flash exposure to freeze the movement at the end of an action and allow an exposure of about 1 sec to produce a controlled blur during the movement. In practice, it may be easier to do this in reverse, making the f lash exposure at the end of the action and moving the subject backwards to create the blur.

8.07 ●●● A pseudo-strobe effect can be created in a similar way by making a series of flash exposures of various stages of a movement on the same frame of film using the camera's multi-exposure setting. Take care to ensure adequate separation of the subject at each stage, so the image does not become too confusing. You will obtain greater clarity and impact when the subject is rim-lit on a dark or black background.

PRACTICAL HINT

- ☐ Use a black, or dark, background and strong rim lighting for the best blur effect. Make tests to determine the speed and duration of the movement and the length of exposure needed.

8.08 ●●● Many soft-focus effects can be created using normal camera lenses, but some of the most subtle and pleasing images are obtained when a poor quality lens or a magnifying glass, or a condenser lens is used. A set of extension tubes or a bellows unit is the ideal means of mounting and focussing such a lens, but it is a fairly simple matter if you have a camera with interchangeable lenses, to construct a crude but workable focussing mechanism using two cardboard tubes, one which will fit inside the other. You can improve the lens quality if required, by cutting a smaller aperture in a piece of black card and mounting it over the lens. ▼

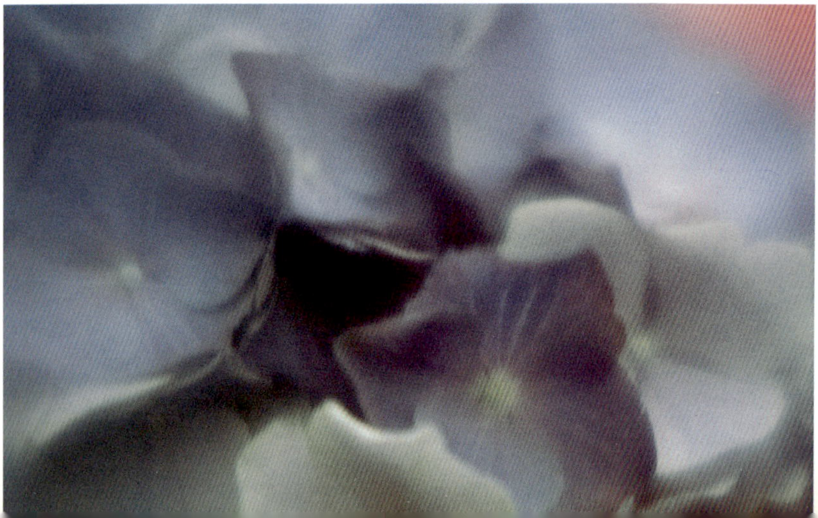

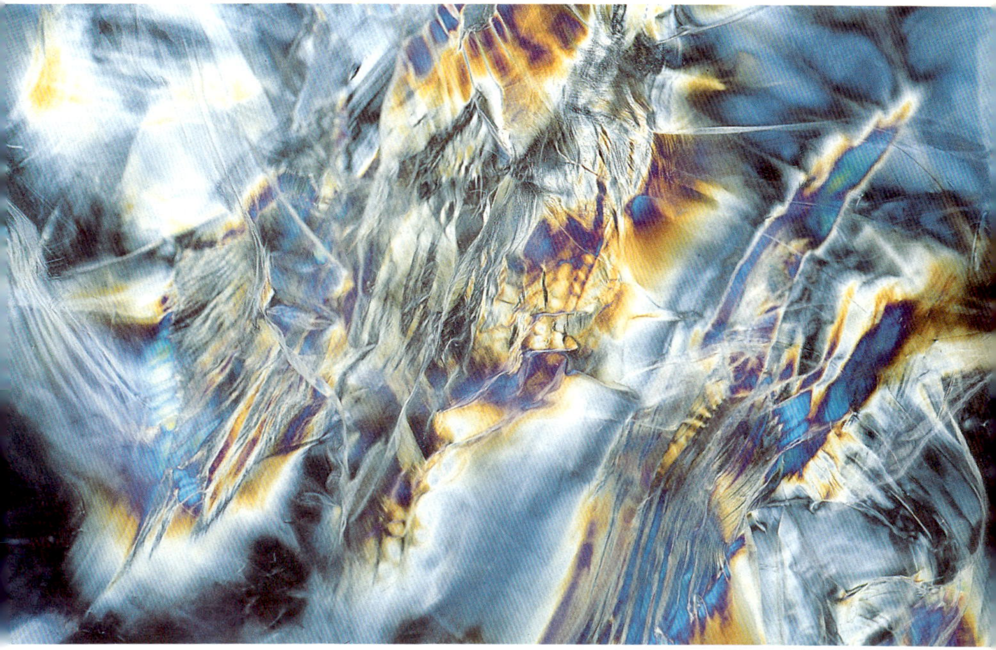

Stressed polythene illuminated by polarised light and photographed using a polarised filter.

8.09 ●●● Create interesting abstract effects using polarised light and clear plastic materials like polythene. When such objects are illuminated by polarised light and then photographed through a polarising filter, the areas of stress where the plastic has been moulded or shaped, will display a range of spectrum colours. Use a light box which is illuminated by polarised light: this can be done by placing the polarising material between the light source and the glass upon which the object rests.

8.10 ●●● You can buy sheets of polarising acetate fairly cheaply from scientific supply stores – the sheets are of low quality, but are quite adequate for this purpose. Adjust the position of the plastic material and rotate the polariser over the camera lens to obtain a range of colourful effects. ▲

PRACTICAL HINT

- To help the composition of multi-exposure shots and make the picture more appealing, include foreground details which will look interesting in silhouette, but be careful to avoid moving objects or people as these will tend to create confusion.

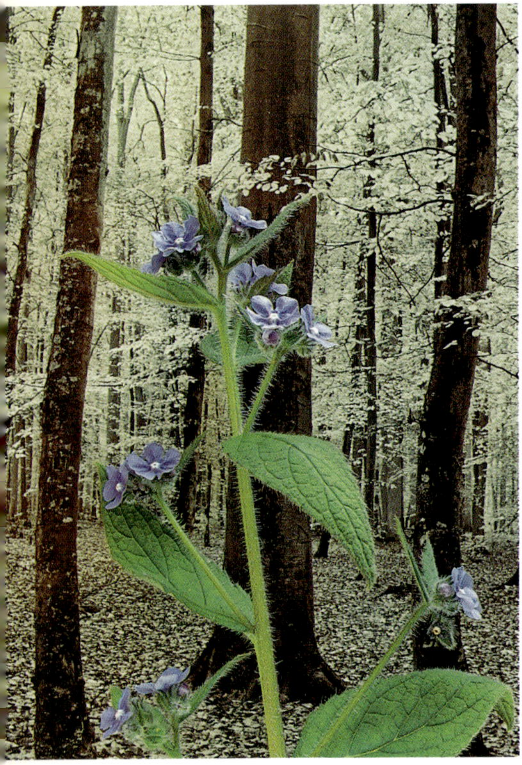

8.11 If you are interested in creating unusual and ambiguous images, the technique of using a photograph within a normal subject can offer some interesting possibilities. Many photographs have a convincing three-dimensional quality, and when this is incorporated into another image the result can be intriguing. Combine a black-and-white photograph with a colourful subject shot on colour film – a cut-out black-and-white print of an apple in a bowl of fruit, for example. You can also use this technique to produce a baffling sense of scale; for instance, a small colour photograph of a model's head could be used as a background for a real hand holding a tea cup. ◀

8.12 Flare often occurs in outdoor situations when shooting into the sun. Light is indiscriminately reflected and scattered within the lens, resulting in effects ranging from a loss of contrast to bright images of the iris being visible within the image. Usually considered a fault to be avoided at all costs, on occasions it can be used in a controlled and creative way to produce atmospheric and interesting effects by lowering the contrast and softening fine detail.

In the studio, lighting can be set up expressly for this purpose. The amount of flare can be controlled by holding a piece of black card in front of the lens to shield it from the light source. Flare can also be induced artificially by angling a piece of optical glass (a square resin filter is ideal) in front of the lens to reflect light from a much brighter area of the scene – the sky in a landscape shot, for example.

TECHNICAL TIP

- Flare will give an artificially high exposure reading, indicating that less exposure is required than is actually needed. For this reason, take the exposure reading from the subject without the flare.

TECHNICAL TIP

- When using a texture screen, to get both the screen and the subject behind it in sharp focus, use the smallest aperture possible and avoid long-focus lenses. You will obtain the maximum depth of field by focussing at a point about two-thirds of the distance between the screen and the subject.

8.13 ●●● Texture screens are devices used mainly in printing techniques, but they can also be used successfully when taking photographs of smaller subjects such as portraits and still-life. You will need to construct a softwood frame somewhat larger than the subject you wish to photograph and to stretch over it a suitable textured material which is partly transparent – muslin, cheesecloth or nylon mesh will all work. Position this in front of the subject, as close as you can manage without restricting the lighting too much.

Frontal lighting is not ideal with this technique, but contrast will be significantly reduced by the texture screen, so it will not matter if the lighting is strongly directional, for instance from the side, although of course, you can experiment with a softer and more diffused light. Glass can also be used as a texture screen if patterned in some way, covered by a fine film of water droplets, for instance, or smeared with clear petroleum jelly. ▶

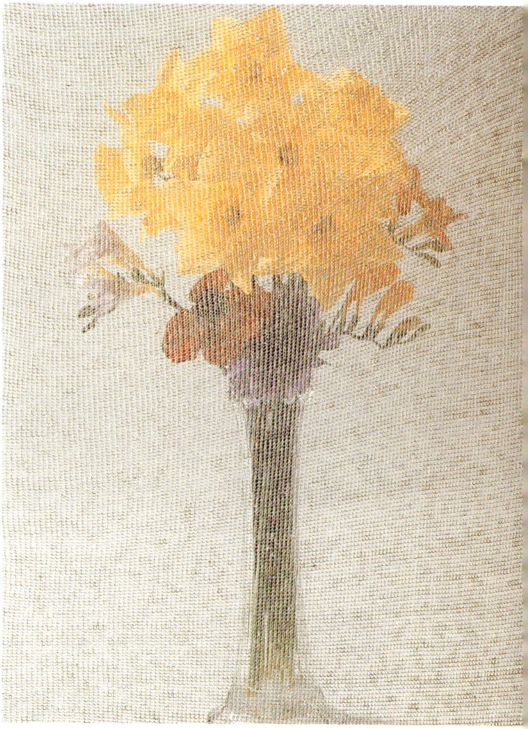

This still-life was shot through a muslin screen.

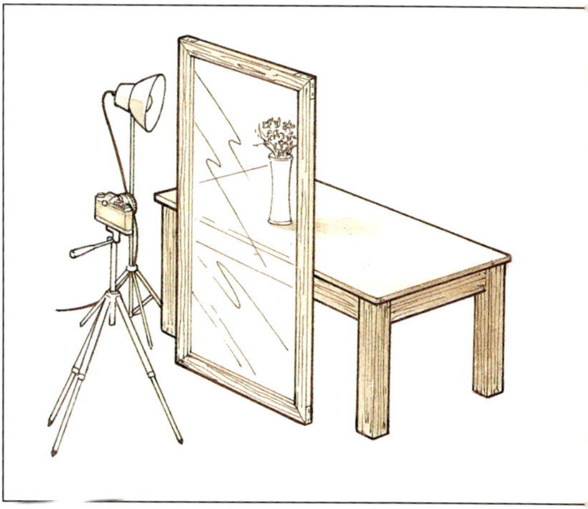

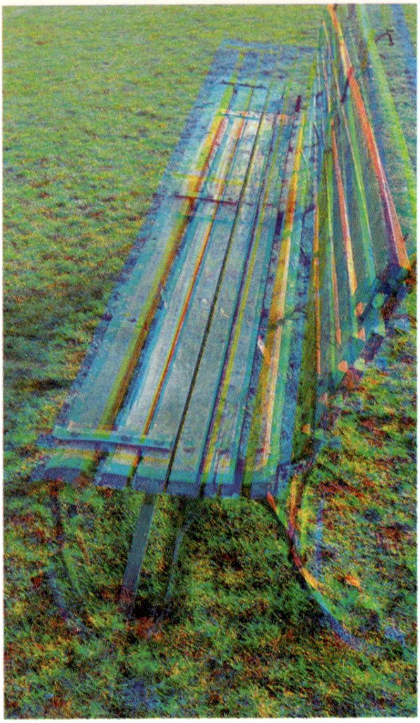

moved between the exposures, there will be bands of colour. Since the filters each have a different factor, you must give three different exposures. Take an exposure reading without a filter and then, with the red filter in place, give the exposure previously indicated. With the green filter give three times the basic exposure, and with the blue give four times the unfiltered exposure. If you use colour negative film, any slight colour cast due to the imbalance of the exposures can be corrected when the print is made. ◀ ▼

8.14 ●● You can create interesting effects with colour photographs by making multiple exposures using colour separation, or tricolour filters. The most suitable subjects are those which are essentially static but contain a moving element – surf flowing over rocks, or clouds in a landscape, for example. Mount the camera on a firm tripod: do not move it or wind on the film until the process is complete. Make three exposures, one through each of the red, green and blue filters; the static element of the image will record as a normal colour but, where the image has

PRACTICAL HINT

- The multiple exposure technique can be used effectively in a variety of ways. Move items between exposures of a still-life, for instance, or alter the lighting so that the position of highlights and shadows changes, or use a zoom lens to alter the image size slightly between exposures.

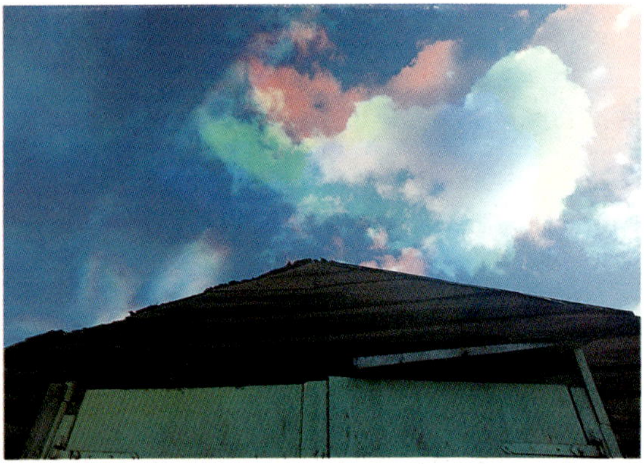

8.15 ●●● With small static set-ups such as a still-life, a projector can provide the means of creating interesting and effective background effects. First, make a wooden frame larger than the background area, cover the frame with tracing paper and place it behind, and as close as possible to, the composition . Position the projector far enough behind the screen to fill the tracing paper completely with the selected image. Switch off all other lighting and take an exposure reading for the projected image.

Now, cover the tracing paper screen with a piece of black velvet, arrange the lighting to illuminate the still-life in the desired way, and take an exposure reading for this. With your camera mounted on a firm tripod, make an exposure for the still-life. Remove the black velvet and extinguish all other lighting then, without moving the camera or winding on the film, make an exposure for the projected image. ▶

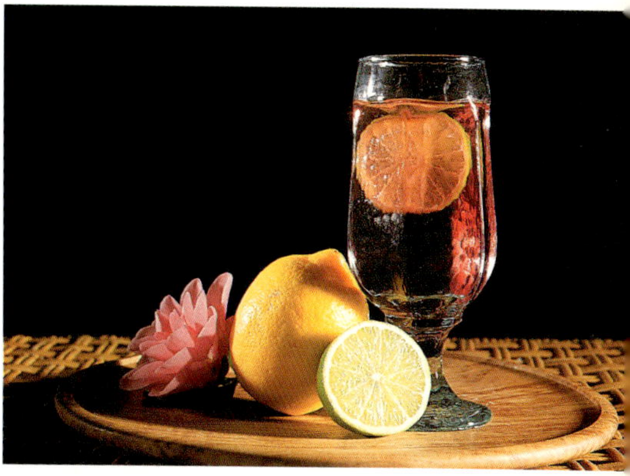

Shot without projected background.

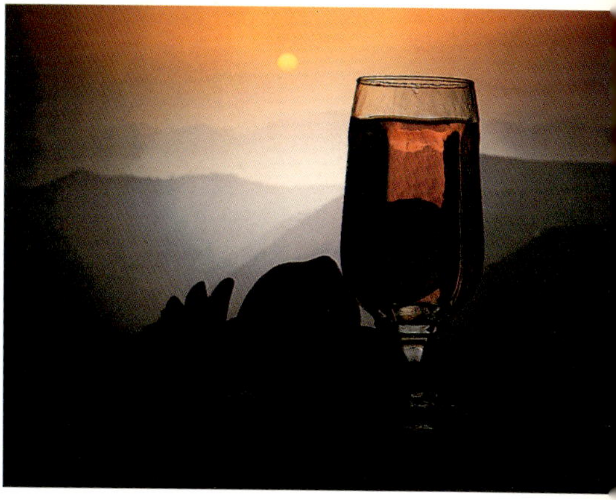

Shot with the still-life illumination switched off.

TECHNICAL TIP

- Tungsten light and artificial light film are best for this technique since they will match the colour quality of the projected image. You can use flash to light the composition, but you must use daylight type film and place an 80A colour correction filter over the projector lens.

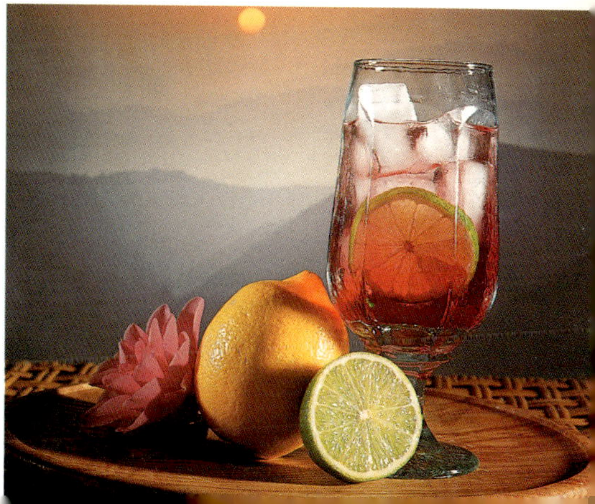

Right: The combined effect of both exposures.

8.16 ●●● Create dramatic and unusual effects by using ultraviolet (UV) light – the type known as black light. Lamps which emit virtually no visible light can be purchased as either filament bulbs or fluorescent tubes from certain electrical stores. This form of UV light causes particular dyes and colours to fluoresce and to radiate intensely bright colours. Many everyday objects and fabrics will react in this way, and you can also use paints or dyes to tint inert materials like glass. Subdue other lighting, as the brightness level of the fluorescence is quite low. Exposures on ISO 200 film with the lamp about 50cm away will be in the order of 1 sec at f5.6. It is best to use daylight type film with a Kodak 2A filter to eliminate unwanted UV light and to make tests or bracket your exposures fairly widely. ▼

8.17 ●●● You can use a projector as a means of altering the quality and nature of an image and to provide ways of making it more abstract. Project the selected transparency on to a light-toned

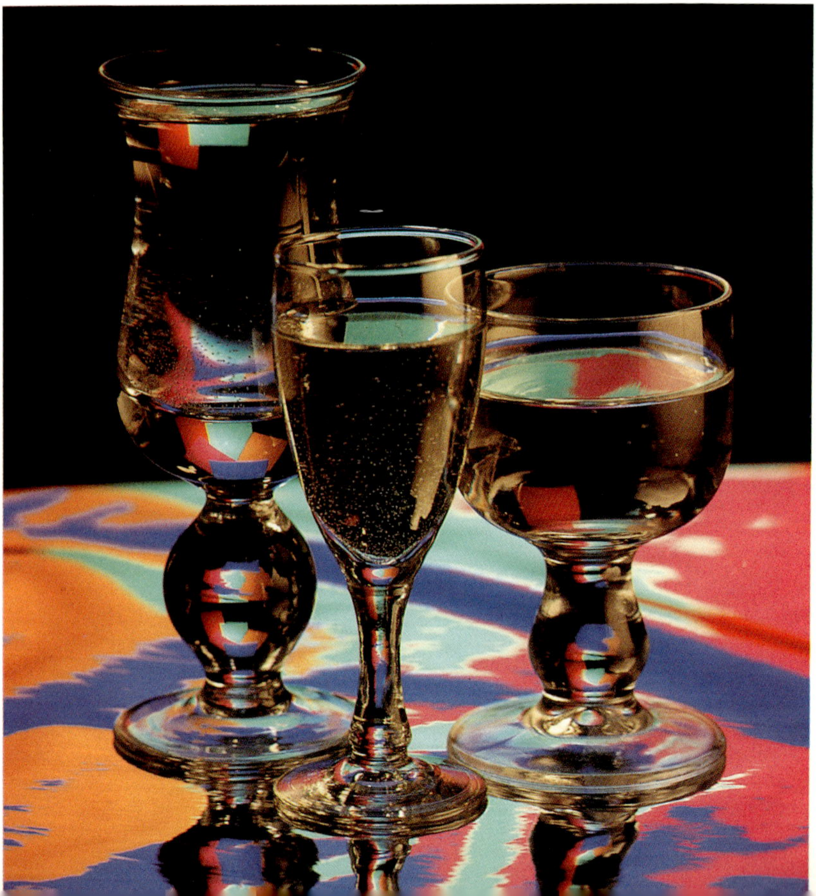

textured surface – hessian or muslin, for instance – and simply rephotograph it. If you use a broken surface, such as crumpled white paper, the effect may be almost abstract. To limit the distortion of perspective you will need to position both the projector and camera lens as close together as possible.

Introduce other forms of interference by back projecting the image on to a tracing paper screen and placing translucent materials (like textured glass or crumpled plastic) in contact with it on the opposite side to the camera. With two projectors you can combine two images and use pieces of card to mask selected areas to control how they blend.

8.18 ●●● In addition to soft-focus techniques, you can use a pinhole to create interestingly diffused images of static subjects including still-life and even landscapes. The technique described here is for an SLR camera with interchangeable lenses.

First, make a small hole with a fine needle in a piece of aluminium foil; the smaller the hole, the more clearly defined the image will be. Remove the lens , tape the foil over the camera's body aperture making sure that the hole is in the centre. This will give a wide-angle view, although a narrower angle can be obtained by using extension tubes or a piece of cardboard tube to hold the pinhole further from the lens.

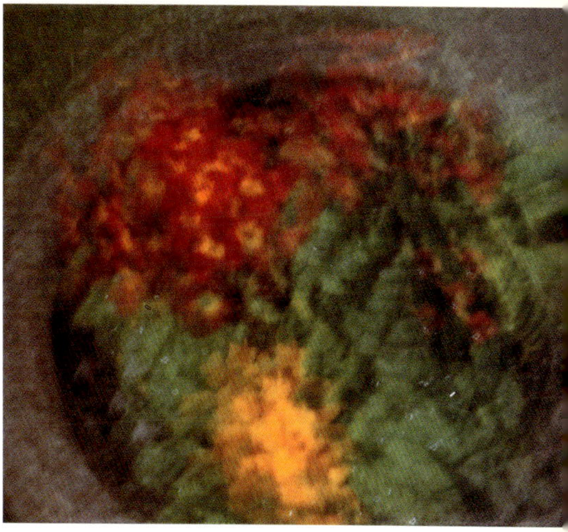

8.19 ●●● Generate abstract images by making two or more holes in a cluster. Providing your camera's TTL meter is reasonably sensitive, you should be able to get a satisfactory reading. ▲

8.20 ●●● The recent rapid developments in digital imaging have made it possible for many photographers who own computers to carry out advanced manipulations with a minimal outlay. The Kodak disc system means that a complete roll of film can be scanned and stored as a series of digital images on to a CD disc as part of the normal developing and printing service. These images can then be loaded into a computer by means of a CD ROM unit and combined, manipulated and enhanced with the aid of a software programme like Adobe Photoshop. The resulting image can be stored on a floppy disc and then used to produce colour prints or transparencies, a service which is offered by a large number of professional colour labs, at a modest price. They also scan and store individual images on to discs.

8.21 ●● The technique known as 'joiners', favoured by David Hockney, involves making multiple shots of small areas of a subject and then pasting the resulting prints together in patchwork fashion to create an overall image of the scene. A contact print mosaic is a variation of this technique; a similar series of photographs is taken in sequence on a single roll of film so that the film can be cut into strips and a contact print made showing the complete scene.

Plan the shots carefully. You will find that it is easier, to begin with, to use a roll-film format so that only about a dozen images are required to complete the picture. Use a tripod with a pan-and-tilt head and work methodically across the image from one side to the other, and then down in strips, or vice versa.

The same technique can be used to create a panoramic view: this has the advantage of not having to be cut and joined. ▼

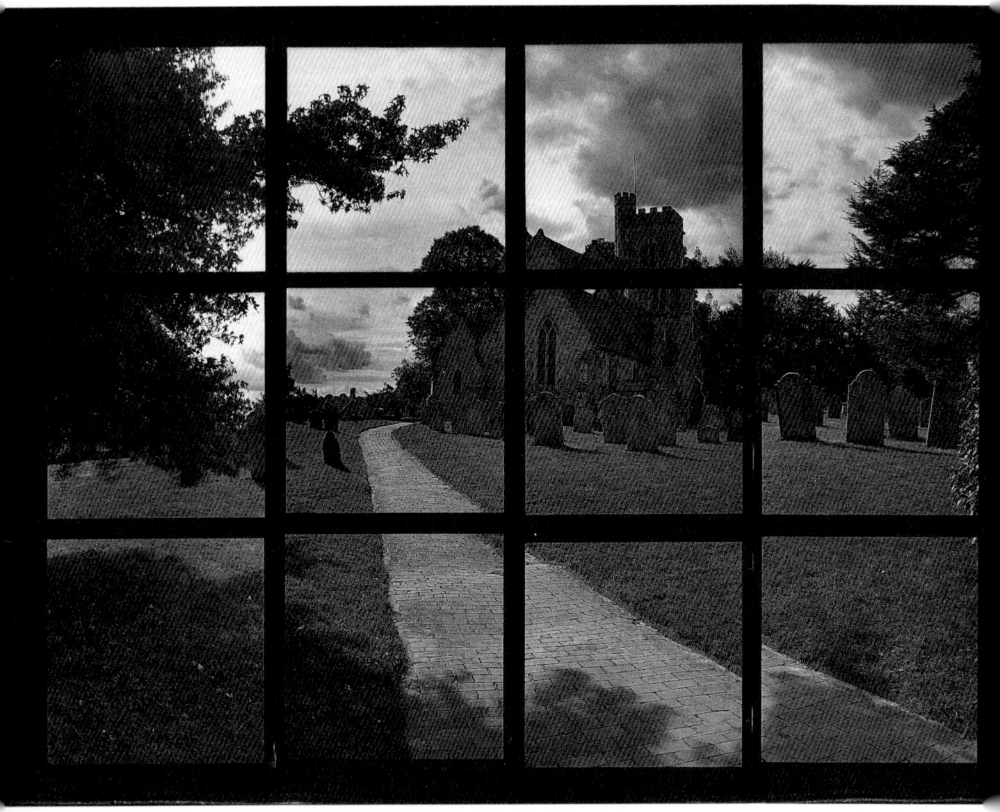

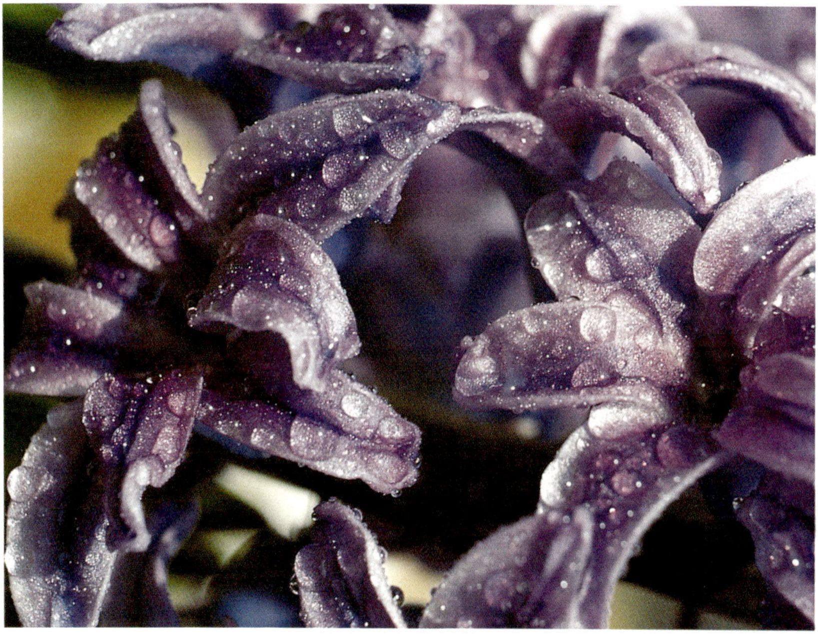

8.22 A small spray gun, the type used for watering house plants, is a useful photographic accessory. A mist of fine water droplets applied to flowers, leaves or fruit can add interest to a close-up image, and heighten the impression of texture. In a similar way, this technique can often be applied successfully to nude and glamour shots where the visual effect of water droplets on oiled, tanned skin can be very powerful. ▲

8.23 When shooting still-life subjects indoors or in the studio, the choice of camera viewpoint and the corresponding perspective effects are often quite limited. You can create a different, and sometimes quite startling, perspective for some of your smaller compositions by shooting from below a subject placed on a raised platform. You can make a platform easily by using stacks of plastic storage or bottle crates to support each corner of a wall flat which has been reinforced by diagonal struts.

8.24 Where objects of similar shapes and size are arranged together in a photograph (a still-life or a group portrait, for example) you can create a better sense of balance and harmony within the image if you select an odd number of objects.

8.25 ● Photography is an excellent way to record your most valuable possessions, should you need to provide details in the event of a burglary or insurance claim, or to document damage caused by an accident.

8.26 ● Sheets of plastic laminate, the type used for kitchen work surfaces, are ideal to serve as backgrounds for still-life arrangements where a plain untextured surface is needed. These sheets can be obtained at builder's merchants in a wide variety of colours and textures. The sheets can be curved easily and wiped clean, when necessary, with a damp cloth.

8.27 ●● Make a useful gadget for supporting small items in still-life arrangements, as well as reflectors or mirrors, by removing the lamp head from a small table lamp with a flexible stem and replacing it with a large bulldog clip. A ready-made alternative is a laboratory stand and clamp obtainable from scientific supply stores.

8.28 ●● An unusual and effective surface for small still-life arrangements is a material called Mirrorflex, obtainable from stationers and art supply stores. It is a thin, flexible plastic foil with a mirror-like surface, which can be wrinkled and curved at will to create a wide range of effects from slightly distorted to the completely abstract. Taped to a panel, the material can also be used to create abstracted reflections of subjects ranging from portraits and nudes to landscapes. ▼

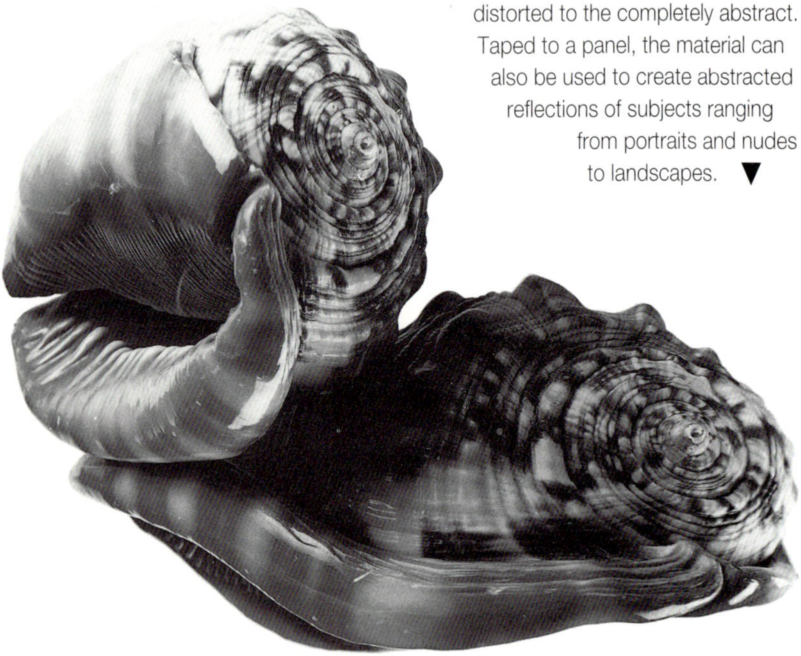

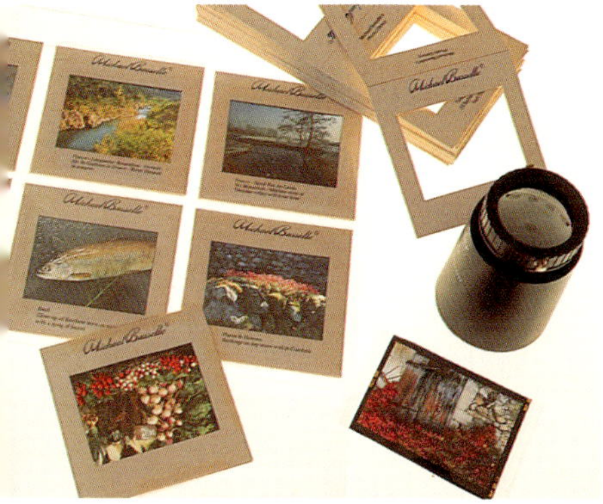

8.29 Never mount transparencies in glass when submitting your work to publishers. Use white card mounts, marked clearly with your name and address, protected by clear acetate sleeves, and then place them inside a viewpack. Include a delivery note which lists the number of images and the subjects sent to ensure they are all returned to you. Do not mount prints on card because the printer cannot scan them. ▲

8.30 Valuable photographs should always be posted by Guaranteed Delivery with Consequential Loss Insurance. This can provide up to £10,000 of cover in the event of loss by the Post Office. Provide adequate protection for your pictures – I use Mailite envelopes, which are padded with bubble plastic – and sandwich the sheets of transparencies between two pieces of corrugated plastic. This gives added protection as well as preventing anyone folding or bending the envelope.

8.31 When submitting work by post, address the package to a specific individual in preference to just 'The Editor' for instance. Unsolicited work should always include return post and packing, but I advise you to telephone first to establish that the pictures you intend to send will be of interest, and are expected.

8.32 Remember the 'Five W' rule when captioning photographs – Where, What, Who, Why and When. Such detail is not always necessary, but the more information a caption contains the wider its potential market. A good picture of a fish, for instance, would be quite likely to sell to an angling magazine, but if it was captioned 'Wild brown trout caught in April on the River Test at Longbridge with a Cat's Whisker fly and a floating line', the number and variety of articles for which the editor might be able to consider its use as an appropriate illustration would be greatly increased. ▼

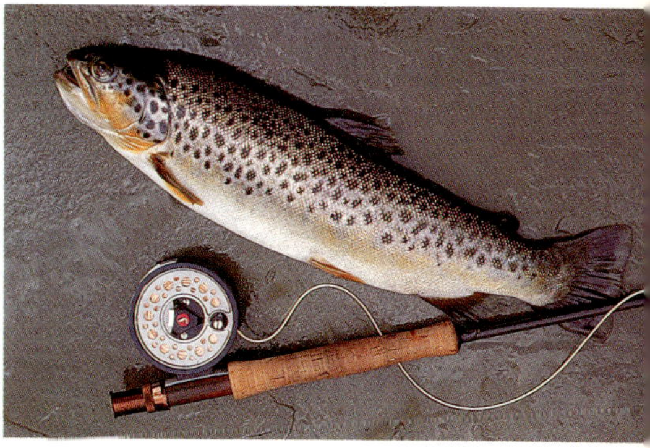

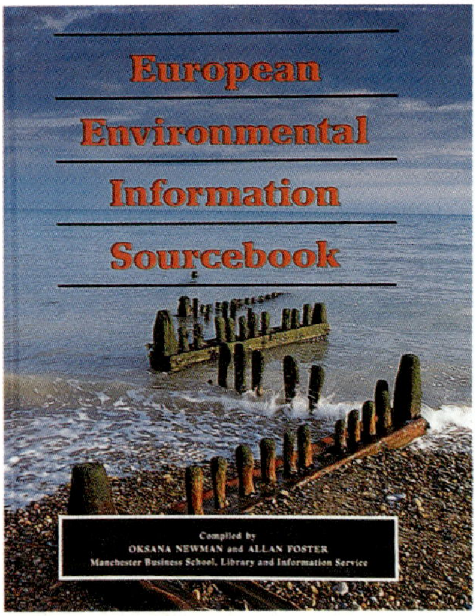

A large area of sky made this ideal for a cover shot.

PRACTICAL HINT

- If you shoot pictures with a publication in mind, remember that the highest fees are usually paid for covers and full page shots, which invariably require a portrait (upright) image. Whenever you have a strong image lined up in your viewfinder, try to frame it as a portrait image, even if it cries out to be a landscape (horizontal) shape. If this means you have to include a large area of sky, it can be a positive advantage because picture editors frequently need photographs where the top third or so of the image is plain enough for type to be superimposed.

8.33 A good photograph is worth more than a thousand words. Certainly photographs can be used most effectively to explain things, and a sequence of clearly understandable images which demonstrate how a technique or process is carried out will stand a good chance of finding a market. There are countless examples: stripping down and repairing a car engine, tying a salmon fly, making a basket, painting a watercolour, preparing a recipe; all of these subjects are in constant demand by book and magazine publishers, and it can be a simple matter to set up and photograph them. In a similar vein, a sequence of good images which describe and give directions for a country walk will also have strong appeal to editors.

8.34 Although exotic locations seem the most tempting subjects to many photographers, it is very often the seemingly obvious and more mundane subjects that are in biggest demand by photo libraries. Some of the top-selling pictures are images of cloudscapes, the Houses of Parliament or traffic jams, while many photo libraries are spoilt for choice with shots of places such as Nepal, the Seychelles and the Australian Outback. ◀

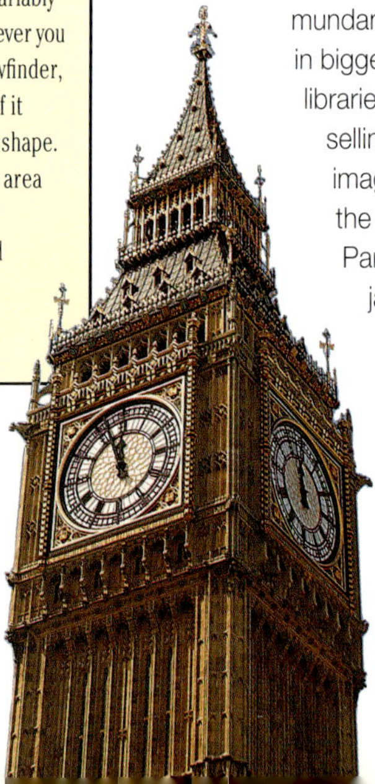

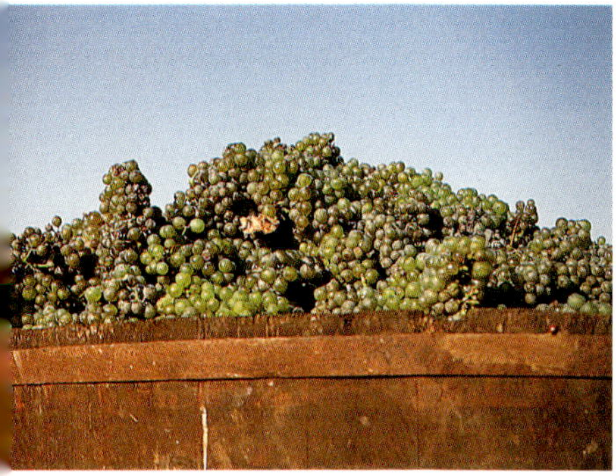

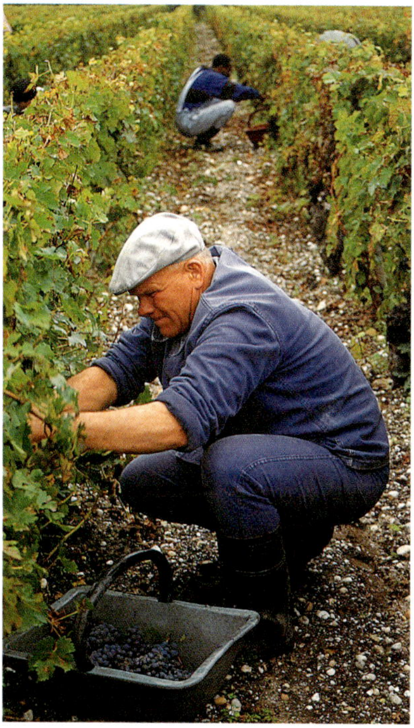

This page: these three photographs are part of a series to illustrate wine making.

8.35 ●● You may find it easier to sell your photographs to a magazine if they are part of an illustrated feature. You need good photographs, some specialist knowledge, experience of the subject and a reasonable ability to write in an interesting and articulate way. An article of about 1000 words, together with a set of well-edited and captioned pictures, will stand an excellent chance of being published if you target the right publications. ▲ ▶

8.36 ●● If you would like to caption and catalogue your work, perhaps with a view to starting a photo library, a computer can be an extremely valuable aid. There are now several modestly-priced database programmes available in both Apple Mac and PC formats which will print self-adhesive caption labels, number and catalogue slides and provide an effective means of searching for images according to descriptions and specific classifications.

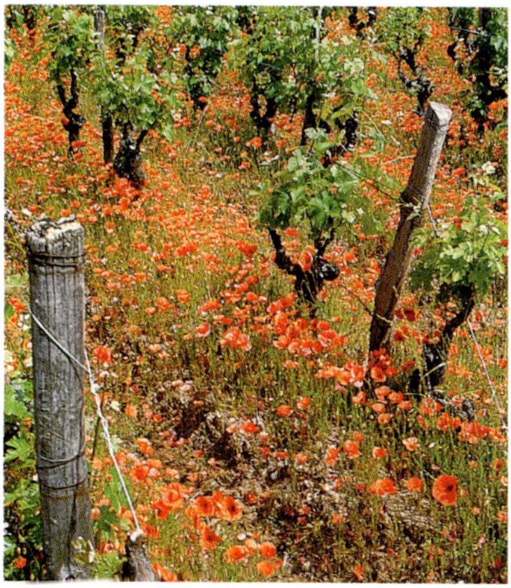

Glossary

Aerial perspective Impression of depth in a landscape photograph, largely created by haze, which renders further planes softer than nearer ones.
Angle of incidence Angle formed between an incoming light ray and the normal (at right angles to the surface).
Angle of reflection Angle formed between the reflected ray and the normal. Equal to the angle of incidence.
Angle of view Optimum angle between two light rays passing through a lens.
Aperture Hole in a lens through which the image-forming light passes. Adjustable in controlled marked steps called f-stops.
Auto-winder Camera attachment that employs a battery-driven motor to wind on film automatically. Simplified form of motor drive.
Average reading metering Camera TTL metering method that measures light over most of the screen area of the viewfinder.
Back projection Projecting a slide (or a film) on to the back of a translucent screen.
Barn doors Hinged flaps for spotlights and flood-lamps to control direction and width of light beam.
Bellows focussing unit Means of flexibility extending the film-to-lens distance. Thus objects much closer than the closest marked distance of the lens can be focussed sharply.
Bounce flash System of reflecting the light from a flash unit to the surface (usually a ceiling), or by directing the flash into a light-coloured umbrella near the subject.
Burning-in Giving extra exposure in enlarging to highlight areas of a print. The remainder of the print is shielded by the hands or a card.
Catch lights Pinpoint reflections of light in the eyes of a portrait subject.
Centre-weighted metering Camera TTL metering method in which the reading is biased towards the intensity at the centre of the viewfinder.
Close-up lens A form of spectacle lens, correctly called a supplementary, in a mount, permitting closer range focussing, according to lens strength.
Computer flash Electronic flash units in which a sensor assesses the strength of light reflected from the subject. Internal circuitry gauges when the amount of light delivered is adequate for a correct exposure.
Contact prints Prints made by direct contact with negatives. Usually used for quick reference.
Contrast Relationship between tones of an image; a print with wide tonal differences is said to be contrasty, one restricted in tonal range is flat.
Depth of field Zone between nearest and furthest parts of a scene extending either side of the focussed subject that reaches acceptable sharpness.
Depth-of-field previewer Button or lever on a reflex camera that stops the lens down to a selected aperture, allowing visual assessment of depth of field.
Depth of focus Very small range of acceptable variation of lens-to-film distance within which critical sharpness can be maintained. Term often wrongly used for depth of field.
Dodging Giving less than the overall exposure to parts of a print which would otherwise appear too dark by interposing an appropriately shaped object in the light path of the area of the image to be dodged during exposure. Also called shading.
Exposure bracketing Taking of extra pictures at exposures more and less than 'correct', to allow for error.
Exposure latitude Tolerance of a film to record satisfactorily if exposure is not exactly correct. Colour films generally have less latitude than black-and-white films, while fast black-and-white films have most latitude.
Fill-in light Additional light to the main light source which directs light to the shadows to cut down contrast. Much used in portraiture.
Filters (optical) Pieces of clear glass, gelatin or other translucent material that modify the nature of light passing through. They may be used at the taking stage, with black-and-white or colour film, or in colour enlarging to give correct colour balance. Also used in darkroom safe lights to give the right light quality for a specific material. Main types are colour compensating, colour conversion, contrast, correction (last two used with black-and-white film), infrared, polarising and ultraviolet.
Filter factor The factor by which exposure must be increased for a particular filter. Usually marked 1½ x, 2 x, etc. on the filter mount.
Fixed-focus lens Lens on a simple camera with focus that cannot be altered. It is set to a distance which will give greatest depth of field.
Focal length Distance from the optical centre of a lens focussed at infinity and the film plane. The longer the length, the more enlarged the image.

Focal point Point on the focal plane where the optical axis intersects it at right angles.
Grey card method Using a Grey Card of 18% reflectance, used to give an average-subject reading for an exposure meter.
High key Photograph using mostly lighter tones, conveying lightness and delicacy in suitable subjects.
Hyperfocal distance The nearest point to the camera giving acceptable sharpness at a given aperture when the lens is focussed at infinity,
Incident light reading Taking a reading of the light falling on (incident on) the subject rather than reflected from it.
Infinity Far distance, and in photographic terms anything beyond 1000m/3330ft. Symbol is ∞.
Infrared film Film that records infrared radiations, those below the red end of the visible light spectrum. It permits photography in the dark if an infrared light source is used. Marked haze penetration when used in conjunction with an infrared filter.
IR mark This, on lens focus mounts, is the focus setting index when using infrared film.
Latitude Extent to which exposure level can be varied and still produce an acceptable result. Usually greater on fast films than on slow films.
Long-focus lens One with a focal length longer than that of the diagonal of negative it covers. Not an interchangeable term with telephoto.
Low key Photograph using mainly the darker tones, conveying sombre impressions or drama.
Macro lenses Prime camera lenses which have the facility for focussing closer than normal lenses, often to a closest focussing distance of 20cm/8in, giving life-size reproduction without accessories.
Mirror lens Compact lens with very long focal length (500mm upwards) which forms the image by means of mirrors rather than lens elements. Has no aperture adjustment.
Orthochromatic Photo emulsion not sensitive to the red end of the spectrum. Now chiefly used for copying work.
Overexposure Action of too much light on the emulsion. An overexposed negative is very dense; an overexposed transparency is too thin.
Parallax error Difference between the field of view seen through a viewfinder and that recorded on the film. Most marked in close-up. SLRs avoid it.
Polarised light Light that vibrates in one plane by being reflected from a surface.
Polarising filter Filter that cuts our polarised light to eliminate reflections from water and shiny surfaces (but not metal). It also darkens blue skies on colour film without altering other colour values.
Push-processing Known as pushing film, this is prolonging development to permit rating of films at faster speeds than recommended. Most successful with fast films on low-contrast subjects.
Soft focus Diminishing of normal definition of a lens to give a soft, romantic appearance to an image. Achieved by special filters, or by diffusing material such as muslin in front of the enlarger lens.
Spot metering Camera TTL metering in which exposure is based on a small area in the centre of the frame.
Standard lens Has a focal length approximately equal to the diagonal of the format it covers. Generally supplied with a camera; for 35mm models it is around 50mm focal length.
Stopping down Decreasing the size of the aperture.
Synchronisation Ensuring coincidence of the flash firing with the shutter's maximum opening.
Telephoto lens Lens of longer than standard focal length, but with shorter physical length than a true long-focus lens.
Test strip Proportionate exposing of a strip of printing paper to assess correct print exposure.
Tonal range Difference in the density between the brightest and the least bright part of an image.
Toning Altering the natural colour of a print by a chemical toning bath. Best known application is sepia toning by sulphide and selenium toners.
TTL metering Abbreviation for 'through the lens'. Common feature of SLR cameras: the internal exposure metering is actuated by light passing through the lens of a cell in front of the film plane.
Ultraviolet Invisible radiation beyond the blue-violet part of the spectrum. Invisible to the eye, it will cause blue cast in colour film. Prevalent at high altitudes, near sea and in misty conditions. Corrected by an ultraviolet filter.
Underexposure Insufficient light has fallen on the emulsion to form a sufficiently strong image. An underexposed negative is too thin, a transparency too dense, a print too dark.
Wide-angle lens Lenses with a wider angle of view than that of standard lenses for the format.
Zoom lens A lens of variable focal length. Variable-focus lenses are similar, but require refocussing after altering the focal length.

Index

Page numbers in **bold** refer to illustrations. Other numbers refer to the paragraphs.